MENTAL REPRESENTATIONS
The interface between
language and reality

How are natural languages interpreted? What is the relationship between an expression of natural language and the object it refers to? Does it involve mediating mental representations? This dynamic collection provides an overview of the relationship between linguistic form and interpretation as exemplified by the most influential of current theoretical approaches – the Chomskian Government and Binding paradigm, the conflicting Situation Semantics paradigm, the Davidsonian programme and, finally, the new relevance theory of cognition and pragmatics. It thus provides a comparative perspective on what are frequently seen as conflicting theories. More ambitiously, it works towards an overall theory of cognition which, the editor believes, has been facilitated by the assumptions and claims of relevance theory.

The contributors to the volume are all well known for their work at the language–cognition interface, and each essay is a stimulating and perceptive consideration of aspects of the problem. The editor's introduction will be invaluable for the background it provides for any reader not fully conversant with current theory. Her concluding essay is a brilliant exposition of the way in which relevance theory can create links whereby apparently disparate views are combined into a unified modular account of language and cognitive processes.

Mental Representations is a work at the forefront of current research. It will undoubtedly be controversial, but at the same time few linguists or cognitive scientists can fail to be stimulated by it.

MENTAL REPRESENTATIONS
The interface between language and reality

EDITED BY
RUTH M. KEMPSON

Department of Phonetics and Linguistics
School of Oriental and African Studies
University of London

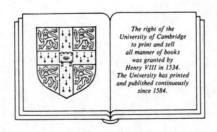

The right of the
University of Cambridge
to print and sell
all manner of books
was granted by
Henry VIII in 1534.
The University has printed
and published continuously
since 1584.

CAMBRIDGE UNIVERSITY PRESS

CAMBRIDGE

NEW YORK   NEW ROCHELLE   MELBOURNE   SYDNEY

Published by the Press Syndicate of the University of Cambridge
The Pitt Building, Trumpington Street, Cambridge CB2 1RP
32 East 57th Street, New York, NY 10022, USA
10 Stamford Road, Oakleigh, Melbourne 3166, Australia

First published 1988

Printed in Great Britain
at the University Press, Cambridge

British Library cataloguing in publication data

Mental representation: the interface
between language and reality.
1. Reality. Perception by man. Role
of language
1. Kempson, Ruth M.
153.7

Library of Congress cataloguing in publication data

Mental representations: the interface between language and reality /
edited by Ruth M. Kempson.
p.   cm.
Includes index.
ISBN 0 521 34251 1
1. Psycholinguistics.   2. Cognition.   1. Kempson, Ruth M.
P37.M36   1988
401'.9–dc19   88–11116   CIP

ISBN 0 521 34251 1

CONTENTS

CONTRIBUTORS

Diane Blakemore, Department of French, Southampton University
Michael Brody, Department of Linguistics, University College London, University of London
Robyn Carston, Department of Linguistics, University College London, University of London
Robin Cooper, Centre for Cognitive Science, University of Edinburgh
Elisabet Engdahl, Centre for Cognitive Science, University of Edinburgh
James Higginbotham, Department of Linguistics and Philosophy, Massachusetts Institute of Technology
Ruth M. Kempson, Department of Phonetics and Linguistics, School of Oriental and African Studies, University of London
M. Rita Manzini, Italian Department, University College London, University of London
Robert May, Department of Cognitive Science, School of Social Sciences, University of California, Irvine
Dan Sperber, Centre National de la Recherche Scientifique, Paris
Deirdre Wilson, Department of Linguistics, University College London, University of London

PREFACE

There is a chain of events leading up to this book. Annabel Cormack and I had been working together for a number of years on quantification and the form of semantic representation funded by the ESRC in the form of two successive grants (SSRC HR6802, ESRC HR8635). During this period, I became convinced that relevance theory, despite the very great generality of its central claims, imposed a surprising number of precise consequences on the form of grammars which seemed to be correct. Moreover these consequences shared an overall similarity with claims of the Chomskian Government and Binding (GB) paradigm, despite substantial differences of detail. As the research project drew to an end, a comparison between GB theory and relevance theory proved to be an increasingly rich source of material for investigating the language–cognition interface. I discovered that Bob Kowalski's work on logic and knowledge bases contained a striking number of claims about knowledge implementation which closely resembled the claims of relevance theory. I became seized with a naive optimism that people working on similar problems within various paradigms might benefit from exposure to each other's ideas. A conference entitled 'Mental representations: properties of logical form' was accordingly held at Cumberland Lodge, Windsor Great Park (also funded by the ESRC as project C00230067), with invited representatives from GB theory, Situation Semantics, relevance theory, psycholinguistics, philosophy of language, and computer science. This book is a direct produce of that conference, though talks given at the conference by John Campbell, Lyn Frazier, Alan Garnham, and Bob Kowalski were unfortunately not submitted as papers for this volume. My optimistic hopes turned out to be at least partly justified, as the articles in this book demonstrate.

As with all books, considerable time has elapsed from the first ideas to the finished product, and the list of thanks is not short. First I wish to express my gratitude to the ESRC for its funding of my research project over a number of years and in various guises. Secondly, I thank Annabel Cormack for the stimulation and pleasure she has provided me throughout the years of our work together, with her perpetual demands for greater rigour. Thirdly, I am thankful that in Deirdre and Dan I have friends who have created a theory of real elegance – so described because precise consequences continue to pour from its general principles – and who have thereby provided me with a continuing stream of intellectual stimuli demanding actions in response, one of which was the organisation of the Cumberland Lodge conference. I thank all those participants at the Cumberland Lodge conference who made it a memorable occasion, and the administrators of Cumberland Lodge who made it such a pleasurable one. Thanks too to all those who have commented on the various sections of the book which are my sole responsibility – Robyn Carston, Wynn Chao, Robin Cooper, Annabel Cormack, Martin Davies, Elisabet Engdahl, Jim Higginbotham, Rita Manzini, Neil Smith, Richard Spencer Smith, and Deirdre Wilson. As always special thanks are due to the publishing team, in this case Penny Carter and her colleagues. They are invariably most efficient in getting books printed to a high standard swiftly through the printing process, and Penny gave me a lot of encouragement through a difficult six months.

Finally, and by no means least, I seize this opportunity to publicly thank Randolph Quirk for having first introduced me to the pleasures of linguistics. Without his enthusiasm and encouragement I might never have had all these years of fun. This book is therefore dedicated to him:

To Randolph, with affection and gratitude.

I

Introduction

The relation between language, mind, and reality

RUTH M. KEMPSON

1 Preliminaries

The hard core of assumptions all theoretical linguists share is remarkably small. They agree on the very general assumption that research on theoretical aspects of language is ultimately directed towards answering the question 'What does knowledge of language consist in?' They also in the main agree that knowledge of language is a faculty discrete from other kinds of knowledge humans have about the world around them, together with its corollary that any explanation of such particular linguistic knowledge (a speaker's competence) must interact in specifiable ways with more general processes of perception, memory, etc., to determine the overall data of language use (a speaker's performance). They all also agree that such language-specific knowledge displays itself in the ability of a speaker to produce and understand an indefinitely large number of strings of words that a speaker treats as systematically divisible into hierarchically structured subgroups. In other words, there is no disagreement that all grammars contain recursively applicable syntactic mechanisms characterising a speaker's knowledge of his/her language.

It is also incontrovertible that speakers use their language to ask questions, convey orders, express opinions, and make assertions about entities in the world around them; so there is also no disagreement that at some point in the overall explanation of language there has to be an articulation of the relation between expressions of a language – simple and complex – and these nonlinguistic entities (which I shall call 'real semantics'). Thus languages are agreed to be used as interpreted formal systems, and not merely arbitrary abstract devices for constructing tree structures in one's head. However, there is very considerable disagreement as to how, or even in the case of the assumptions about real semantics, whether these agreed assumptions should be implemented as part of a grammar of a language.

The burden of this introduction is to present some of the paradigms within which these general assumptions have been variously implemented, to evaluate the extent to which these paradigms conflict, and to place each paradigm in an overall cognitive perspective. In effect I am presenting the reader with a sketch of the state of the art with respect to current theories of language and mind. In addition, this sketch is intended to fill in whatever background assumptions individual readers may lack in the various fields of philosophy of language, formal semantics, formal syntax, and pragmatics. My hope is that this introduction will enable readers to appreciate the papers as contributing different answers to essentially the same question: What is the relation between language, mind, and reality?

2   The rationalist theory of mind

By far the most influential paradigm of modern times has been that of Noam Chomsky. The central task, according to his view, is to explain the psychological problem of how children, despite very wide heterogeneity in the language input and in their general learning skills, all acquire a language, and hence an internalised grammar within the same short span of years. Furthermore, in no case does a child's competence correspond to a description of the sentences to which they have been exposed; for their internalised competence mechanism has a demonstrable generative capacity which far outstrips this finite corpus, a corpus which plays the subsidiary role of providing evidence against which their internalised grammar is confirmed or disconfirmed. Chomsky takes this as indicative of the innateness of the language faculty, by definition one for which a cognitive system is preset to develop, requiring only appropriate triggering from the environment for the ability to be released.

The Chomskian view is summarised in Chomsky 1986:

The language faculty is a distinct system of the mind/brain, with an initial state S_0 common to the species (to a very close first approximation, apart from pathology, etc.) and apparently unique to it in essential respects. Given appropriate experience, this faculty passes from the state S_0 to some relatively stable steady state S_s, which then undergoes only peripheral modification (say, acquiring new vocabulary items). The attained state incorporates an I-language [internalised language] ... UG [Universal Grammar] is the theory of S_0; particular grammars are theories of various I-languages. The I-languages that can be attained with S_0 fixed and experience varying are the attainable human languages.

The change from the initial state (UG) to the acquired grammar (an individual Core Grammar) is a process of enrichment of the language faculty as constrained by the UG template. This template is itself modular in the sense of having several theories as modules – case theory, binding theory, bounding theory, control theory, X theory, and theta theory, all of them an interacting set of constraints on configurations and relations between configurations allowed by natural language grammars. The substance of both the initial and final states thus rests in the syntactic properties of the associated system, not in any semantic properties. The real-semantic properties of UG and of Core Grammars are, indeed, not interestingly different. In both, there are expressions used as names, as predicates, as connectives and as operators. So Chomsky's claim about the nature of the mind and its acquisition of language skills centres on formal structural properties of the faculty, and not on the semantic properties of the system. Indeed, Chomsky considers the real semantic relation between linguistic expressions and objective entities in the world to be no property of grammar at all (see Chomsky 1981 and elsewhere).[1]

Fodor's Representational Theory of Mind (RTM) is in the same rationalist tradition (Fodor 1981, 1982). According to this view, cognitive mechanisms extract information from the outside world, and process, store, and retrieve such information via an internalised system of representations called the language of thought. Each cognitive mechanism has a number of input systems, e.g. visual, aural, and by claim the language faculty, whose task is to map any incoming information from its physical form into a representation in the language of thought in which form it can then interact with information either stored in memory or retrieved from other input systems. These internal representations have real semantic content in the sense that they are representations of entities external to the cognitive mechanism. However, internal cognitive operations governing behaviour are internal to the organism; from which near-tautology, it follows that relations between internal representations have to be stated in terms of their formal, syntactic properties and not their externally definable semantic content. Suppose for example, I see John with his head on his hands as he listens to me, with his eyelids drooping. On the basis of this visually present information I decide that John is tired. If from my memory I then extract a further piece of stored information that if John is tired he always feels badtempered, I will deduce that John feels badtempered. Each of these steps involves an activity of the cognitive mechanism; and one of these is making the inference. As an activity of the cognitive mechanism the step involved in making the inference has – according to the theory – to be stated in terms internal to the cognitive mechanism. It is not captured in terms of the real-semantic relation holding between me, my belief-state and John, but in terms of the form of the representations entertained internally by the cognitive mechanism – in this case, schematically, 'P, if P then $Q \vdash Q$'. Hence the characterisation – representational theory of mind. Thus for different reasons, both Chomsky and Fodor espouse theories which articulate formal properties of representations internal to the human mind. They make different claims about the language faculty – for Chomsky, it is a discrete cognitive subsystem, for Fodor it is an input system – but both are agreed on the essentially syntactic character of the generalisations to be made.

3   Linguistic theory and truth conditions

Many philosophers have, however, addressed the problem of language capacities not by looking at formal properties of natural language but rather their semantic properties. They have constructed answers to the question 'What is it that a speaker has to know in order to understand a language?' All attempts to answer this question in recent years have been in the shadow of the devastating argument of Quine (1961) that any definition of a concept of meaning for linguistic expressions is hopelessly circular, and hence empty.

3.1   Davidson and truth theory

In the wake of Quine's attack, philosophers tried to explain the concept of understanding a language without invoking any entity such as the meaning of an expression. Davidson in particular set up the paradigm of truth-theoretic semantics for natural language. Davidson (1967) claimed that theories of natural-language content (and hence understanding), rather than implementing the schema 'S has meaning p' should be constrained to entail sentences of the form 'S means that p', and he claimed that this requirement is met by theories which entail sentences of the form 'S is true iff p' with additional formal and empirical constraints to guarantee that p is indeed a correct interpretation of S. Thus he argued that the correct basis of a theory of meaning for a natural language was a truth theory for that language, recursively enumerating sentences such as ' "Snow is white" is true iff snow is white' via the concepts of reference, extension, satisfaction, and truth familiar from Tarskian semantics for first-order formal languages, and with, notably, no invocation of meanings of individual expressions as such.

Several difficulties are presented by Davidson's account of natural language content. One apparent difficulty is the so-called 'opaque' contexts, a set of phenomena where more appears to be needed in determining the semantic value of the complex expression than the mere extension of its parts. Thus for example, though in a non-opaque context such as is demonstrated by (1):

(1)   John dropped a book on relevance-theoretic semantics
the truth of the whole expression depends exclusively on the extension of each constituent expression, in particular on there being a non-null extension to the expression 'a book on relevance-theoretic semantics', in an opaque environment such as (2):

(2)   John is looking for a book on relevance-theoretic semantics
the truth-value of the whole cannot be straightforwardly computed from the extension of the expression – for the expression can have a null extension and yet the sentence be true. So the combinatorial projection of truth-values for a sentence from the values assigned to its constituent parts has to be more than just extensions assigned to those parts. For otherwise there is no basis for predicting the difference between (1) and (2). So the argument goes (cf. Davidson 1968–9 for an attempt to incorporate such sentences within his account and Higginbotham 1986 for a linguistic application of this view).

3.2   Montague and model-theoretic semantics

An alternative framework which retains the truth-theoretic approach to content, and which also eschews meanings as nonreducible entities, is model-theoretic semantics as applied to natural languages (Montague 1974). In this framework, the concept of possible world (or index – by definition a world-time pair) is added to the repertoire of extension, reference satisfaction, and truth, but otherwise the semantics provided is rigorously extensional. Even the concept of index itself has no more conceptual content than assigned it in the model – it has a set of extensional values stipulated as assigned to the individual elementary expressions of the language at that index, and this is the only content attributed to the construct. Indeed, though expressions are assigned meanings, the construal given to these meanings is not in any sense conceptual – the sole concept of content for an expression is a function from indices (world-time pairs) to extensions (called the 'intension' of the expression). The combinatorial projection of truth-values from the values assigned to its constituent parts then depends not only on the extensions assigned to the parts, but the assigned intensions, crucially in the case of (2). However, there is still no invocation of representations of meaning as such.

What both the Montague and the Davidsonian approaches to natural language reconstruct is the compositional basis of natural language interpretation – how it is that semantic values of elementary expressions combine together in a rule-governed (recursively specified) way to determine semantic values of an indefinitely large number of compound expressions. In the Montague framework in particular, which enriches a modal logic with the construct of intension and combines this with the lambda calculus of Church (1940) to provide an explicit compositional semantics for natural language, a wide variety of expressions which had resisted analysis within a purely extensional framework appeared to be subject to an elegant formal characterisation. The assumption that Davidson and Montague shared, emphasised most strongly by Montague, is that natural languages do not have uniquely defining characteristics of any interest, but are interpreted systems of the same type as formal, constructed languages, and are characterisable by the same descriptive techniques. In particular, the interpretation of natural languages is identical to that of formal languages, a relation between expressions of the language and the nonlinguistic entities which they refer to or denote (whether in an extensional Tarskian way as advocated by Davidson, or in a model-theoretic way as advocated by Montague). According to this view, a grammar contains (i) a set of rules for characterising the expressions of the language each with its associated structure, and (ii) a set of semantic rules which determine compositionally from the values assigned to the terminal elements (the lexical expressions) the extensional value of the expression as a whole. And the value of the sentential expressions is assumed to be that of a truth-value – true or false.

The combined force of Quinean scepticism and the technical virtuosity of model-theoretic semantics led to a very widespread critique of the characterisation of content in the form of representations of linguistic meaning as had been favoured by linguists within the transformational paradigm, such as Katz (1972) and Jackendoff (1972). As Lewis (1970) dismissively puts it:

Semantic markers [a representational construct used by Katz] are symbols: items in the vocabulary of an artificial language we may call Semantic Markerese. Semantic interpretation by means of them amounts merely to a translation algorithm from the object language to the auxiliary language Markerese. But we can know the Markerese translation without knowing the first thing about the meaning of the English sentence: namely the conditions under which it would be true. Semantics with no treatment of truth conditions is not semantics. Translation into Markerese is at best a substitute for real semantics, relying either on our tacit competence (at some future date) as speakers of Markerese or on our ability to do real semantics at least for the one language Markerese. Translation into Latin might serve as well, except in so far as the designers of Markerese may choose to build into it useful features – freedom from ambiguity, grammar based on symbolic logic – that might make it easier to do real semantics for Markerese than for Latin.

3.3   Semantics and the Chomskian paradigm

As a result of this onslaught, most linguists took one of two options. Either they made no attempt to consider real semantics in articulating properties of grammar, and assumed that every (nonphonological) representational construct in the grammar was a construct of syntax, or they adopted model-theoretic semantics as the basis for investigating semantic properties of natural language systems. The former move is characteristic of the Chomskian paradigm (Chomsky 1981, 1986). Considerations of systematic restrictions on interpretation provided by natural language, such as quantifier interpretation, anaphor–antecedent relations, construal of infinitive constructions, etc., are treated as syntactic problems subject to configurational solutions. Thus for example, the interaction between the interpretation of quantifying expressions and the interpretation of pronouns is reconstructed via a level of logical form (LF) at which the interpretation potential of quantifying expressions can be reflected in a branching syntactic structure discrete from that of the surface sequence. This configuration is assumed to be a structural configuration of the same language, albeit at an abstract level. It is constructed by an operation of quantifier raising (QR) which moves NPs from their argument position to the front of the sentence to create a structural configuration analogous to the structures of predicate calculus, a syntactic process which provides a level from which the scope facts of quantifying expressions can be predicted from their configuration (May 1977 and this volume). There are therefore three levels of syntax – D-structure, S-structure, and LF.

This level of LF is defined as the level at which certain specified constraints hold, and these are all constraints on interpretation. The binding principles (Chomsky 1981) constitute one such set of constraints. These legitimate only certain assignments of indexing, the assignments then constraining the interpretation of anaphoric dependence. They are defined as filters on LF configurations, requiring (a) that an anaphor be bound (coindexed with some c-commanding expression) within its governing category (roughly a clause containing a specified subject) as in the indexed string (3):

(3)   Joanna$_i$ scratched herself$_i$

(b) that a pronominal be free (not bound) within its governing category, precluding for example the indexed string (4):

(4)   Joanna$_i$ scratched her$_i$

(c) that a name be free, precluding for example the indexed string (5):

(5)   She$_i$ scratched Joanna$_i$

Another such constraint is the theta criterion. This now has various versions, but its effect is invariably to guarantee that every verb has the appropriate number of logical arguments (specified in the lexicon as 'theta-roles'), each uniquely satisfied by a distinct syntactic expression. In Chomsky 1981 this was stated as:

(1) Each theta-role is assigned to one and only one argument

(2) Each syntactic argument is assigned one and only theta-role

In Chomsky 1986 this was revised to make explicit the link with case theory:

Each argument α appears in a chain containing a unique visible theta-position P, and each theta-position P is visible in a chain containing a unique argument α.

For this latter formulation we need the concepts of D-structure, chain, and visibility. A chain is a set of nodes forming a history of movement from a given D-structure position, a set whose head is a case-marked NP and whose most deeply embedded member is assigned a theta-role. An element is visible for theta-marking only if it is assigned case, and this assignment of case is at S-structure. So it is chains then that are uniquely assigned case and a theta-role. The theta criterion now guarantees that any given theta-role specification is uniquely associated with an NP visibly assigned case at S-structure (either by its morphology or in virtue of its syntactic configuration). This, then, formally reconstructs the intuition that the interpretation of predicate argument structure derived from verb noun-phrase configurations must be recoverable from S-structure.

The three levels of the grammar – D-structure, S-structure, and LF – are further constrained by the requirement that syntactic information projected from the lexicon must be present at all three levels of syntax. No information can get lost in moving from one level of structure to another. This is the so-called projection principle. Thus the theta criterion holds not merely at S-structure, but at D-structure and LF as well.

Put together, the binding principles, the theta criterion, case theory, and the projection principle, jointly guarantee the mapping of a syntactic analysis of a sentence onto an unambiguous, indexed structural configuration at LF from which the real semantic interpretation of the sentence can be derived. In effect an LF structure is the updated analogue of Katz's Markerese representations, *sans* any definitional account of lexical items and with the advantage that the syntactic properties of such structures are relatively familiar and well understood – it is a structured indexed configuration which provides the basis for interpretation but does not itself constitute that interpretation.

3.4 The problem of indexicality

A grammar with no account of real-semantic interpretation of its elements may seem an impoverished beast; and many linguists, granting the force of Lewis's taunt, adopted the view that real-semantic explanations were an essential part of a formal characterisation of natural languages, and accordingly investigated the potential of model-theoretic semantics as a component of grammar. However, truth-theoretic paradigms are not without their own problems, as emerged from the consequent detailed study of natural languages (e.g. Kaplan 1979, Cresswell 1979). One of the most pressing of these is the problem of indexicality, the term given to the phenomenon whereby the value that an expression has is dependent in some way to be analysed on the context in which it is uttered. In outlining his programme of truth theory as a basis for natural language semantics, Davidson referred to this problem as 'the fly in the ointment' (Davidson 1967). It is a fly that has turned out to be persistently troublesome.

With words such as *I*, *here*, and *now*, dependency on context is explicit and relatively straightforward, and the extent of the phenomenon of context-dependency was not immediately recognised. It is in fact pervasive, and not reducible to observable discourse entities such as speaker, hearer, time, and place of utterance. Take, for example, pronouns. The value a pronoun has is always assumed to be recoverable in the speech context – either as in (6) referring to some independently identifiable individual (though not someone necessarily visibly identifiable in the utterance situation), or as in (7) referring to some individual already previously referred to:

    (6)   He fainted

    (7)   A man walked in. He fainted

The interpretation of tense too is dependent on context, and in exactly parallel ways. Either the tense is assumed to be fixed as some identified time previous to the time of utterance, as in (6), or as in (7), the time is fixed via the time reference of the previous sentence. Like pronouns, time reference can also be dependent on a preceding quantifying expression as in (8):

    (8)   Whenever Rob saw blood, he fainted

Definite NPs present the same problem. They are traditionally assumed to refer uniquely to one and only one entity (Russell 1905). But this is known to be a context-sensitive phenomenon. An utterance of (9)

    (9)   The fridge door is open

does not assume that there exists one and only one fridge door; but rather that some fridge door is uniquely identifiable in the context. As with pronouns, this context-sensitivity is not restricted to the discourse scenario, and it can be set up by antecedent sentences, either explicitly as in (10) or implicitly as in (11):

    (10) John bought a fridge and just a day later the fridge door wouldn't close

    (11) John bought a fridge and just a day later the door wouldn't close

Even the interpretation of predicates as to what set of entities are to be taken as their extension is dependent on context in exactly parallel fashion. Thus *students* in (12)

    (12) Most students failed

is not necessarily construed as the total set of students in the entire domain of individuals – it can be assumed within the speech situation to be interpreted as denoting some particular set of students, for example the students taking my logic exam this year. And self-evidently, those students do not have to be present in the scene of the discourse. Moreover, just like the anaphoric use of pronouns, the set intended as the extension may be recoverable from the (immediately) previous discourse as in (13):

    (13) I set a particularly hard logic exam this year and most students failed

The dependence of a sentence's real-semantic content on some notion of context is thus all-pervasive, and an understanding of the process involved in determining contextual values is essential to explaining the relation between sentences and such truth-theoretic content (see Carston, chapter 7, for a detailed account).

The problem this poses for truth-theoretic semantics is not merely a descriptive one. For the Davidsonian programme, it is particularly poignant (though for a partial reply, see Higginbotham this volume). This programme sought to explain what is involved in language understanding without invoking meanings for any construct. The route taken was to require the theory to yield truth conditions for sentences as a characterisation of their interpretation. This cannot literally be correct, for we have to add the parameter of a context against which the sentence is evaluated. What is then required if the Davidsonian goal is to be achieved, is a characterisation of context which determines values for elementary parts which is independent of any concept of linguistic meaning. But this is where the rub comes; for the selection of context which determines such values is not antecedently fixed independent of the content of the sentence. On the contrary it may depend critically on the linguistic content of the sentence itself. Consider (14):

    (14) I set a hard logic exam this year and the invigilators were kept busy escorting panicking students out of the exam hall

Suppose the examination hall where logic exams are taken is a room named Ridgeley Hall. It is not the extensions of the expressions that are themselves in the context for evaluating either the first or second conjunct of (14) in any sense independently. Neither Ridgeley Hall nor the people involved in invi-

gilating have to be independently identified by speaker and hearer as part of
the information they bear in mind in evaluating either conjunct. The hearer
may well not have thought about either the place or the method of taking
examinations at the onset of the second conjunct, let alone the first. It is that
Ridgeley Hall is described by the phrase *exam hall* that determines that
Ridgeley Hall provides the referential value of the expression – it is the very
choice by the speaker of the expression *exam hall* that links it to the antecedent
use of the expression *a hard logic exam*. Worse, invigilators are by definition
people who help administer exams and it is this definitional property which
guarantees that the referent of *the invigilators* is uniquely identifiable as the
invigilators of the logic exam for the purpose of evaluating the truth-value of
the whole proposition asserted. But this is the manipulation of linguistic
content to determine referential values for terminal expressions which the
Davidsonian programme cannot countenance.

More generally, if we grant that natural-language sentences systematically under-determine their truth-theoretic content, this being partly fixed by
contextual parameters, but if further we require that some account be given
of how the output strings of a grammar contribute to determining their truth-
theoretic content, then we have to specify the input that they provide to this
process. And this in itself is an individuation of intrinsic linguistic content for
an expression which is not its reference, nor its extension, nor a truth-value.
From this it follows that an articulation of truth-theoretic content for sentences modulo the contribution of contextual parameters has to assume a
concept of linguistic meaning – it is that which contributes to reference and
extension assignment, disambiguation, etc.

3.5   Situation Semantics

The problem of context-dependence has been approached recently within a
formal semantic framework known as Situation Semantics devised by
Barwise & Perry (B&P) in the face of their growing realisation of the
inadequacies of orthodox model-theoretic approaches (Barwise & Perry
1984). Situation Semantics preserves the central claim of truth theory that
the only possible concept of content for natural language semantics is the
articulation of a direct relation between language tokens and objective
reality, but in all other important respects, it diverges from model theory.
Among the claims made in Barwise & Perry 1983 are:[2]

(1) It provides a formal reconstruction of reality which is language
independent [unlike model theory, in which a model is articulated only as
values assigned to a set of expressions of a given language]. This takes the
form of a theory of situations.

(2) This theory of situations then provides a set of entities which
sentences can be said to denote. Contrary to all truth-theoretic semantics
stemming from Frege in which sentences denote a truth-value, sentences
denote situation types, and can therefore be distinguished according to their

associated situation type, a means of distinction that is much more fine-grained than the classical analysis.

(3) The cornerstone of the theory of situations is the articulation of relations between situation types and constraints on those relations. These constraints on situations are used to articulate a so-called ecological theory of meaning in which all information-carrying processes are analysed as relations between situations. Content for linguistic expressions is merely one such case – the meaning of utterance U is a relation between the situation in which U is uttered and the situation described by U, a conventional relation between situations to which speakers of the language are said to be attuned.

(4) Given (3), it follows that human retrieval of information from the environment does not – or at least does not necessarily – involve internal cognitive representations (contra Fodor), but may constitute just another uniformity between situation types. Situation Semantics thus appears to set its face against the syntactic theory of mind of Fodor and, indeed against Chomsky's form of rationalism.

(5) Barwise & Perry (B&P) take seriously the under-determinacy of linguistic content *vis-à-vis* propositional content, which they call 'the efficiency of language', and articulate a whole range of factors (called 'parameters'), which play a part in determining the interpretation of an expression when uttered – so-called 'resource situations', 'speaker's connections' etc. These provide independent input to implementing the schematic relation between situation-types provided by the linguistic meaning of an expression. Thus for example, the expression 'my wife' is said to be a 4-place relation between the discourse situation, speaker's connections, resource situations, and objects, a relation which can be further specified (in apparently sixteen different ways) depending on how the discourse situation and connections are fixed. (Detailed exemplification of this under-determinacy of linguistic meaning and its further specification by fixing such parameters is given in B&P 1984 and Engdahl this volume.) There is, however, no attempt in the Situation Semantics paradigm to provide an account of what constrains the selection of resource situations or speaker's connections. So the account of context-dependence is a purely formal one (see Hornstein 1985).

3.6 Situation Semantics and the rationalist programme

The emphasis on its ecological approach places Situation Semantics firmly in the post-Quine tradition of characterising the content of representational systems without positing meanings as such. Moreover, B&P appear to have set their approach in direct conflict with Fodor's rationalist theory of mental representations. However, despite initial appearances, it is not obvious to what extent Situation Semantics conflicts with Fodor's Representational Theory of Mind (RTM), or with Chomsky's rationalism. The initial appearance of incompatibility stems from two aspects of the theory: (i) the characterisation of beliefs as complex events, (ii) the characterisation of linguistic meaning as a set of conventional constraints. The RTM, recall, claims that all mental states, including beliefs, essentially involve structure, and that cognitive operations such as inference are defined exclusively in terms of the form of such states. Beliefs for B&P, however, are said to be complex event types, 'efficient bodily conditions (about which virtually nothing is known) that have enough structure to account for the complex information-retaining and behaviour-guiding capacities that we use them to explain' (B&P 1984: 242). The question is how much intrinsic structure should be attributed to these 'bodily conditions'. An example given by B&P is the characterisation of Joe's belief that Jackie is biting his dog Molly. This is represented as a situation type in which the belief relation holds between an individual Joe and an event-type E, where E itself involves the relation of biting, the role of biter being filled by the dog Jackie, and that of being bitten by the dog Molly who belongs to Joe.

In this characterisation of belief, there is nothing which imparts structure to the mental state of Joe himself – the belief state is merely a complex situation type in which there is a relation of the belief type between Joe and Jackie, Molly, and the situation type in which the one dog bites the other. Those working in Situation Semantics have indeed taken care to emphasise that it is the structure inherent in reality which provides the interpretation of information-bearing states rather than any cognitive representation of that structure (e.g. Engdahl, chapter 3 of this volume). However, rhetoric apart, there is nothing to preclude the attribution of such intrinsic situation-type structure to the mental state of the believing organism if it turns out to be necessary 'to account for the complex information-retaining and behaviour-guiding capacities that we use them to explain' (Cooper discusses this issue in chapter 2 of this volume). And if Fodor's RTM-stance is correct, the attribution of such structure to the mental state of the organism is indeed necessary. The conclusion would then be that the theory of situations does not preclude a system of mental representations. On the contrary, it could be used to provide a semantics for constructs of this language of thought, a set of representations transparent with respect to inference, which more or less directly reflect the situation types they represent.[3] There is therefore room for peaceful coexistence between Situation Semantics and Fodor's RTM. And in Perry's recent work, there seems to be a movement in this direction. For in Perry (1986), there is no denial of the existence of mental representations when necessary, but merely the denial that they are invariably necessary for the retrieval of information.

Moreover, this conclusion seems to be the move that B&P must make in order to allow an account of the acquisition of meanings for lexical items. Given B&P's premise that the contents for expressions of the language are a set of conventional constraints on reality to which a community is attuned, it is hard to see how a child can progressively acquire the lexical base of a language system, the one aspect of acquisition which involves a progressive hypothesis formation process. If the association of content with an expression is invariably a convention, then that association must be the property of a community of individuals, for a convention is by definition the property of a multi-membered set of individuals, at least given Lewis's account of convention.[4] With this characterisation of linguistic content, it follows that the expressions of a child's language have content only in so far as he/she is attuned to community-determined processes. But what community is the child attuned to in assigning contents to his words – a single individual doesn't constitute a community, so private hypotheses as to the content of a word are ruled out a priori. Thus the progressive acquisition of contents for lexical items by a process of hypothesis formation subject to disconfirmation is precluded in principle. The only possible account of acquisition of lexical contents is a 'brute-causal' explanation, the acquisition emerging by some method direct from the environment to which the child is exposed.[5]

Now something extremely close to this view is not implausible. Indeed with the addition of one premise, this view is Fodor's view. The additional premise is that words name expressions of the language of thought, the large majority of these being concepts, n-place predicates in this internalised language of thought. Fodor's view (1982a) about semantic properties of acquisition is that concepts (crucially, not words) have exactly the property to which a Situation Semantics account of language acquisition seems committed. Concepts are not acquired by a rational learning (hypothesis-formation) process. To the contrary, the cognitive mechanism has an innate device, a 'sensorium', for individuating concepts on the basis of information presented by the environment. This sensorium leads an individual to acquire concepts 'brute-causally' from the environment as suitably triggered by it. An important part of that environment is the language community to which the child is exposed so his sensorium device will be exposed to the concepts individuated by this community. The concepts a child acquires will therefore in large measure be determined by the community in which he develops. Hence, Fodor concludes, concepts are innate (by definition, not learned by any rational process) and yet culture-specific.

The relevance of this argument to the apparent non-existence of a semantic acquisition process upon Situation-Semantic premises, is that it provides a basis for predicting just the right amount of hypothesis formation in the language acquisition process. In Fodor's view, the problem of acquisition of content for a word in his language is reduced to hypothesising what individuated predicate of the language of thought the word names. The rest – the relation between concept and the portion of reality it denotes – is brute-causal, determined by the sensorium as activated by the environment, a process incidentally constrained by the community of which the child is a member. Whether this relation between concept and what we might now call situation type is a convention can now remain an open question. Nothing in the Fodor individualistic programme demands that it have the force of convention, but it is not precluded either. Even if the means of fixing this relation were conventional and dependent on the community in some essential way, it would not provide evidence for an externalised, non-individualistic view either of natural languages or (fortunately) of the language of thought. The means of establishing the relation between concept and situation type is irrelevant to the articulation of natural-language grammars according to this view – even the specification of that relation is not a property of grammars. And any conventions associated with the way in which concepts are fixed in an individual's system of mental representations would be a mere heuristic – a strategy that guarantees maximally efficient manipulation of the sensorium for communication purposes. It would not therefore be reflected in the specification of that system of representations.

The direction of the argument is that the Situation Semantics programme needs to posit an intermediate level of cognitive representation in order to give any account of the semantic acquisition of language; and the intermediate level provided by the language of thought hypothesis gives just the right, minimal, level of hypothesis formation required. Such a proposal would then fall into line with the Chomskian account of language acquisition that what a child learns is a lexicon – the lexical items of his language with their associated syntactic and phonological properties, and – we might now add – the concept that the item names. Postulation of the language of thought thus enables the Situation Semantics account of language content to remain (almost) intact, at the same time resolving what would otherwise be a foundational conflict between Situation Semantics and the entire Chomskian rationalist programme.

4   Relevance theory

Into this medley of conflicting views about the necessity of mental representations and the status of real semantic content has come relevance theory (Sperber & Wilson 1986), with a first claim to explain the full complexity of context-dependence in language understanding. Like Chomsky's philosophy of language and Fodor's philosophy of psychology, Sperber & Wilson's approach (S&W) is unrepentant cognitive psychology, providing simultaneously a theory of central cognitive processes and a theory of communication. S&W adopt the Fodor RTM assumptions (i) that the cognitive system perceives and processes information from the world around via the construction of propositional representations in the language of thought, and (ii) that language is an input mechanism, a vehicle for interpreting utterances as propositional representations. Being an input mechanism, a grammar is taken to be a device mapping surface strings onto expressions of the language of thought. The only content ascribed to a sentence by the grammar is accordingly its so-called logical form, this being a representation (often incomplete) in the language of thought compositionally determined from the concepts the individual expressions name and their associated logical configuration as determined by the syntactic structure of the string. In other words, it has all the translation characteristics rejected by Lewis 1970. According to this view natural languages are unlike formal languages in not being directly truth-theoretically interpreted, for there are (at least) two levels of representation intermediate between the syntactic characterisation of a sentence as a construct of grammar and characterisation of real-semantic content, levels which are essential to the translational characteristics of natural language, definitional of input mechanisms. There is not only the logical form of the sentence but also the completed proposition (its 'propositional form'), a representation of the real-semantic content associated with the sentence upon that use.

The algorithm mapping sentences on to language-of-thought formulae provided by a natural language grammar is, S&W claim, partial in the sense that sentences are mapped onto incomplete formulae: the interpretation of a sentence as an utterance invariably involves a process of hypothesis formation, subject to disconformation – there is no fully deterministic procedure for mapping sentences onto their propositional contents (see S&W 1986 and Carston this volume). This process involves taking the logical form of the sentence uttered as a basis for constructing a hypothesised representation of the proposition the speaker is intending to convey (its propositional form), and combining this with selected representations of additional premises to lead by a deductive process to further information (called 'contextual effects'). The hypothesised propositional form and the selection of additional premises are all made on the basis of represented information accessible to the hearer at the time, as triggered by the form of the sentence uttered. And it is the additional information which is added to the logical form of the sentence to form this hypothesised proposition which is the basis of the context-dependency intrinsic to the determination of real-semantic content (Carston this volume discusses this point in detail).

The entire process of utterance interpretation, as all other cognitive processes, is constrained by that of relevance, this being defined as effecting the balance between the conflicting pressures to derive information (contextual effects) and yet engage in minimal processing effort (Blakemore and Carston, both of this volume, give more detailed accounts). Contextual factors which display the context-dependence of propositional content are then predicted to include any representation accessible to a hearer at minimal cost during the utterance process. This process is exemplified by (15):

(15) He's sick

According to this view, (15) would have a logical form with the argument position unfilled, but constrained to be satisfied by an argument predicated of the property 'male'. In Kempson 1986b this is formalised by the use of

distinguished variables, $\beta_1, \beta_2 \ldots$, which are place-holders for the argument
to be substituted:

Present (sick (β_i))

male (β_i)

the sex specification being a constraint on the value to be selected. The value
of β and the additional premises the hearer selects as context are driven by
the need to draw information inferentially at minimal processing cost – i.e.
by the requirements of relevance. Suppose the concept of Hugh, Ruth's son,
is accessible in that there has just been talk of Ruth's concern for him.
Relevance considerations will predict that identifying the argument position
of the predicate 'sick' as representing Hugh will conform to relevance
requirements, for this choice triggers the accessibility of such a premise as
(16)

(16)   If Hugh's sick, Ruth will stay at home

to yield the inference (17)

(17)   Ruth will stay at home

this in its turn, say leading to the further inference (18) via the additional
premise (19)

(18)   We won't have a lecture

(19)   If Ruth stays at home, we won't have a lecture

Adequate contextual effects have been achieved with minimal processing
cost, and the construal of (15) is confirmed.

The kinds of examples so problematic for the Davidson paradigm are
unproblematic in this representational theory of context in which a context is
constructed by the hearer as part of the process of utterance interpretation
from representations accessible to him at the time. Such an account predicts
that among the representations accessible to the hearer will not only be
representations of entities present (and prominent) in the discourse scenario
(the directly referential cases such as (6) and (9) above) but also representations associated with linguistic expressions just used (the coreference cases
exemplified by (7) above) and those associated with the very linguistic
expression being used (e.g. (11), (13) and (14) above). Thus the analysis of
examples (6)–(14) on relevance-theoretic assumptions is essentially unitary –
there is no difference in principle between understanding pronouns as indexically or anaphorically fixed, interpreting the domain of extension of predicates indexically or via the representation assigned to preceding linguistic
expressions, or deciding on the reference of definite NPs via their linguistic
content. Interpretation by a hearer invariably involves deciding on a
representation in the language of thought onto which the linguistic expression is to be mapped. And in all cases in which the linguistic content under-
determines propositional content, of which pronouns, definite NPs and
domain selection are paradigm examples, the selection of the propositional
value of the expression is predicted to make use of any representation of
information accessible to the hearer as constrained by relevance.

The centrality of representations as themselves providing interpretations of linguistic objects is a pivotal claim of Sperber & Wilson. There are, they point out, two kinds of relationship between a representation of some object and that object – it can be based either on truth (as is familiar) or resemblance. So too Sperber & Wilson argue with utterances. In the former case we have familiar descriptive uses. In the latter case, the so-called 'interpretive' use, an utterance is interpreted by the propositional representation it resembles. So for interpretive use, even the propositional form of the utterance is not truth-theoretically interpreted directly, for it is 'interpreted' by a discrete propositional form it may only loosely resemble. This resemblance relation, they argue, lies at the heart of many natural language phenomena (cf. Sperber & Wilson 1986 and Wilson & Sperber this volume).

4.1 Relevance theory and truth-theoretic semantics

Despite the sketchiness of these outlines, some of the similarities and differences between the theories are already apparent. Relevance theory shares with Situation Semantics a recognition of the extent of the problem of context dependence in determining truth-theoretic content for sentences. But the two theories reconstruct the phenomenon from a conflicting set of premises as to the nature of language and of the mind – the one a real-semantic account, the other a syntactic account (though if Situation Semantics concedes the existence of mental representations for a cognitive explanation of at least some forms of inference, then the extent of the incompatibility is much reduced – see Cooper this volume). Further, Situation Semantics adopts the orthodox stance that context somehow provides pre-assigned values (for which it is assumed no theory is available). Relevance theory in contrast provides an explanation of the enrichment process, analysing the phenomenon of context dependence as a constructional/syntactic process, building a propositional structure the utterance is taken to express on the basis of the (incomplete) form provided by the grammar. From this relevance account, it follows that the only sense in which natural language sentences are truth-theoretically interpreted is indirectly (via the propositions the sentence is used to assert), and it follows too that real-semantic interpretation is not a part of grammar. It is the language of thought which is semantically interpreted, not the natural language expressions. Put crudely, it is our beliefs which are directly about the world we live in, not the sentences of our language.

4.2 Relevance theory and the Chomskian paradigm

The theory with which relevance theory shares most assumptions is the Chomskian paradigm. Chomsky and S&W agree that the concept of content to be articulated in a grammar is purely representational. They agree that such a representation of content, the logical form of a sentence, provides a partial basis for interpretation. However, there is disagreement over the status of the logical form representation, itself a reflection of the important Chomsky–Fodor disagreement over whether the human language faculty is a central cognitive system or merely an input mechanism to the central cognitive system. On GB assumptions, the LF of a sentence is a construct of the same type as the S-structure from which it is derived, one of a set of indexed, labelled bracketings which jointly constitute the syntactic analysis of the sentence. By contrast, the logical form of a sentence on relevance-theoretic assumptions is an incomplete expression of a different formal system, that of the internalised language of thought, an inferentially transparent system whose completed formulae display all the properties of formal systems devised to reconstruct inference – no ambiguity, no indexical elements.

From GB assumptions, it follows that if the interpretive potential of natural language expressions displays structural properties, this has to be characterised as a syntactic property of grammars of natural language. From relevance assumptions, it does not – it remains an empirical matter whether the structural properties so displayed are structural properties of the natural language or of the internalised representational system, the language of thought. I shall sketch three such examples. First, in GB we find invisible empty categories postulated as syntactic constructs of natural language grammar to provide arguments for predicates (e.g. PRO as a syntactic subject of infinitives). According to a relevance theory backdrop, this is not a move which has to be made a priori, as there remains the option that natural language expressions are mapped on to fully specified argument–predicate structures without this full specification being a configurational property of the natural language syntax (see Kempson this volume for some discussion). Secondly, against GB assumptions the binding principles constraining the interpretation of anaphors, pronominals and names operate over natural language configurations as defined either at S-structure or at LF: no other level of structure is provided for. According to relevance assumptions, a further possibility opens up – that binding principles might be sensitive not so much to natural language configurations as to language of thought configurations, a distinction which would be observable in any case where it could be demonstrated that the mapping from natural language configuration to language of thought configuration is nontrivial (see Kempson forthcoming). Thirdly, quantifier scope: in GB this is reconstructed as QR, a movement rule applying to quantifying expressions in argument position to provide a natural language configuration in which scope can be determined geometrically. On the assumption that a logical form of a sentence is a language of thought configuration, we have the alternative that scope is defined over configurations of this system, and not over natural language configurations. According to this alternative, QR does not have to be construed as a movement process relating structural configurations of a single system, but could be construed in one of two alternative ways. It might be a process relating structural configurations of the language of thought, or it might be a process mapping configurations of one language, the natural language, onto configurations of another, the language of thought.

These sketches of relevance-theoretic proposals are not intended as arguments even in outline. In each case, the debate has yet to be entered into. Indeed it might turn out that the input to the mapping onto the relevance-theoretic level of logical form is not S-structure but the GB level of LF (but see Kempson forthcoming for an argument that reconstruction phenomena provide deciding evidence in favour of a direct mapping from S-structure to the relevance defined level of logical form). But it is an empirical one, with clear answers at least in principle, depending on the details of the evidence. And the success of the arguments either way will be of more than local interest. For the outcome of such arguments will have consequences for the more important question of whether the language faculty is a central cognitive system in its own right with no other representational system to interpret it, or is an input mechanism interpreted via the postulated language of thought.

5 The current state of the art

Leaping ahead in intellectual time with sketches of possible arguments may be fun; but one cannot prejudge the future, nor effect agreement between theories by mere pronouncement. And the present state of the art is in general unrelentingly tribal as the chapters of this volume display, each researcher articulating and evaluating solutions within the confines of their own selected paradigm. Higginbotham adopts the background assumption that natural language grammars contain rules directly assigning truth-theoretic interpretations, and in direct response to the challenge posed in this introduction argues that the phenomenon of context-dependence does not pose a serious problem for the Davidsonian approach to semantics. He goes on to compare model-theory and Davidsonian semantics, arguing that model-theory needs to have restrictions imposed on it which render it not interestingly distinct from Davidsonian assumptions. Like Higginbotham, Cooper directly addresses the issues raised here, but within the perspective set by Situation Semantics assumptions. He is concerned to answer the question of whether the Situation Semantics characterisation of facts and their structure is itself a representation and hence involves the attribution of mental representations to the speaker, despite the supposed Situation Semantics anathema to mental representations. The problem he focuses on is whether in positing negative, conjunctive and disjunctive facts, the analyst is imposing such language-like structure on reality that it can no longer be construed as reality directly but has itself to be construed as a representation with language-like form.

There are two papers on pronominal anaphora, each against a different set of theoretical assumptions. Engdahl, who like Cooper adopts Situation Semantics assumptions, proposes an account of what she calls the 'relational' interpretation of pronouns which makes crucial use of so-called 'parameters' – variable-like entities which have a range of values. Despite their language-like characteristic, Engdahl argues that they are genuine semantic constructs, and not indicative of any intermediate level of representation. Within the broad framework of the GB paradigm, adopting the assumption that pronominal anaphora is interpreted via a richly specified LF configuration, May combines his own theories of dominance and scope (May 1985) with Pesetsky's theory of paths (Pesetsky 1982) to demonstrate that there is a range of cases of pronominal anaphora in which the pronoun is directly bound by a quantifier and not via some intervening empty category (a phenomenon broadly denied within the GB paradigm).

Like May, Brody & Manzini build on recent work in the GB paradigm. Adopting assumptions drawn from Chomsky 1986, Manzini 1983, and Brody 1985, they propose a syntactic solution to the problems of interpretation posed by 'implicit argument' phenomena. These so-called 'implicit arguments' are particularly suggestive of the view that interpretation of natural language is not specified over natural language structures because they are aspects of interpretation which are not represented at any of the levels specified in GB syntax – D-structure, S-structure or LF. But Brody & Manzini argue that an explanation of implicit arguments can only be given in terms of interaction between case theory and (a revised version of) the projection principle and is therefore an essentially syntactic phenomenon.

There are four chapters adopting relevance-theoretic assumptions. Wilson & Sperber introduce some basic concepts of relevance theory. In particular they distinguish between descriptive and interpretive representation, and argue that loose talk and metaphor, echoic utterances and irony, and interrogative and exclamative utterances can be successfully analysed as instances of interpretive rather than descriptive representation. Carston shows how adoption of relevance assumptions solves two unrelated problems – the problematic status of so-called 'generalised conversational implicatures', and the pervasive problem of context dependence in the articulation of truth-theoretic content (as sketched in this introduction). In neither case is the process either algorithmically driven with a predetermined set of values (characteristic of processes internal to the grammar), or part of the implicated content of the utterance (definitional of indirect information conveyed by an utterance). Yet the information conveyed by the utterance in both cases depends on the same process of pragmatic enrichment from a linguistic content to the associated propositional form. Carston concludes that the explanation given buttresses the relevance-theoretic claim that it is only the language of thought to which truth-theoretic content is ascribed, ascription of interpretation to an expression in a language merely articulating the mapping from linguistic forms onto logical forms. Blakemore also adopts the premises of relevance theory and demonstrates that linguistic meaning cannot be delimited as contributing exclusively towards the truth-theoretic content expressible by a sentence, since some aspects of linguistic meaning encoded in the grammer constrain the other main aspect of utterance interpretation – the selection of a context. Finally, Kempson discusses the relation between properties of UG and properties of the central cognitive system. She argues that there is closer interaction between principles of UG and principles of relevance theory than might at first appear. Indeed the properties of UG can be seen either as general principles constraining the cognitive system or as faculty-specific instantiations of the general constraint imposed by the search for relevance.

In our various ways then, we all have answers to the general questions 'What does knowledge of language consist in?' and 'What is the nature of mental processes?'; but the evidence for and against those answers depends – as these chapters display – on articulating and answering more specific questions. Detailed solutions have to be implemented within individual paradigms, and so like the blind men describing the elephant, we can only hope that our theories and their detailed proposals will gradually increase our understanding of these general issues.

NOTES

1 Not all those working in the Chomskian paradigm agree. In particular Higginbotham argues explicitly for a Davidsonian interpretation of LF structures as a part of the grammar of language (see Higginbotham 1986 and this volume).

2 I retain here the concepts and vocabulary of Barwise & Perry 1984. But reader, beware. This is an evolving theory in which concepts and notation are subject to revision.

3 There is a slight caveat to be added here, but it turns out to buttress the need to pair situation semantics with Fodor's RTM. In discussing the notoriously problematic Twin-Earth cases where the intensions of the two constructed cases are identical but their extensions are different (see Putnam 1973), Fodor argues that Earth-water and Twin-Earth-water are identical in intensional (truth-theoretic) content except in so far as context contributes to determining their extension (Fodor 1986). The concept of context invoked is not that associated with indexicality but that of properties holding of the situation/set of circumstances independent of language against which the thought is evaluated. Thus the intensional content of an expression for Fodor is that which determines its extension *sans* this new concept of context. In order to give substance to such a proposal, Fodor needs to turn to a theory of situations which is independent of language itself. And situation theory is the first contender for such a theory. Thus the extent to which the intensional content of a concept fails to determine its extension fully turns out to be a further argument for pairing RTM with a theory of situations.

4 A convention C is a regularity R of behaviour amongst a group of individuals with the following properties. (1) Everyone involved conforms to R and (2) believes that others also conform. (3) The belief that others conform to R gives all involved good reason to conform to R. (4) All concerned prefer that there should be conformity to R. (5) R is not the only possible regularity meeting the last two

conditions. (6) Finally everyone involved knows (1)–(5) and knows that everyone else knows (1)–(5), etc. (taken from Davidson 1984).

5 One way to diffuse this argument (suggested to me by Robin Cooper) is the riposte that it is not the Lewis sense of convention which is intended. But by any definition, a convention is a social construct, involving interaction between more than one individual.

REFERENCES

Barwise, J. & Perry, J. 1983. *Situations and attitudes*. Cambridge, Mass.: MIT Press.

Blakemore, D. 1986. Semantic constraints on relevance. Ph.D. thesis, University of London.

Brody, M. 1985. On the complementary distribution of empty categories. *Linguistic Inquiry* 15: 505–46.

Chomsky, N. 1981. *Lectures on government and binding*. Dordrecht: Foris.

Chomsky, N. 1986. *Knowledge of language: its nature, origin and use*. New York: Praeger.

Church, A. 1940. A formulation of a simple theory of types. *Journal of Symbolic Logic* 5: 56–68.

Cresswell, M. 1979. Adverbs of space and time. In F. Guenthner & S. Schmidt (eds.) *Formal semantics and pragmatics for natural languages*. Dordrecht: Reidel, 171–99.

Davidson, D. 1967. Truth and meaning. *Synthese* 17: 304–23.

Davidson, D. 1968–9. On saying that. *Synthese* 19: 130–46.

Davidson, D. 1984. Communication. In D. Davidson *Inquiries into truth and interpretation*. Oxford: Oxford University Press.

Fodor, J.A. 1981. *Modularity of mind*. Cambridge, Mass.: MIT Press.

Fodor, J.A. 1982. *Representations*. Cambridge, Mass.: MIT Press.

Fodor, J.A. 1982a. The current state of the innateness controversy. In J.A. Fodor 1982.

Fodor, J.A. 1986. Individualism and supervenience. *Proceedings of the Aristotelian Society Supplementary Volume* LX: 235–62.

Higginbotham, J. 1986. Linguistic theory and Davidson's program in semantics. In E. LePore (ed.) *Truth and interpretation*. Oxford: Blackwell, 29–48.

Hornstein, N. 1985. Review of Barwise & Perry 1983. *Journal of Philosophy*.

Jackendoff, R. 1972. *Semantic interpretation in generative grammar*. Cambridge, Mass.: MIT Press.

Johnson-Laird, P. 1983. *Mental models*. Cambridge: Cambridge University Press.

Kamp, H. 1984. A theory of truth and semantic representation. In J. Groenendijk *et al.* (eds.) *Truth, interpretation and information*. Dordrecht: Foris.

Kaplan, D. 1979. On the logic of demonstratives. In P. French, T. Uehling & H. Wettstein (eds.) *Contemporary perspectives in the philosophy of language*. Minneapolis: University of Minnesota Press, 401–12.

Kempson, R.M. 1986a. Ambiguity and the semantic–pragmatic distinction. In C. Travis (ed.) *Meaning and interpretation*. Oxford: Blackwell, 79–103.

Kempson, R.M. 1986b. Definite NP's and context-dependence: a unitary theory of anaphora. In T. Myers, K. Brown & B. McGonigle (eds.) *Reasoning and discourse processes*. London: Academic Press.

Kempson, R.M. forthcoming. Logical form: the grammar–cognition interface. *Journal of Linguistics*.

Lewis, D. 1969. *Convention*. Cambridge, Mass.: Harvard University Press.

Lewis, D. 1970. General semantics. *Synthese* 22: 18–67.

Manzini, M.R. 1983. On control and control theory. *Linguistic Inquiry* 14: 421–46.

May, R. 1977. The grammar of quantification. Ph.D thesis, Massachusetts Institute of Technology.

May, R. 1985. *Logical form: its structure and derivation*. Cambridge, Mass.: MIT Press.

Montague, R. 1974. In R. Thomason (ed.) *Formal philosophy*. New Haven: Yale University Press.

Partee, B. & Bach, E. 1984. Quantification, pronouns and VP anaphora. In J. Groenendijk *et al.* (eds.) *Truth, interpretation and information*. Dordrecht: Foris.

Perry, J. 1986. Thought without representation. *Aristotelian Society Proceedings Supplementary Volume* LX, 137–52.

Pesetsky, D. 1982. Paths and categories. Ph.D thesis, Massachusetts Institute of Technology.

Putnam, H. 1973. The meaning of 'meaning'. In K. Gunderson (ed.) *Language, mind and knowledge*. Minnesota Studies in Philosophy of Science VII. University of Minnesota Press.

Quine, W.V. 1961. Two dogmas of empiricism. In *From a logical point of view*, 2nd edn. Cambridge, Mass.: Harvard University Press.

Russell, B. 1905. On denoting. *Mind* 14: 479–93.

Sperber, D. & Wilson, D. 1986. *Relevance: communication and cognition*. Oxford: Blackwell.

II

On the direct interpretation of natural languages

Contexts, models, and meanings:
a note on the data of semantics[1]

JAMES HIGGINBOTHAM

In natural languages, or more precisely in human first languages, the meaning of an expression on an occasion of its use is determined partly by its form, and partly by features of the scene that are exploited more or less actively in conjunction with that form so as to arrive at as full an interpretation as the circumstances may warrant. The rules of semantics, since they relate forms to meanings, are independent of context; but they come alive only in use. Disentanglement is therefore necessary: we can arrive at what is context-independent about meaning only by judicious comparison of context-bound cases.

One way to factor out the effects of context is to look for features of sentences that vary together. If it is true in any context that if A then B, then we may be sure that something context-independent about A and B is responsible for the truth of the conditional. Data of this kind lead to the fruitful enterprise of looking for invariants, as interpretations, or models, are allowed to vary.

If the above remarks are common coin, there is much else in current practice that is not. The notion of independent rules of semantics has in particular been criticised, and model-theoretic methods have been seen not merely as a useful abstract investigative tool, but also as giving rise to a conception of semantics itself. To a number of researchers, including Kempson (this volume) it has seemed that the absolute semantic notions of reference and truth, or at least the standard attempts at execution using these notions, are irremediably defective as applied to natural languages.

A problem that is common to many varieties of semantic research is the nature of the data, or the facts that semantic theory aims to account for. Whatever these facts are, they do not appear to us except as cloaked in the haze of usage. Abstraction being essential, it is not surprising that different points of view should emerge. It may, therefore, be worthwhile to reflect on the question of semantic data.

The purposes of this chapter are chiefly clarificatory. My first aim will be to explain one point of view on semantic theory, conceived as the theory of reference, in which we may, it seems to me, exploit the advantages of the usual truth-theoretic paradigm without running afoul of contextual entanglements; my second will be to clarify the role of the theory of models within a semantic theory for ordinary human languages. I would not have either aim if I did not think that there was some confusion on these matters in the current literature; however, my citations will be sparse, although the literature cited is, I think, typical.

One subject anterior to both of those stated above is that of clarifying the intentions with which I will use the familiar, 'disquotational', paradigm of semantic data. This subject is the topic of section 1 below. In section 2 I will turn to the question of how to modify that paradigm in the service of segregating the context-dependent and context-independent features of a sentence. This question will be discussed with respect to one type of construction, that of the (singular) incomplete definite description or demonstrative (an expression like *that book* or *the woman*, incomplete in the strong sense that everyone knows that there are many things satisfying the nominal predicate of the description). The method that I will advocate is a modification and extension of that of Burge (1974); it takes into account some more recent discussion, especially Lycan (1984) and Soames (1986). In section 3 I advert to some questions of the role of model theory in semantics. My aim here is deflationary. I shall argue that an exposition of the semantics of an actual or possible human first language in model-theoretic terms is at best superfluous. By the time the model theory is supplemented with enough to deduce things that speakers actually know about their languages, the reference to models drops out; it could have been absent from the beginning. Finally, in a more critical vein, I will argue that model-theoretic methods are, at least as usually understood, too coarse for linguistic purposes, if those purposes include at least a partial explanation of the basis for the acquisition of language and the form in which knowledge of language is realised in the mature speaker.

1 Disquotation

The first data for the semantics of one's own language include the *disquotational* facts, exemplified in (1)–(3):

    (1) *Snow is white* is true$\longleftrightarrow$snow is white

    (2) *snow* refers to snow

    (3) *is white* is true of $x\longleftrightarrow x$ is white

Strictly speaking, (2) and (3) are more 'theory-laden' than (1): that the notion *refers* applies to *snow*, and *true of* to *is white* are facts established by surveying the roles of these expressions in sentences generally. However, I believe that these facts, and many others like them, are thoroughly established, and therefore deserve to be taken as among the facts to be deduced from an adequate semantics for English.

In a context-dependent language, there are limits to what disquotation can do. As Davidson has remarked, we can assert disquotational statements in any *given* context, as in (4):

(4)   *She is lazy* is true⟷she is lazy

But these facts will not reveal how truth conditions vary systematically from context to context.

Our basic question will then be, what modifications in the disquotational scheme will yield statements that are both acceptable as data and sufficiently detailed to reveal the range of knowledge of native speakers about their languages? Before proceeding to this question, I will consider the sense in which the disquotational data *are* revealing, and some further issues about what goes into linguistic knowledge.

A person who knows a language knows, as one says, the truth conditions of its sentences. The substantive in the notion of knowledge of truth conditions is knowledge, not truth conditions. Truth conditions need not be viewed as things that sentences of a language HAVE, or possible states of affairs that they answer to; rather, I will interpret the statement 'the truth condition of S in L is that p' as, 'speakers of L come to know, by knowing the semantic principles that govern L, that S is true just in case p'. From this point of view, disquotational statements of truth conditions are significant for their combination of depth and obviousness: the whole lot of them are among the things one knows when one knows a language, and they remain a touchstone of adequacy even while theory is elaborated.

It should not, in my opinion, be supposed that everything that is to be explained of knowledge of language is a simple disquotational fact. In particular, there are many cases where we ought to delve into the meanings of words (and therefore go beyond the disquotational data about them), in order to understand the hypotheses about their meaning that people form and use in sentences containing them. For instance, it seems to me that we should analyse the word *missing* as it occurs in one interpretation of (5), an example due to Irene Heim.

(5)   The spare tyre is missing from this car

The sentence is ambiguous, since it may be understood as true even where there is no thing x such that x is missing. To understand the ambiguity, we should consider more closely what *missing* means.

The fact is, that *missing* involves *failing to have what one ought to have*, and is so understood in (5). For an F to be missing from x, then, can be for x not to have an F, when it ought to have an F. If we then understand the subject NP as object of *have*, but within the scope of the negation shown in the explanation of *missing*, then the ambiguity comes out just as expected.

Note that the issue is not just one of finding some notation that allows (5) to be ambiguous, but rather of probing the reasons why it should appear with a verb like *missing*. As several authors have noted, a survey reveals that some notion of possession, or of having, and often a normative component, is involved in verbs admitting ambiguities of this kind – thus *lack*, *need*, as well as the notorious *seek*, *look for*, *hunt*, and others. Such a phenomenon can hardly be an accident, and is not to be bypassed in favour of a purely technical solution, of the sort that was advocated by Montague, at least in his later writings.[2]

At just this dialectical point, a cloud appears on the horizon. In saying that missing something involves failure to have that thing, or, as I would also say, that for a thing *x* to need something involves reference to a normal or flourishing state appropriate to *x*, to which *x* can be restored only if it gets that thing, have not certain connections between words effectively been classified as analytic, at least in the familiar linguistic interpretation of that term? If entered into the lexicon, as it apparently must be if (5) is to turn out, as it should, to be ambiguous, our interpretation of *missing* will lead to our being able to prove *if x is missing y, then x doesn't have y* within semantic theory alone. If so, then what limits are there on lexical entries? And wherever the limits are set, what justifies them?

It is my impression that some investigators have responded to our question by simply abstaining from saying anything about the meanings of words (or, alternatively, by setting down any number of 'semantic postulates'). Others, to be sure, have embraced that analytic–synthetic distinction with eyes open. The view that I should like to advance is an attempt to pull the string from the issue, by considering more closely what motives of inquiry are behind the elaboration of lexical entries, such as that for *missing*. First, I will consider the question in a more general setting, that of the disquotational facts of semantics itself.

Let the true statements

s is true$\longleftrightarrow p$

whether disquotational or not, be called *equivalences*. In semantics one aims at an explicit theory such that the equivalences known explicitly or tacitly to native speakers are consequences of that theory. Evidently, the equivalences that people come to know far outstrip those that a theory of knowledge of language aims to deduce. Furthermore, any theory that proves all of the equivalences that people *do* know will also prove many that they *don't* know, including some that they are disposed to deny. To some extent, the disparity between what is proved and what is known disappears under natural idealisation. But not all of it will go away; and there will be, in any articulated account, some distinction between knowledge that flows from linguistic principles alone and knowledge whose deduction requires other information. Where do we draw the line?

I am sceptical that there is any line that needs drawing. As Chomsky especially has emphasised, language is a relatively tractable object of study to the degree that it involves an independent system of principles, principles that take root in each learner on the basis of divergent and scattered exposure to the community. What belongs to language, then, will be what belongs to this system of principles. We need not, and in fact cannot, draw the boundaries of the system in advance of inquiry. In semantics, we should distinguish between those systematic phenomena that belong to what we might call the design features of the language from those that have no interaction with the linguistic system. The phenomenon of the verb *missing*, as I have remarked, is only one example of a lexicalisation that is understood with reference to having or not having a thing. Hence, we have good reason to assign the properties of this verb to the faculty under study; and the question of analyticity does not even arise.

The distinction between what is linguistically systematic and what is unsystematic, or can be filled in any old way, far from coinciding with the analytic–synthetic distinction, actually cuts across it. For instance, there is no reason I am aware of to include old chestnuts like *vixens are foxes* among the things that semantic theory ought to deduce, this allegedly analytic sentence having no role to play in the design of language. On the other hand, some sentences that are at the very least strong candidates for syntheticity, say *foxes aren't people in disguise* do have a role to play in the linguistic system, as is shown by any speaker's reaction to an NP like *the fox whom I met*. Briefly: it is not whether something is analytic or synthetic, but where and how it gets used that counts.

To summarise this section, I have suggested that disquotation is a vital source of data both for sentences and for some of their parts; but I have also urged that we should not balk at making our theories responsive to facts that are not disquotationally apparent, whenever these facts bear on the overall design of language considered as a systematic faculty, the principles of whose organisation we aim to uncover. With this much preliminary, I turn to some questions of the limits of disquotation.

2   Normal forms

A major issue in adapting disquotational facts to the study of natural languages is that of preserving both the richness and the obviousness of such facts, while accommodating contextual relativity. Richness and obviousness are aims that pull in opposite directions. At one extreme lies a method that would attempt to build all possible contextual parameters, together with the variety of contributions that they might make, into the specification of contexts C. This method, which would preserve richness at the cost of obviousness, is scouted and rejected in Lycan (1984), and has been despaired of by others. Lycan himself sketches a method that goes the other way, toward obviousness at the cost of richness: let the relevant referents and extensions of parts X of an expression be represented in any context by parts $C(X)$, which have whatever reference or extension they may have, and then run a compositional semantics off the $C(X)$. This method abstracts altogether from the contents of lexical items, and in any case cannot be expounded generally until the logical grammar is fixed.

Although I have no universal balm to offer, it seems to me that in many cases we can do better than adopt either of the suggested extremes. My starting point will be the discussion of definite descriptions and nominal demonstratives in Burge (1974). Consider a personal pronoun used demonstratively, as in (6):

(6)   She is lazy

If everything goes right, then the speaker of (6) will have referred to a thing x by using the pronoun, and the utterance will be true if x is lazy, false otherwise. Simplifying a bit, and only in ways not essential to the present discussion, the semantics for (6) comes out as in (7):

(7)   If x is referred to by *she* in the course of an utterance of (6), then that utterance is true just in case lazy(x)

The statement (7) is an instance of a general scheme for giving the truth conditions of context-dependent utterances, a scheme that may be displayed as in (8):

(8)   If u is an utterance of S such that $A(x, y, z, \ldots)$, then u is true just in case $B(x, y, z, \ldots)$

The view suggested in Burge is that (8) is the normal form for linguistic data about the truth conditions of whole sentences. If so, then truth values are to be thought of as predicated absolutely of utterances, and the contextual features on which interpretation may depend are to be enumerated in the antecedent of a conditional, one side of whose biconditional consequent registers their effects on the sentence as uttered. It might be hoped that such a method will present the semantic data in a way that makes them obviously correct, and is productive of consequences; clearly the method does well for (6), as shown in (7).

Personal pronouns, proper names, demonstratives, and definite descriptions are a rich analytical laboratory for Burge's idea, and occupy a major part of his article. As I said, I will focus here chiefly on incomplete definite descriptions. Before proceeding, however, I will offer a distinction and a (minor) correction, both of which seem to me to underscore the versatility of Burge's type of account.

First, the distinction. At least since Kaplan (1977) notice has been taken of the difference between *indexicals*, such as I, and *demonstratives*, such as *this*. Intuitively, Burge's notion of what the speaker is referring to (the object of the speaker's 'act of reference', in the terminology of his article) is ill-suited to the first-person pronoun. There is nothing I have to DO to refer to myself with I (nor can I refer otherwise), any more than there is anything I have to do to refer to snow with *snow*. Context-dependent though it is, the reference of the first-person pronoun is fixed by its form, whereas the reference of a neutral demonstrative is not.

Acts of reference in the sense of Burge mark the fact that indexicals and demonstratives alike have no reference apart from contexts in which they are actually used. But no act apart from use is required to give an indexical a reference. Distinctions along the indexical–demonstrative axis begin to show more clearly when we reflect that most context-dependent items are neither purely indexical nor purely demonstrative, but show features of both. The second-person pronoun MAY refer to anything the speaker chooses to address, but MUST refer to some such thing. So much belongs to its linguistic meaning.

We can, and should, make a broad distinction between those features of an expression that constrain its reference, what we might call the *linguistic component* of that expression, from what the expression leaves open for the speaker's exploitation. Indexicals occupy one extreme, in that nothing at all is left open; demonstratives occupy the other, the only constraint on a word like *this* being that the speaker refer with it to something or another.

For the normal forms of the data for semantic theory, the effect of the distinction just drawn is to separate into two parts the conditions in the antecedent, whose consequence is the statement of truth conditions. For the case of (6), the normal form becomes (9), a refinement of (7):

> (9)   If x is referred to by *she* in the course of an utterance of (6), and x is female, then that utterance is true just in case lazy(x)

To refer to a male as *she* is to have misspoken, even if we might charitably regard 'what was said' as true if whoever was referred to is lazy.

The distinction just drawn will be put to further use when we come to consider incomplete definite descriptions. In the meantime, it may be worth observing that it allows a pronoun like *she* to be used demonstratively, without assigning the conditions on its reference to 'pragmatics'; in this way, I think, we can answer the worry expressed in Lycan (1984), chapter 3.

I have elaborated a distinction within Burge's way of looking at context-dependent constructions. Using this distinction, it is possible to make a small but not insignificant correction to his view about proper names. Burge starts with the idea that proper names are fundamentally general terms, that is, nouns, not NPs. He observes that they may, unlike pronouns, be put in construction with determiners (*a Mary*, *that Mary*), and that they may be modified (*the Mary I met last year*). Further confirmation of this point of view comes from the fact that proper names of people can undergo noun-incorporation. NPs can never be incorporated: so we have *I'm going tree-chopping*, but not **I'm going that tree chopping*, or **I was it-chopping*. But proper names can be incorporated, even when it is widely known that they refer to just one thing: we have *Stalin-hater*, *Reagen-baiting*, and many other such forms.

The above observations lead to the proposal that utterances of *Mary* unaccompanied by any overt determiner are in effect utterances of *that Mary*, where the nominal is silently converted into a singular term. But this proposal is wrong. Different truth conditions are to be assigned to (10) and (11):

(10)   That Mary had fish for lunch

(11)   Mary had fish for lunch

On seeing a woman emerge from the seafood restaurant, and taking her for my friend Mary, I might volunteer either (10) or (11). Suppose that the woman is *a* Mary, but not my friend Mary. Then (10) is true if the woman had fish for lunch, but (11) is not verified thereby.

Other observations support the distinction just made. Examples (12) and (13) differ in that in (12), but not in (13), the adjective can be understood restrictively or appositively:

(12)   that unhappy Mary

(13)   unhappy Mary

We should conclude that proper names of people, when they occur without determiners, become singular terms in a way that has yet to be brought out. After considering incomplete descriptions, I will revert to the question just posed.

Consider an incomplete definite description in a context where the speaker refers to something by means of it, as in one use of (14):

(14)   The dog wants out

The linguistic component of the description includes the content of the nominal head; the thing to which the speaker refers should be a dog. It also includes *singular number* (conversely, it includes multiple reference in case the description is plural). Finally, the contribution of the definite article is seen in the requirement, noted in traditional grammar, that the referent be obvious or familiar (for a sophisticated development of this point of view, see Heim (1982)). Fully labelled, the normal form for (14) is as in (15):

(15)   If x is referred to by *the dog* in the course of an utterance of (14), and (i) the speaker does not refer to any $y \neq x$ with that phrase; (ii) x is a dog; (iii) x is obvious or familiar, then that utterance is true just in case wants out(x)

Thus the linguistic component even of so simple a phrase as *the dog* contains several independent features.

Of course, there should be no pretence that our order of understanding an utterance is parallel to the order suggested by the conditional in its normal form. In interpreting an utterance of (14), for instance, we do not have to first see what the speaker is talking about, then see whether it satisfies the linguistic component of the referential phrase, then determine the truth conditions of what is said, and then judge whether it is true. On the contrary, it is obvious that we often work in very different orders. Sometimes, assuming that what was said *is* true, we determine the conditions that must be satisfied for it to be true, and then cast about for objects reference to which would fulfill those conditions. Numerous other orders, and interleavings of reasoning about context and assertion, are commonplace. We infer backgrounds from truth conditions as much as we infer truth conditions from backgrounds, and the 'information' that we gather varies in consequence, to no great surprise.

Returning to the distinction observed between proper names used with and without determiners, we may conjecture that some further feature of the linguistic component of the name as used apart from a determiner, over and above those features that flow from the name as a common noun, are responsible for the different judgements in (10) and (11), or the properties of modification in (12) and (13). This feature must follow from the fact that the name, as used alone, is an NP; it would not do to posit a 'hidden' determiner in (11), since that would fail to capture the absence of restrictive modification in (13). Moreover, the feature does not stem from restrictions on the context in which utterances using a proper name are to be evaluated, say with those in which there is a unique Mary around; evidently, one can say things like *Mary is talking to Mary*, referring to two different Marys.[3]

Suppose that (11) fails to be true because, although the person to whom I referred with the name *Mary* is a Mary, she is not the Mary that I thought she was. The antecedent of the normal form for the semantic data for (11) then includes a further condition, absent from the antecedent of the normal form for (10), whose non-satisfaction implies a failure for the truth conditions of (11) to be delivered through the biconditional consequent. In support of this further condition, it may be observed that where a speaker is in a position to apply a proper name, but has no prior opinion about the identity of the referent, the name is in order. For instance, if the person I saw emerging from the restaurant were wearing a conventioneer's name tag (presumed accurate) reading 'Hello, my name is Mary', (11) appears to be true, provided that she had fish for lunch. The use of names to refer to persons otherwise unknown to the user is common in the military, where prominent labels showing one's surname are worn as part of one's uniform. The condition governing the use of a proper name without a determiner is not a strong condition, requiring that the speaker know the referent, but a weak one, requiring that the speaker's opinion about the identity of the referent is not mistaken. The weak condition nevertheless serves to distinguish the proper name *Mary* from the description *that Mary*.

If the above or any similar suggestion is correct, then the antecedents of the normal forms for data for sentences containing proper names will make reference to the cognitive states of speakers. Links to these states are part of the meaning of the name; i.e., they are part of the conditions attaching, as a matter of linguistic form, to the name when used without a determiner.

Thus far, I have suggested that a distinction between the linguistic components of an expression and the aspects of its interpretation that are left open for the speaker, articulated within a modified form of Burge's account of context-dependence, gives us normal forms for the theory of reference and truth that are a rich source of data, and obvious enough that they can be taken AS data for a theory to work with. However, the context-dependent constructions that we have considered up to now have all been *referential* in character, in a sense that seems to me sufficiently close to Donnellan's original usage to justify the name I give them here; that is, the contribution of these constructions has been assumed to belong to the antecedent of the normal forms of the sentences in which they occur. Incomplete definite descriptions of an *attributive* character have been studied in Soames (1986), and I will conclude this section with a discussion of these. First, however, I will observe some consequences of the discussion to this point (some of which were pointed out in Davies (1982), including some data involved in Taylor (1980)).

Consider a description with a demonstrative, accompanied by ostension, as in (16):

(16)   John likes that book (pointing to a book)

Such a description may contain a pronoun whose antecedent lies outside it, as in (17):

(17)   *John* likes that book *he* read (pointing)

But the antecedent cannot be a quantifier, as in (18):

(18)   **Every man* likes that book *he* read (pointing)

Ambiguities between strict and non-strict identity are possible with incomplete definite descriptions, as in (19):

(19)   *John* likes the book *he* read, and so does Bill

where we may complete the second main clause as *Bill likes the book John read*, or as *Bill likes the book he, Bill, read*. The ambiguity disappears in the demonstrative case:

(20)   *John* likes that book *he* read (pointing), and so does Bill

In (20), the second clause can be completed only as *Bill likes the book John read*. This example is significant, since it shows that it is not because of some intrinsic semantic incoherence that (18) is impossible with the pronoun bound by the quantificational subject. Why shouldn't (20) be understood as (21) is?

(21)   *John* likes that book *he* read (pointing), and *Bill* likes that book *he* read (pointing to the same book)

We should conclude, with Davies, that the demonstrative description, if used ostensively, has its content outside the clause where it occurs; for the phenomena just considered follow *in toto* on this assumption, which Burge's account suggests naturally anyway. In particular, there is no prospect of a pronoun shifting its reference under VP-deletion in (20): the VP is in effect *likes x*, from which the pronoun has disappeared. This modest success still leaves us with the attributive definite descriptions, to which I now turn.[4]

I will understand the attributive use of a description to correspond to the case where the speaker does not (attempt to) refer to an object by means of it. The content of the description is then interior to the statement of the truth conditions of the utterance in which it occurs. One can therefore bind a pronoun contained in such a description to an expression of generality out-side it, as in (22):

(22)   *Everyone* likes the book *he* read

where the description remains incomplete, or empty, for the various choices of value for *he*. Incomplete though it be, the description inherits the purport of uniqueness from its definite article: if somebody (of the sort one is talking about) read two books (of the sort in question), then a person who asserts (22) will acknowledge, and is antecedently prepared to acknowledge, that he or she has misspoken.

In some cases, incomplete descriptions are elliptical for complete des-criptions that the speaker would be able to give on demand. For instance, a person who spoke of 'the square root of two' might grow testy if reminded that two has two square roots, for it should have been evident that one was speaking only of positive roots. But, as Soames carefully explains, ellipsis is surely not the answer in all cases. Often, there is just no saying what the speaker might have had in mind as a completion for the description. How, then, is it to be completed for the purpose of obtaining a reference?

Notice first that we need not address ourselves to the case where the description simply IS incomplete, at the point in the communicative transac-tion where it occurs. A case of such incompleteness is illustrated in (23), where the description evidently has an anaphoric function:

(23)   A man entered the room. The man was wearing a hat

No referent has yet been established here. Also, it is not part of our aim to explore all the cases where a referent is established without having been properly determined. We are assuming that the reference is completed, and asking how this is done: if it is not done at all, we just have sloppy (or sly) speech, with which we deal as best we can.

By narrowing the issue in the way suggested, I have perhaps made the answer obvious. What is required is that we express a restriction on the nominal head, *book he read* in the case of (19) or (22), such that in proper, non-anaphoric, and attributive use of the description the restriction has just one object in its extension, but leaves it open how it is intended or made manifest. This purpose will be served by second-order variables. As, following Burge, we introduced the notion of a speaker referring to a thing x by means of an NP, so we shall introduce the notion of a speaker *confining the range of* an N to things x such that X_x. For the notorious example (24), we obtain a datum as in (25):

(24)   The murderer (whoever he is) is insane

(25)   In any utterance of (24) in which the speaker confines the range of *murderer* to things x such that X_x, that utterance is true just in case insane$((\iota x)$ (murderer(x) and $X_x))$

Notice that the notion of range-confinement is necessary anyway, because in many utterances the domains over which expressions of generality range are proper parts of the ranges to which they are restricted by the nominal heads with which they appear. In such cases, as in (26):

(26)   Many arrows missed

we take the quantifier-word to be doing its work in conjunction with a restricted range within the extension of *arrows*. Similarly, I think, we should take the attributive incomplete description as a function of its parts, namely the definite article and a restriction on the range of the associated complex noun. The scheme (25) evidently takes in ellipsis as a special case; but the case is special, in that the speaker's confinement of the range of the noun might not be due to any decision the speaker has made, but due to the circumstances in which the speaker is placed.

Binding of pronouns is allowed within an incomplete attributive description; hence also, we obtain the possibility of non-strict identity in (19).[5] There are further applications of second-order variables to plural constructions, as shown in Boolos (1984). Finally, it seems to me that the notion of range-confinement should also be applied to tense and time-reference, yielding distinctions in this realm as well, within an overall account of the sort that Burge originally suggested.[6]

In this section, I have explored with reference to a few examples the idea that the normal forms for data in semantics are conditionals, whose consequents spell out the truth conditions of utterances of sentences with given structure, assuming that the antecedents are fulfilled. We have seen that the effects of linguistic form – the phenomena that constitute the subject-matter of semantics – are found in both antecedents and in consequents. For the vindication of semantic theory, it is not required that we expound common-sense linguistic communication, a project that seems swiftly to turn hopelessly anecdotal anyway; but the contributions of linguistic forms must be a theoretically tractable object of study, empirically testable with reference to what people are observed to do. I should like to believe that some version of what is here advocated promotes semantic theory in this sense, without leading into the morass of communicative context.

3   Models

Many researchers in semantics describe their methods as model-theoretic. Davidson (1973) contrasted model-theoretic with what he called 'absolute' semantics, and argued that the two concepts were appropriate to different enterprises. Criticisms of model-theoretic semantics has come more recently from LePore (1983). Model-theoretic approaches have been elaborated and defended in Gupta (1980) and Dowty, Peters & Wall (1982), among other work. A further survey of the literature, and several personal communications, have suggested to me that the relations between model-theoretic and absolute methods stand in some need of clarification, to which it is the purpose of this section to contribute.

For any conception of meaning that may be advanced, it is obviously a requirement on semantic theory according to that conception that appropriate facts about a language, known routinely to its native speakers, be derivable within the theory. Above, I have followed Davidson in assuming that all disquotational facts about truth and reference should be derivable; but I have also indicated where a more extensive conception of data seems to me appropriate. What are the data appropriate to the model-theoretic conception? From the literature, one may get the impression that model-theoretic methods are concerned above all, and perhaps exclusively, with quantification, truth-functions, validity, and other notions that figure in logical theory. This view seems to me arbitrary at best, and mistaken at worst, for reasons given below. At the same time, I think it would be incorrect to defend an absolute conception of semantics against a model-theoretic one: once the misleading impressions are corrected, we might well see conditions on truth in terms of conditions on models (although it is not clear to me that there are more than heuristic reasons for doing so). Finally, I will offer some reasons for thinking that model-theoretic semantics, at least as it is usually practised, is too coarse for many purposes of linguistic theory. But these last observations, if correct, have application to absolute semantics as well.

First, I will underscore a familiar point about semantic knowledge, emphasised especially by LePore. Consider a simple predicate of the grammar of a competent speaker of English, say the noun *apple*. Using *English* as a name of this person's grammar, we take up the disquotational fact, that for this person the word *apple* refers to apples, as shown in (27):

(27) true of(English, *apple*, x)$\longleftrightarrow$apple(x)

In model-theoretic semantics, one typically does not produce theories that will have statements like (27) among their consequences. But there are model-theoretic counterparts to such statements. Using *English syntax* as a name for the syntactic part of our speaker's grammar, I believe that (28) is a satisfactory rendering of what the model-theorist would have in mind as such a counterpart (or see Dowty *et al.* (1982)):

(28) *apple* is an N, true of a thing x in the universe (of individuals) of a model M for English syntax just in case the subset M_{apple} of individuals that M assigns to *apple* includes x

The statement (28) is not insubstantial, since it requires that the interpretation of *apple* be a subset of the domain of M. But (28) obviously does not come to the same thing as (27); for example, given some knowledge of English syntax and model theory, a monolingual speaker of Chinese who knew about *apple* only that it was an ordinary English noun would know (28), but not (27), whereas you and I know (27).

It follows that model-theoretic semantics, if restricted as it usually is, cannot prove simple facts available to native speakers. At this point, one often hears it suggested that (28) can be extended to a variant of (27) by designating some particular, perhaps 'intended', model M^* as the value of the variable M. Take English to be the ordered pair (English syntax, M^*), thus bringing the notion *true of* as it occurs in (28) into line with that of (27). Now, M_{apple} also depends on M, and so the result of instantiating M to M^* will be (29), the left-hand side of which, by our stipulation about English, abbreviates (30):

(29)   true of(English, *apple*, x)$\longleftrightarrow x \varepsilon M^*_{apple}$

(30)   true of((English syntax, M^*), *apple*, x)

Obviously, nothing has been gained: M^*_{apple} could be anything. To complete the picture, we need to say what the 'intended model' *does* assign to *apple*, as in (31):

(31) $x \varepsilon M^*_{apple} \longleftrightarrow$ apple(x)

where x ranges over whatever the domain of M^* is.

But then the whole route through models has been the merest diversion. We might as well have stated (27), and let it go at that. The path through the 'intended' M^* is also misleading: what has been stipulated in (31) is just (32):

(32)   For any admissible model M for English syntax, true of((English
         syntax, M), *apple*, x)$\longleftrightarrow x$ is in the domain of M, and apple(x)

Anyway, what one refers to by *apple* is obviously prior to whatever model one may 'intend'.

I have laboured over a simple example, considering the difference between a model-theoretic and an absolute semantics for an ordinary English substantive. I have therefore dealt with the lexical, as opposed to the structural, side of semantics. But this feature of the example was completely inessential.

To see this, first look again at (28). This statement is a partial determination of the role of the word *apple* in English (it says that word is a predicate of individuals), and by the same token a partial determination of the notion *model for English syntax* (it says that only those models are admissible that make the word *apple* a predicate). The latter notion, initially empty, grows in significance as the theory is filled out. One gets from this notion just what has been put into it. If model-theoretic semantics seems to say more about structures than about words, that is because more substantive conceptions have been put into the former, and withheld from the latter.

Consider now an absolute statement within the realm of structural, or combinatorial, semantics, as in (33):

(33)   An English S=NP–VP is true in English if and only if the
         reference of NP in English is a thing x such that VP is true in
         English of x

(here and below, disregarding pleonastic subjects). What is its model-theoretic counterpart? Assuming that the theorist recognises elementary sentences like *John left* as instances of the structure NP–VP, it may be as in (34):

(34)   If S=NP–VP, then for any model M for English syntax, S is true
         in M if and only if M_{NP}, an object in the domain of M, is an
         element of the set M_{VP} of objects in M that M assigns to the VP
         of S

Following the abbreviations used above, (34) may be simplified to (35)

(35)   true(English, S=NP–VP)$\longleftrightarrow M^*{}_{\text{NP}}\varepsilon M^*{}_{\text{VP}}$

where M^* is the proper model for English syntax, and English=(English syntax, M^*).

Certainly, (35) is informative: it tells us, just as (33) does, that syntactic combinations NP–VP express predication. However, what tells us this is the ε of (35), or *is an element of* of (34). That *this* substantive notion should be admitted is all to the good: we get more information with it than without it. But the same is true of the substantive notion *apple*(x). True, the predicate ε has to do with sets, and the predicate *apple* with fruits; but from the point of view of characterizing what people know about their languages, this difference hardly warrants a distinction of semantic principle.

The point just observed may be recast in another form. Suppose we assume that the structures of human languages are over a broad range *narrowly compositional*; that is, that the interpretation of constituents $A=B–C$ is a function of the interpretations of B and C. Assuming only compositionality, one would be entitled in a model-theoretic framework to write not (35), but only (36):

(36)   true(English, S=NP–VP)$\longleftrightarrow M^*{}_{\text{NP-VP}}(M^*{}_{\text{NP}}, M^*{}_{\text{VP}})$

where $M^*{}_{\text{NP-VP}}$ is some function or other. It is the further determination of this function as (the characteristic function of) ε that gives us what speakers actually know about this mode of syntactic combination.

We can easily conceive of languages whose combinatorial semantics was sensitive to empirical matters, for instance languages in which NP–VP expressed predication if NP referred to apples, but not otherwise (in fact, English is itself such a language, if views of adjectival modification of the sort suggested in Higginbotham (1985) are on the right track). Conversely, while many lexical items have straightforward empirical content, others, such as the logical constants, are abstract, and in fact are standardly explicated in model-theoretic semantics. We should dismiss the idea that model theory is intrinsically involved in the structural, and absolute semantics in the lexical, aspects of language.

I have argued, then, that (36) is to (35) as (31) is to (29); in other words, that the specification of the meaning of particular modes of syntactic combination completes our understanding of such modes in just the way that the specification of the meaning of a word completes our understanding of that word.

Now let the word whose meaning we wish to give belong to logic. I think that it has often been supposed that semantic theory illuminates the meanings of the logical words in a way that it does not illuminate the meanings of ordinary empirical predicates. Let our logical word be *every*, where competent speakers of English know such things as (37):

(37)   A sentence S=$_{\text{NP}}$(every) N)–VP of English is true if and only if everything x such that N is true of x is a thing x such that VP is true of x.

For a model-theoretic counterpart to (37), we might, taking into account the category to which quantifiers answer, assume (38):

(38)   For any admissible model M for English syntax, a sentence $S = (_{NP}(\text{every}) \text{ N})\text{–VP}$ is true in M if and only if $M_{every}(M_N)$ $(M_{VP}) = \text{truth}$

However, (38) as conspicuously fails to reveal what speakers of English know about *every* as (28) fails to reveal what they know about *apple*. What is wanted is an indication, cast in terms of admissible models, of what *every* in fact means. Such an indication might be given by (39):

(39)   For any admissible model M for English syntax, M_{every} is that function F such that, for every ordered pair (X,Y) of subsets of the domain of M, $F(X,Y) = \text{truth}$ if and only if everything in X is in Y

There are, to be sure, alternative ways of specifying F; but some such way must be adopted if we are to progress from the statement that *every* is an expression of generality to the statement of which expression of generality it is.[7]

Why, then, is model-theoretic semantics for natural language thought to be so intimately tied to logic, and to structural meaning? Evidently, the meaning of anything, in so far as it can be specified at all, can be specified in terms of conditions on models. By allowing oneself precisely the vocabulary of logic and mathematics, one can put limits on what can be said in one's semantic theory; but one can also impose limits in any number of other ways.

In fact, our last example does seem to reveal a definite role for abstract model-theoretic semantics (that is, for model-theoretic semantics limited to a certain vocabulary). This honourable role, which is exploited for logical vocabulary beyond the usual in the field of abstract model theory, is that of a special department of lexicography concerned with the meanings of those expressions that remain invariant under various morphisms and permutations of the domain of discourse. Such expressions constitute a small, but vital, part of language. That, however, cannot be a reason for abstaining from the rest. There seems to me nothing in the model-theoretic conception that would justify segregating the lexicon of English in this way.

It seems to me that a persistent source of misunderstanding on the points made above may be a tendency to think of *models* interchangeably with *possible interpretations*, and, compounding matters, to think of both of these as possible worlds. A *model* is a model for a syntax. It is not a 'possible interpretation' of *English* if that means 'the language we speak'; for that language is not just a syntax, and has whatever interpretation it, in fact, has. Furthermore if our language, or aspects of it, are to be understood in the terms of possible-worlds semantics, then the possible worlds and the things in them are elements of some *given* interpretation, and by no means alternative interpretations of what we say.

For an example where things seem to get muddled, perhaps in the way

I have suggested, I consider some remarks from Dowty *et al.* (1982). They allow nonlogical expressions to vary across models, and take all of the ordinary logical constants as invariable, remarking that 'these words are usually said to have a fixed interpretation' (p. 11). On the same page, they continue:

That invariance is, after all, what we would expect of the constants of a particular logic: we can easily imagine different situations in which the set of snorers varies, but it is difficult to imagine a situation in which *and* means something other than what it does in our world.

On literal reading, the discussion is not coherent. It makes no sense to ask which words *of a person's language* have a 'fixed interpretation': for they all do; and the question whether *and* is a logical constant has nothing to do with whether it could 'mean something other than what it does in our world' (which, of course, it could). Finally, even if the snorers should remain invariant by God's decree across counterfactual situations, that would not elevate *snorers* to the status of a logical constant, for it does not respect permutations of the universe of discourse.

In harping as I have on the above passage, my purpose is not to decry a lapse in an elementary and very effective textbook. My point, rather, is that deep involvement with one set of issues has led to a spurious, and invidious, distinction between the contributions of lexical and structural semantics or between logical and empirical notions, to the theory of meaning.

Semantic theory contains statements like (27), (33), and (37), or their model-theoretic counterparts, now understood as including sufficient information to be recognisably as informative as they. These statements are supported by what they imply about whole sentences, and ultimately by what is observed about normal persons and their environments. I have supposed that these statements are advanced not only as true, but also as tacitly known to native speakers, and as underlying other tacit and explicit knowledge that they possess. It therefore follows that these statements need not be theoretically equivalent to other statements that coincide with them extensionally, or even are provably coextensive with them. Native speakers of English, apart from the pathological or the deprived, know that *apple* is true of x if and only if x is an apple. Only a few of them know that *apple* is true of x if and only if x is an apple and Pisa is near Florence; and if in general they know that *apple* is true of x if and only if x is an apple and $7+5=12$, that is because they know independently that $7+5=12$. Within any semantic theory, statements of reference and truth conditions will be finely discriminated.[8]

Given the interpretation that I assume, model-theoretic semantics is too coarse for linguistic purposes. The methods of model theory home in on English or other languages by placing progressively more restrictive conditions on the class of their admissible models. But a person can learn more about the meaning of a word or a construction without this knowledge being reflected in the admissible models; at least this will be so if the ignorant speaker uses a word with the same intension as the more knowledgeable, as Hilary Putnam and others have argued. It seems that a less than fully competent speaker, or a speaker less than fully competent in some respect (as we in fact all are), not only uses words with the same intension as the more competent, but also knows that this is so, and intends it to be so. If that is right, then there are aspects of knowledge of meaning that are more fine-grained than what can be expressed in terms of the progressive acquisition of a proper or admissible model.

The point may be emphasised by taking a certain analogy with syntax. A syntax determines, for each category, what expressions belong to it. For the purposes of some abstract investigations, a syntax, or uninterpreted language, can be regarded as a sequence of sets of expressions, each position corresponding to a category. But for linguistic theory, which is concerned with how syntactic systems are apprehended and acquired, the means of specification of categorial membership is the essence of the subject. As these means of specification, the rules of syntax, are more finely discriminated than their outputs, so the principles of semantics are more finely discriminated than the classes of models that they determine.[9]

Let model-theoretic semantics then be redescribed as the theory, not of admissible models, but of the conditions on them, known to native speakers. With this emendation, the model-theoretic framework can distinguish among different accounts of linguistic knowledge that yield the same classes of admissible models.

The question comes to mind whether the model-theorist is not attributing, contrary to fact, tacit knowledge of set theory; but I doubt that this observation carries much force as an objection, if only because the vocabulary of any significant part of linguistics is theoretical anyway.

I have argued that model-theoretic semantics, except when understood as a format for investigating certain parts of the lexicon, is at best a circumlocution. But then, if due qualifications are made, is it not at worst harmless? If it WILL be insisted that interpretations be specified in terms of conditions on models, we should be able to eliminate the reference, provided that those conditions have been specified sufficiently to display what speakers know. *Pace* confusions such as that between models and possible worlds, there need be no radical distinction between absolute and model-theoretic methods. On the other hand, the latter methods must break out of the mathematical vocabulary if they are to express what we in fact know about meaning.

NOTES

1 For discussion and encouragement, I am particularly indebted to Akeel Bilgrami, George Boolos, Richard Larson, and Scott Weinstein.

2 Montague might be understood as an extreme disquotationalist, inasmuch as he proposed that semantic rules should not distinguish among the members of a syntactic category.

3 For extended discussion of this point, see Soames (1986).

4 Examples of the sort discussed here are considered in Taylor (1980). He cites (i) as a reason for keeping the content of the description inside its clause:

(i)   someone loathes *that* denigrator of his

I regard (i) as ungrammatical (with *his* bound to *someone*). An appearance to the contrary may come from failing to distinguish the case where the indefinite is used to make a reference to a thing from the case where it is purely quantificational; in the first case, *someone* behaves like *John*, so that the counterexample is only apparent.

5 See Reinhart (1982) for the comparison of non-strict identity with quantificational contexts.

6 For the past tense in particular, Burge shows that simple quantification over past times is almost never appropriate. However, Burge's proposal that the speaker *refers* to a past time or interval seems too strict, in that it misses the fact that past-tense assertions are existentially general. Thus I would prefer to say that in using the past tense speakers confine the range of the temporal variable to times t such that T_t, and within such confinement assert that there are t such that $A(t)$, where A is the rest of the statement. In general, the point of range-confinement is to allow relativity to other things than individual objects of reference.

7 As Harman (1986) has noted, different specifications may differ in what they attribute to speakers, even if elementary logic proves them equivalent in their assignments of truth values. See below for some discussion of a related point.

8 Consistently with fine discriminations within a theory, there remains the possibility of alternative whole theories of persons and their languages. If these exist, then we should regard the reality to which semantic theory corresponds as whatever is invariant among such theories. (I am indebted here to unpublished work by Akeel Bilgrami; he, however, is not responsible for the use that I make of it.)

9 For discussion of related points, see the early and late sections of Chomsky (1986). I am indebted to Tyler Burge for comments on an earlier draft of this article.

REFERENCES

Boolos, G. 1984. To be is to be a value of a variable (or to be some values of some variables). *The Journal of Philosophy* 81: 430–49.

Burge, T. 1974. Demonstrative constructions, reference, and truth. *The Journal of Philosophy* 71: 205–23.

Chomsky, N. 1986. *Knowledge of language: its nature, origin and use.* New York: Praeger.

Davidson, D. 1973. In defense of convention T. In D. Davidson *Inquiries into truth and interpretation.* Oxford: Oxford University Press, 1984.

Davies, M. 1982. Individuation and the semantics of demonstratives. *Journal of Philosophical Logic* 11: 287–310.

Dowty, R., Peters, S. & Wall, R. 1982. *Introduction to Montague semantics.* Dordrecht: Reidel.

Gupta, A. 1980. *The logic of common nouns.* New Haven: Yale University Press.

Harman, G. 1986. The meanings of logical constants. In E. LePore (ed.) *Truth and interpretation: perspectives on the philosophy of Donald Davidson.* Oxford: Blackwell.

Heim, I. 1982. The semantics of definite and indefinite noun phrases. Ph.D thesis, University of Massachusetts, Amherst.

Higginbotham, J. 1985. On semantics. *Linguistic Inquiry* 16: 547–93.

Kaplan, D. 1977. Demonstratives. Ms., UCLA.

LePore, E. 1983. What model-theoretic semantics cannot do. *Synthese* 54: 167–87.

Lycan, W. 1984. *Logical form in natural language*. Cambridge, Mass.: Bradford Books/ MIT Press.

Montague, R. 1974. *Formal philosophy*, ed. R. Thomason. New Haven: Yale University Press.

Reinhart, T. 1982. *Anaphora and semantic interpretation*. London: Croom Helm.

Soames, S. 1986. Incomplete descriptions. *Notre Dame Journal of Formal Logic* 27: 349–75.

Taylor, B. 1980. Truth-theory for indexical languages. In M. Platts (ed.), *Reference, truth, and reality*. London: Routledge and Kegan Paul.

2

Facts in situation theory: representation, psychology, or reality?[1]

ROBIN COOPER

0 Introduction

The first part of this chapter will sketch a treatment of the interaction of negation, conjunction and disjunction in Situation Semantics that will involve the use of fact algebras. The second part will discuss whether the objects used in the analysis are to be thought of as part of a logical representation or as mental objects or as objects of non-psychological reality.

1 Negation, conjunction, and disjunction

Barwise & Perry (1983) mention that sentence negation, as opposed to VP negation, is a problem for Situation Semantics as they describe it in their book. (1) contains some well-known kinds of examples from English which can be used to argue that sentence negation is necessary for an adequate semantic analysis of natural languages.

(1) a. Not every student passed the test
    b. A child hasn't been born in this town for two years
    c. It's not true that Reagan will be re-elected and that the US will have a coherent foreign policy

In the normal predicate calculus type representation of each of these sentences the negation would have scope over the whole sentence. The *not* in (1a) must have scope over the universal quantifier. In (1b) the only sensible reading is where *not* has scope over the existential. It is not normal to interpret this sentence as meaning that there is some child who has not been born in the town, whereas there may have been several others who were successful in this enterprise. Finally, in (1c) the *not* has scope over a conjoined sentence.

However, one could argue in each of these cases that, while the scope relations are as we have suggested, this does not support the claim that there is syntactic sentence negation in English. Rather English uses negation of constituents other than sentences to achieve the effect of what would be sentence negation in a predicate calculus-like representation. In (1a) one could claim that *Not every student* is the negation of a generalised quantifier (cf. Barwise & Cooper 1981 and Keenan & Stavi 1986). To account for the scope relationship in (1b) while still maintaining that VP negation is involved, one could claim with Montague in 'Universal grammar' (in Montague 1974) that VPs are predicates which apply to a generalised quantifier in subject position. (See Bach 1980 for a discussion of this.) What we have in (1c) is, of course, a standard trick for representing the kind of sentence negation that you can get in logic in a natural language by embedding the conjoined sentence in a VP and then negating the VP.

Given that the syntax of these examples suggests that English uses negation over constituents other than sentences to achieve the effect of sentence negation, one might think that Barwise & Perry were on to a good thing. One might say that a theory which has trouble with sentence negation might be precisely the right one for natural language. I will concentrate on examples of conjunction like (1c) and show why it is that we need something like sentence negation in order to account for examples like (1c), even if they do not involve sentence negation syntactically.

Developments since Barwise & Perry (1983) have lead to the project of creating a general theory of situations which we could use in place of set theory to formalise grammar. Situation theory as currently conceived (see, for example, Barwise & Peters, forthcoming) introduces an algebra of facts which provides the tools for accounting for this kind of wide scope negation. I will discuss one version of this here which deviates in some ways from the way the algebra is defined in other places.

Rather than talking of declarative sentences as being true or false in possible worlds, Situation Semantics talks of them as describing situations. Situations are thought of as situation-theoretic objects which among other things (e.g. like being embarrassing) support certain facts. We use the notation

$$s \models \sigma$$

to say that the situation s supports the fact σ.

Facts[2] are also situation-theoretic objects. Examples of facts are represented in (2).

(2) a. $\langle\!\langle \ell, \text{see}, \text{John}, \text{Mary}; 1 \rangle\!\rangle$

b. $\langle\!\langle \ell, \text{see}, \text{John}, \text{Mary}; 0 \rangle\!\rangle$

Such facts have a location, ℓ (a chunk of space-time which represents where and when the fact holds), a relation of a certain number of places (e.g. the two-place relation *see* – relations are basic unanalysed objects in situation theory), an appropriate number of individuals which are the arguments to the relation and finally a polarity value which indicates whether the fact is positive or negative. We talk of sentences describing a situation when a certain fact is supported by the situation. Thus the semantic rules will be designed in such a way that the statements in (3) are true.

(3) a.   *John saw Mary* describes situation s

iff $s \models \langle\!\langle \ell, \text{see}, \text{John}, \text{Mary}; 1 \rangle\!\rangle$

(where ℓ is a location temporally prior to the location of discourse)

   b.   *John didn't see Mary* describes situation s
        iff $s \models \langle\!\langle \ell, \text{see}, \text{John}, \text{Mary}; 0 \rangle\!\rangle$
        (where ℓ is a location temporally prior to the location of discourse)[3]

In the examples that I discuss in the rest of the paper locations will be irrelevant so I will leave them out and make the simplifying assumption that we can make statements as in $(3')$.

$(3')$ a.   *John saw Mary* describes situation s
        iff $s \models \langle\!\langle \text{see}, \text{John}, \text{Mary}; 1 \rangle\!\rangle$

   b.   *John didn't see Mary* describes situation s
        iff $s \models \langle\!\langle \text{see}, \text{John}, \text{Mary}; 0 \rangle\!\rangle$

Here is one simple proposal for the interpretation of sentence conjunction and disjunction in these terms. It is a simple adaptation of the rules for interpreting these connectives in propositional logic which was suggested in Barwise & Perry (1983).

(4) a.   A sentence S_1 and S_2 describes situation s iff S_1 describes s and S_2 describes s

   b.   A sentence S_1 or S_2 describes situation s iff S_1 describes s or S_2 describes s

(4a) will mean that the sentence *John saw Mary and Mary saw John* will describe a situation which supports both of the facts in (5).

(5) a. $\langle\!\langle \text{see}, \text{John}, \text{Mary}; 1 \rangle\!\rangle$

   b. $\langle\!\langle \text{see}, \text{Mary}, \text{John}; 1 \rangle\!\rangle$

(4b) will mean that the sentence *John saw Mary and Mary saw John* will describe a situation that supports at least one of the facts in (5). So far, so good. Now let us move on towards our negative sentence (1c). It seems a reasonable assumption to say that our semantics should be designed in such a way that (6) holds true.

(6) *It is true that S* describes situation s iff S describes s

Now what should we do with the negation of such sentences? A possibility that offers itself is that represented in (7).

(7) *It is not true that S describes situation s* iff S does not describe s

This is a possibility for encoding semantic sentence negation which is independent of whether the negation is represented syntactically as sentence negation or VP negation. It is a possibility that Barwise & Perry do not pursue since they realise that it has problems.

Notice first that it is a very different kind of negation to that sketched for simple sentences. The sentence *John didn't see Mary* required that a specific negative fact be supported by the described situation. This would mean that the situation would be inconsistent with John seeing Mary (at the same location). If you tried to add the corresponding positive fact to the situation you would have an inconsistent situation. (An inconsistent situation is one which supports two facts which are the same except that their polarity values are different. Inconsistent situations are not to be found in the real world.)

The kind of negation we have sketched in (7), however, does not require the presence of any particular fact in the described situation. It merely requires that the sentence S should not describe the situation. Under this semantics a sentence like

    It is not true that John saw Mary or Mary saw John

would require that the described situation should not support either of the facts in (5). But it would not require that the situation support any negative facts. Thus some of the situations it describes could be extended to a consistent situation which supports one or both of the positive facts. Consider the situation *s* which is completely characterised by saying that it supports the fact that Bill saw Mary and Mary saw Bill. According to our semantics the sentence

    It is not true that John saw Mary or Mary saw John

would describe this situation since it does indeed not support either of the facts of John and Mary seeing each other. Now consider consistent extensions of *s*. Any extension of *s* will support all the facts that *s* supports and, if it is a proper extension, some additional ones. There should be nothing to prevent a consistent extension of *s* from supporting the fact of John seeing Mary or of Mary seeing John. Of course, such an extension could not, according to our semantics, be described by the sentence *It is not true that John saw Mary or Mary saw John.*[4] This is what makes the analysis conflict with our intuitions about the meaning of the sentence.

The problem is that our analysis of negation here is not providing us with any negative facts supported by the situation that would make such extensions inconsistent. What negative facts could sentences of the form *It is not true that S* require? Clearly if *S* is simplex it could be the negative fact corresponding to *S*. If *S* is a disjunction of two simplex sentences then we could require that the negative facts corresponding to the two disjuncts are supported by the situation. Similarly if *S* is a conjunction of two simplex sentences then we could require that at least the negative fact corresponding to one or the other of the disjuncts is supported by the situation.

As we have stated this here it is not a compositional treatment since you have to look at the internal form of *S* before you can decide precisely what rule to apply for *It is not true that S*. It would not work when either of the conjuncts are themselves conjoined. There *is* no corresponding negative fact for conjoined sentences because there is no single fact corresponding to conjoined sentences given the kind of semantics suggested in (4). One solution to this problem is to revise the semantics of conjunction and disjunction so that there are situations which support facts corresponding to conjoined sentences.

In order to do this we will introduce an algebra of facts with operations corresponding to *and, or* and *not.* Thus we will have facts like those in (8).

(8) a. $\langle\!\langle\text{see, John, Mary; 1}\rangle\!\rangle \wedge \langle\!\langle\text{see, Mary, John; 1}\rangle\!\rangle$

   b. $\sim(\langle\!\langle\text{see, John, Mary; 1}\rangle\!\rangle \vee \langle\!\langle\text{see, Mary, John; 1}\rangle\!\rangle)$

According to this idea, the sentence *John saw Mary and Mary saw John* as well as the sentence *It is true that John saw Mary and Mary saw John* would require that (8a) be supported by the described situation. The sentence *It is not true that John saw Mary or Mary saw John* would require the negative fact (8b) to be supported. Thus on this analysis the case where negation has scope over a conjoined sentence would require the presence of a negative fact just as much as if the embedded sentence had been simplex. It is the presence of this negative fact which will make the situation inconsistent with additional facts which might contradict it.

But how exactly do we get the contradiction? We said earlier that an inconsistent situation is one which supports two facts which are exactly alike except that they have different polarity values. According to our intuitions a situation which is completely characterised as in (9) should be contradictory, but it is not contradictory according to this simple definition.

(9) $s \models \sim(\langle\!\langle\text{see, John, Mary; 1}\rangle\!\rangle \vee \langle\!\langle\text{see, Mary, John; 1}\rangle\!\rangle)$

   $s \models \langle\!\langle\text{see, John, Mary; 1}\rangle\!\rangle$

Rather than change the definition of inconsistent situation I am going to employ another device from Situation Semantics, that of *structural constraint*. Structural constraints play something of the role that meaning postulates played in earlier semantic theories, though they account not only for logical or necessary inferences. (Barwise & Perry 1983 have a detailed discussion of them.) The kind of constraints that we will talk about here will say that if one kind of fact is supported by an actual situation (i.e. a real situation which is part of the world) then another fact or facts must also be supported by an actual situation (not necessarily the same one). We use the notation $\models\sigma$ to say that σ is a fact supported by an actual situation. (10) contains structural constraints for the operators in our algebra.[5]

(10) If $\models \sigma_1 \wedge \sigma_2$, then $\models\sigma_1$ and $\models\sigma_2$

   If $\models \sigma_1 \vee \sigma_2$, then either $\models\sigma_1$ or $\models\sigma_2$

   If $\models \sim\langle\!\langle\text{r, ...; i}\rangle\!\rangle$, then $\models\langle\!\langle\text{r, ...; i}'\rangle\!\rangle$ ($0'=1$, $1'=0$)

   If $\models \sim(\sigma_1 \wedge \sigma_2)$, then either $\models\sim\sigma_1$ or $\models\sim\sigma_2$

   If $\models \sim(\sigma_1 \vee \sigma_2)$, then $\models\sim\sigma_1$ and $\models\sim\sigma_2$

Armed with these constraints we can define the notion of a situation which is *full* with respect to them, i.e. a situation (whether or not actual) which supports all the facts required by the constraints. (We might say that such a situation is 'closed under the constraints'.) For example, if such a situation supports $\sigma_1 \wedge \sigma_2$ then it must also support σ_1 as well as σ_2. A more precise characterisation of fullness is given by the definitions in (11).

(11) a. A s-specific version of a constraint is obtained by replacing each '$\models$...' in the constraint by '$s \models$...'

   b. A situation s is *full* with respect to a set C of constraints iff s obeys s-specific versions of the constraints C

c. A *logically full* situation must be full with respect to (at least) the constraints (10) on $\wedge$, $\vee$ and $\sim$

We see now that a logically full extension of the situation characterised in (9) must be characterised as in (12).

(12) $s_E \models \sim (\langle\!\langle \text{see, John, Mary; } 1 \rangle\!\rangle \vee \langle\!\langle \text{see, Mary, John; } 1 \rangle\!\rangle)$

$s_E \models \langle\!\langle \text{see, John, Mary; } 1 \rangle\!\rangle$

$s_E \models \sim\langle\!\langle \text{see, John, Mary; } 1 \rangle\!\rangle$

$s_E \models \sim\langle\!\langle \text{see, Mary, John; } 1 \rangle\!\rangle$

$s_E \models \langle\!\langle \text{see, John, Mary; } 0 \rangle\!\rangle$

$s_E \models \langle\!\langle \text{see, Mary, John; } 0 \rangle\!\rangle$

But (12) is, of course, an inconsistent situation according to our simple definition. We can, then, define consistent situations to be those which have a consistent logically full extension according to the simple definition.

This solves the problem. With this machinery we will be able to have the kind of semantic sentence negation with scope over conjunctions which we seem to need to account for the semantics of natural language, even though it is arguable that there is no syntactic sentence negation. But what have we done in order to achieve this? Have we not encoded part of the *syntax* of propositional logic in the *semantic* situation-theoretic objects? Have we not furthermore introduced something like part of a proof theory for propositional logic into our calculus of situation-theoretic objects by our use of constraints?

2   What are the facts?

It is disquieting to discover that one of the very aspects of Situation Semantics that is appealing, the fact that it gives us structured objects called situations where we used to have unanalysed blobs called possible worlds, is making our situation-theoretic objects look very much like bits of a semantic representation language. Is Situation Semantics really just a (heavily?) disguised representational theory?

The first thing to point out is that, although it may appear that we have built the syntactic inference rules of classical propositional logic into our theory of situations, we have not done precisely that. The structural constraints will require that if $\sigma_1 \wedge \sigma_2$ is supported by an actual situation, then both σ_1 and σ_2 are. But it does not go the other way. This will have as a consequence that a situation which is full with respect to these constraints will support the two individual facts if it supports the conjunction, but that a situation can be full with respect to these constraints if it supports the individual facts but not the conjunction. Similarly a situation which is full with respect to these constraints can support a fact without supporting the disjunction of that fact with any other arbitrary fact. The structural constraints correspond to one of the conditionals in the biconditionals which are the corresponding rules of inference in classical propositional logic. The constraints allow you to infer less complex facts from more complex ones but not the other way around.

These structural constraints are basically the same as rules which Hintikka used to define *model sets* in the fifties and sixties[6] (see Hintikka 1973, chapter 1 and the references therein). Hintikka's model sets were to be thought of as partial descriptions of possible worlds which could be tested for consistency in the same kind of way as I have suggested testing for the consistency of a situation here. It is Hintikka's result which provides support for the claim that this is a reasonable way to talk about consistent situations. What Hintikka could show was that any set of sentences which leads to a consistent model set would also lead to a consistent complete description of a possible world and vice versa. Thus model sets could be used to test for consistency in general. The great advantage of model sets over complete descriptions of possible worlds is that model sets can be small finite collections whereas complete descriptions of possible worlds get unmanageably large. It is, however, hardly consoling to the nonrepresentationalist that Hintikka's model sets are sets of *sentences*.

The notation for facts we have used may look a lot like expressions of logic, but facts are nevertheless to be thought of as non-syntactic objects about which the axioms of situation theory provide a theory. It is instructive to compare facts with sets, about which the axioms of set theory provide a theory. We use the notation

$$\{a,b,c\}$$

We can think of this as an expression of the language of set theory, if we want. But that would not mean that sets themselves are syntactic expressions of a language. What exactly sets are is a matter of debate which is really independent of the building of an axiomatic set theory. Two people can work with the same set theory and have different beliefs about what kind of objects sets are. A platonist might believe that there are real objects in the world which are sets in addition to the basic elements. A formalist might believe that only the basic elements exist in the world and that in talking about sets mathematicians are placing structure on the collection of basic elements which is not really there. An everyday working mathematician who is interested in proving theorems might ignore the whole issue since the theorems will hold whatever kind of object it turns out she is talking about. So it is, I think, with situation theory. We use the notation

$$\langle\!\langle r,a,b;\, 1 \rangle\!\rangle$$

We can think of this as an expression of the language of situation theory. But that would not mean that facts themselves are syntactic expressions of a language. What exactly facts and situations are is a matter of debate which is really independent of the building of an axiomatic situation theory. Two people can work with the same situation theory and have different beliefs about what kinds of objects facts and situations are. A platonist might believe that there are real objects in the world which are facts and situations. A formalist might believe that the theory places some structure on the world which is not really there. An everyday working linguist who is interested in providing situation-theoretic semantics for fragments of natural languages might ignore the whole issue as the relationship she proposes between language and situation-theoretic objects will hold good whatever kind of object it turns out to be.

Note that viewed in this light the issue is not one of representation language versus reality but a question of the status of the objects of situation theory in reality. The question of facts being identical with the language we use to denote them need not arise. If we were to take this view, it would correspond to an extreme formalist view in set theory which regards it as a theory which is not about anything, except perhaps a theory of syntax for the language of set theory.

There is an important element involved in situation theory which makes the parallel with set theory less clean than we have suggested here. Situation theory is a theory oriented towards problems of cognition and information. This introduces psychology. One consequence of this is that the ordinary working situation theorist or semanticist is less likely to keep her fingers away from the big questions about the precise nature of situation-theoretic objects. Another consequence is that one can be something like a formalist and a platonist at the same time. One can say that the expression of situation theory

$$\langle\!\langle r,a,b;\ 1\rangle\!\rangle$$

really represents an expression in another language, the language of mental representation. Such a claim would not, of course, be saying that the language of situation theory is to be found in people's heads. Rather it would be saying that the subject matter of situation theory is mental objects (expressions of a mental language) and not a theory of non-mental objects in the world. On this view, one would be a platonist in that one would be thinking realistically about a mental representation language and one might simultaneously be something of a formalist by claiming that there are no non-mental objects which are facts or situations.

Barwise & Perry (1983) are platonists in the sense that they regard the objects of situation theory such as facts and situations[7] as part of the non-mental world. (This is not to say that they are not platonists with respect to mental objects as well. Mental states are important situation-theoretic objects. However, mental states are not the same things as facts and situations.)

The semantic realism in Barwise & Perry (1983) is greatly influenced by the ecological realism of Gibson (1979). The notion of a uniformity or invariant across situations is very important. Facts can, I think, be thought of as invariants across situations. Consider situations where Claire sees Anna. All of those situations have something in common, which enables us to perceive them as similar situations. There is a uniformity, or regularity, which holds across all of those situations. This invariant is the situation-theoretic object which we would call the fact of Claire seeing Anna and is represented in the language of situation-theory as

$$\langle\!\langle \text{see, Claire, Anna; } 1 \rangle\!\rangle$$

Notice that the claim is that the fact is something that various situations have in common. It is not claimed that the invariant is any kind of mental object. However, it is an invariant which human beings are attuned to. That is, it is one of the facts that we can use to distinguish situations from one another and to group situations together as being similar. Facts about microwave radiation on the other hand are not invariants that we are attuned to, at least not with our unaided biological perceptual apparatus. There may be many facts to which no cognitive being or machine is attuned. We do not know about them, of course, but that does not mean that they do not exist. The theory of situations is not in principle limited to facts to which people are attuned. It is not a theory of mental representation or perceptual categories.

What status does such a view give to the kind of complex facts which we introduced in the first part of this chapter? Does it make sense to say that a disjunctive fact or a negative fact is an invariant across situations? The answer must surely be 'yes'. There is something which remains invariant across all situations in which Claire sees Anna or Anna sees Claire. Similarly there is something which remains invariant in all situations in which Anna does not see Claire. To say that such invariants are not there and that disjunction and negation are only linguistic phenomena seems to be missing some important generalisations about situations. If we accept disjunctive and negative facts as true invariants across situations then it is presumably not hard for us to accept conjunctions as such also.

Linguists often talk about generalisations rather than invariants, uniformities or regularities. They often think of generalisations as not being in the world but as residing in people's heads. After all, it seems natural to say that it is people who make generalisations. Nevertheless, true generalisations must correspond to a uniformity in the data. If there is no corresponding uniformity, then the generalisation is at best false, if it is a generalisation at all. Linguistic generalisations correspond to invariants to which the speakers of a natural language are attuned. But, of course, the fact that human beings are attuned to precisely those invariants is something very important about human cognition.

Let us explore an example which Lyn Frazier described to me in discussion.[8] Consider an acoustic filter which takes noise as input and gives a sine wave as output. Surely, one might argue, the sine wave is not there in the data. Is it not created by the filter? So surely what we have been calling invariants across situations, simple facts, disjunctive facts, etc. are like the sine wave. They are something that our cognitive filter creates from the noisy world that is presented to our perceptual apparatus.

Can the sine wave be regarded as a uniformity across noises? Can it be

regarded as something which is present in the data, even though it is impossible to perceive it in the data without the filter? The noise must support the
sine wave in the same kind of way that we have been saying that situations
support facts. If you had not had appropriate data as input the filter would
not have been able to extract the clean wave form. A filter which extracts a
sine wave from noise is such a radical filter that we are tempted to say that its
output is really something quite different from its input. In the case of a less
radical filter, say, one that removes a certain band of high frequencies, we
would be less likely to say that the output was not present in the original
data. Filters by their nature preserve something of their input data, but some
filters are more radical than others. Some filters are so radical that the output
bears, according to our (pre-theoretic?) intuition, so little resemblance to the
input that we are tempted to say that the input did not contain the output.
Viewed from this perspective the difference between representationalist and
realist theories of meaning might be seen as one of degree. The debate could
be seen as concerning how radical the cognitive filter can be.

How can we decide how radical the cognitive filter can be? It is even
not entirely clear what it would mean for it to be more or less radical in the
semantic domain that we were discussing in the first part of this chapter.
Presumably one that will extract disjunctive or negative invariants is more
radical than one that will not. This is what our pre-theoretic intuition tells
us: we find it harder to conceive of disjunctions or negations as being part of
the world.

I do not think that the study of semantics alone will provide us with the
right kind of data to understand fully how radical the cognitive filter might
be or what the consequences would be of claiming that there is a language of
mental representation as opposed to a radical cognitive filter. What is needed
is some more concrete data on the nature of our perception of invariants
across restricted kinds of situations. The study of phonetic perception viewed
in this light seems to be a very important domain in this respect. As speakers
of a language we are attuned to phonetic invariances across speech situations. This view has been pursued in some of the phonetic literature. Despite
the relatively concrete nature of phonetics (compared with semantics), the
nature of coarticulation makes the isolation of phonetic invariants corresponding to the sounds we actually perceive a non-trivial matter. Both
scholars influenced by Gibson (e.g. Fowler *et al.* 1980 and Fowler & Smith
1986) and those arguing for a specific cognitive module specialised for
phonetic perception (e.g. Liberman & Mattingly 1985) have argued that the
regularities are to be found not in the acoustic signal but in articulatory
gestures. This makes the perception of speech from entirely acoustic data a
rather more abstract business than one might have expected and it therefore
becomes relevant to ask whether our phonetic perception involves a mental
representation of sounds. An attempt to consider this more concrete problem

with the kinds of tools we use in semantics might prove to be revealing about how innocent or realistic we can expect our semantics to be.[9]

3 Conclusion

In the first section of this chapter we presented a semantics for negation, conjunction, and disjunction which appeared to make semantic objects which we called facts look like syntactic objects. The result is reminiscent of work by Russell (1918) and Wittgenstein (1921) on logical atomism. In particular Russell (1918), Lecture III was concerned with the problems we have addressed of whether there should be negative or disjunctive facts. In the second part of the paper we tried to breathe reality into these semantic objects by regarding them as invariants across situations. We suggested that there was no reason that such invariants should not be negative or disjunctive facts. But however we view facts in terms of reality, are we not running into a problem that seemed to plague logical atomism, namely that the world begins to look like a language if we claim that there are complex facts. The view of facts as invariants is something that distinguishes the situation-theoretic view from logical atomism. The claim with respect to cognition is that we are only attuned to certain invariants, and only some of those will be relevant to the interpretation of language. In talking of the invariants relevant for the interpretation of language we are by no means characterising the whole noise of the world and there is no suggestion that the facts we need for the interpretation of natural language represent the whole world. Viewed in this light it might be quite surprising if the invariants relevant for linguistic meaning did not bear significant structural similarities to the syntax of our language. Why else would we have disjunctions if not to talk about disjunctive invariants in the world? At any rate, we can rest assured that there is much more in the world besides these syntax-like invariants and that we are therefore in no way reducing the world to language.

NOTES

1 I would like to thank Elisabet Engdahl and Ruth Kempson for commenting on previous drafts of this paper. I have benefited a great deal from discussing various ideas in this paper with Jon Barwise, Michael Byrd, Lyn Frazier, David House and Alvin Liberman. Part 1 of the chapter is a revised version of Cooper (1984). Part 2 builds on material from a talk I gave at Lund University during the spring term of 1986 entitled 'Situation Semantics and the psychology of perception'. I am grateful to Michael Heinz for transcribing that talk. This research has been supported in part by a Romnes Fellowship from the University of Wisconsin, Madison and a Guggenheim Fellowship.
2 Actually, as was made clear to me by Dietmar Zaefferer, the German word *Sachverhalt* is better than the word *fact* as a name for these objects since it does not imply that they actually hold in the world. Douglas (1986) points out an interest-

ing discussion of the term in Ajdukiewicz (1979) who says that a *Sachverhalt* is 'what is stated by a sentence', 'whether true or false'. It is 'neither a linguistic expression, nor a psychological act of thinking, nor any "ideal meaning", but something that belongs to the sphere of objects to which a given sentence refers'. *Sachverhalt* is normally translated as *state of affairs* and indeed this term has been used in the situation-theoretic literature for what we call facts. However, *state of affairs* seems to me an unfortunate term since it at once suggests a state as opposed to an event and also something more like a collection of facts, i.e. something more like what we are considering as a situation.

3 The condition on ℓ in the negative sentence is only one of a number of alternatives. As this is not at issue here, the reader may substitute a condition like 'for any ℓ temporally prior to the location of discourse' if s/he wishes.

4 i.e. the sentence would not be persistent.

5 In other versions of this what we are giving here as constraints are given as part of the definition of the algebra of facts.

6 I am grateful to Michael Byrd for pointing this out to me.

7 Or rather the objects that would later be viewed as situation-theoretic objects.

8 Frazier holds a very different view of what the example shows from the view I will try to argue for here.

9 From the perspective of a situation-theoretic approach to language, it seems that a useful way to view phonetic perception is in terms of both articulatory and acoustic situations. What speakers must be attuned to are the constraints that hold between these situations. Thus one would expect the invariants to be found in the relationship between articulation and acoustic data, but not necessarily in either one or the other.

REFERENCES

Ajdukiewicz, K. 1979. Proposition as the connotation of sentence. In J. Pelc (ed.) *Semiotics in Poland 1894–1969*. Dordrecht: Reidel.

Bach, E. 1980. Tenses and aspects as functions on verb-phrases. In C. Rohrer (ed.) *Time, tense and quantifiers*. Tübingen: Niemeyer Verlag.

Barwise, J. & Cooper, R. 1981. Generalized quantifiers and natural language. *Linguistics and Philosophy* 4(2): 159–220.

Barwise, J. & Perry, J. 1983. *Situations and attitudes*. Cambridge, Mass.: MIT Press.

Barwise, J. & Peters, S. forthcoming. Naive situation theory. Ms., CSLI.

Cooper, R. 1984. Sentence negation in situation semantics. In J. Drogo (ed.) *Papers from the Twentieth Regional Meeting*, Veena Mishra and David Testen, Chicago Linguistic Society.

Cooper, R. in preparation. *Introduction to situation semantics*.

Douglas, I. 1986. *Discourse, diegesis and the real: an integrative theory of meaning*. Ph.D thesis Murdoch University.

Fowler, C.A., Rubin, P., Remez, R.E. & Turvey, M.T. 1980. Implications for speech production of a general theory of action. In B. Butterworth (ed.) *Language production*. London: Academic Press.

Fowler, C. & Smith, Mary 1986. Speech perception as 'vector analysis': an approach to the problems of invariance and segmentation. In Joseph Perkell and Dennis Klatt (eds.) *Invariance and variability in speech processes*. Hillsdale, NJ: Erlbaum.

Gibson, J. 1979. *The ecological approach to visual perception*. Boston: Houghton Mifflin.

Hintikka, J. 1973. *Logic, language-games and information: kantian themes in the philosophy of logic.* Oxford: Oxford University Press.

Keenan, E. & Stavi, J. 1986. A semantic characterization of natural language determiners. *Linguistics and Philosophy* 9(3): 253–326.

Liberman, A. & Mattingly, I. 1985. The motor theory of speech perception revised. *Cognition* 21: 1–36.

Montague, R. 1974. *Formal philosophy: selected papers of Richard Montague,* edited and with an introduction by Richmond H. Thomason. New Haven: Yale University Press.

Russell, B. 1918. The philosophy of logical atomism. *The Monist,* reprinted in Russell: *Logic and knowledge,* edited by R.C. Marsh. London: Allen and Unwin, 1956 and Russell: *The philosophy of logical atomism,* edited and with an introduction by David Pears. La Salle, Illinois: Open Court, 1985.

Wittgenstein, L. 1921, 1961. *Tractatus Logico-Philosophicus,* originally in *Annalen der Naturphilosophie,* published in 1961 with a new translation by D.F. Pears & B.F. McGuiness and with the Introduction by Bertrand Russell. London: Routledge and Kegan Paul.

3
Relational interpretation

ELISABET ENGDAHL

1 Introduction

In this chapter I will be concerned with a type of relational interpretation of noun phrases that shows up in a variety of contexts.[1] I will first provide some illustrations of how these relational readings arise. Then I will argue that they are not simply variants of certain wide scope interpretations. I then address the issue of how these readings can be expressed semantically and outline an analysis within the framework of Situation Semantics which I believe permits an illuminating account of how these readings arise and interact with the interpretation of other constituents. This account uses notions like setting of parameters and in the final section I turn to issues having to do with parameters and mental representations.

2 Relational readings

2.1 Relational readings of interrogative quantifiers

Consider the question in (1) together with the three ways one could conceivably answer it.[2]

(1) Which book did *every author* recommend?
    a. War and Peace   (individual answer)
    b. Bellow recommended Herzog, Heller
       recommended Catch-22, . . .   (pair-list answer)
    c. *His* most recent book   (relational answer)

The answer in (1a) provides a title of a book; hence every author recommended the same book and I will refer to this reading as the **individual reading**. The answer in (1b) reflects a reading where *every author* takes wider scope than the interrogative phrase *which book*. On this reading, the question in (1) is equivalent to a set of questions; one for each author in the relevant set of authors. I will refer to this reading as the **pair-list reading** since the answer often takes the form of a list of pairs supplying values for both of the quantifiers involved. The third type of answer illustrated in (1c) illustrates what I will be referring to as the **relational reading** of the question. Here the interrogative quantifier *which book* apparently has wider scope than the sentence internal quantifier *every author* as shown by the fact that we get a single answer. Nevertheless, this answer does not pick out an individual book as in the (a) reading, since the choice of book will vary with the authors.

The question that arises now is whether relational answers are just a convenient way of abbreviating pair-list answers or whether they express a distinct reading which is not reducible to the pair-list reading. I will briefly provide some arguments that relational readings are in fact not reducible to pair-list readings.[3]

First, let us consider questions with negative quantifiers, as illustrated in (2):

(2)   Which book did *no author* recommend?

     a.   War and Peace

     b.   *Bellow didn't recommend Herzog,

          Heller didn't recommend Catch-22 . . .

     c.   *His* most recent book

Since negative quantifiers don't easily take wide scope, there doesn't seem to be a way of interpreting (2) with *no author* taking wider scope than the interrogative phrase. This is reflected in the fact that pair-list answers illustrated in (2b) are not available to this question. Nevertheless, a relational answer as in (2c) makes perfect sense. Note that we apparently get an answer with a bound pronoun, despite the fact that the antecedent *no author* does not take scope outside the sentence. A similar but perhaps even clearer example is given in (3).

(3)   Who does *no man* love?

     His mother-in-law

Suppose (3) is asked in a world where every woman has a son who loves her. In this world, there will be no true individual answer since every woman is loved by at least one person. A pair-list answer is also not available since that would involve interpreting *no man* with wider scope than the interrogative quantifier. A relational answer seems to be the most natural.

We can make the same point with questions which contain narrow scope indefinites as in (4).

(4)   How can I find *a book* in this library?

     By looking under *its* author's name in the main catalogue

It seems to me that I can very well ask the question in (4) without having any particular book in mind. What I want to find out is a general procedure for finding any book in this library. The relational answer provides precisely such a procedure.

A second argument against reducing relational answers to pair-list answers is provided by questions into opaque contexts, as shown in (5):

(5)   Which book would you expect *every author* to recommend?

     a.   War and Peace

     b.   I would expect Bellow to recommend Herzog, and Heller to

          recommend Catch-22 . . .

     c.   *His* most recent book

All three types of answers are possible with this question. The pair-list answer in (5b) presumably requires that the addressee knows each author and is interpreting (5) as a set of questions, one for each author. On the readings illustrated by the answers in (5a) and (5c), on the other hand, *every author* remains under the scope of *expect* and consequently under the scope of the interrogative. Still the relational answer is possible whereas a pair-list answer isn't possible without giving *every author* wide scope.

We have seen how an interrogative phrase like *which book* may get a relational interpretation if there is a quantifier phrase inside the question. We can make this more explicit by letting the interrogative quantifier contain an **overt** dependent element, for instance a bound personal pronoun as in the following variant of (1).[4]

(6)   Which of *his* books did *every author* recommend?
   a.   *War and Peace   (individual answer)
   b.   Bellow recommended Herzog, Heller
        recommended Catch-22 . . .   (pair-list answer)
   c.   *His* most recent book   (relational answer)

On the interpretation where *his* is bound by *every author*, there is clearly no single book that all authors recommend which explains why an individual answer isn't possible whereas both the pair-list answer and the relational answer are possible.

The question–answer pairs in (1)–(6) thus provide us with a set of examples where the initial interrogative phrase is answered in a relational way, i.e. the answer does not pick out an individual *per se* but rather a set of individuals who are dependent on the interpretation of some quantifier inside the question. What is particularly interesting is that these readings arise even in cases where the antecedent quantifier can be shown to have narrower scope than the interrogative quantifier. We thus seem to have a case of mismatch between position and scope.

Within most versions of generative grammar, e.g. the Government-Binding theory, it is customary to assume that a phrase can have scope only over constituents that it c-commands.[5] The requirement that a quantifier must have wider scope than any phrase which is dependent on it is usually required to hold at Logical Form (LF) (cf. Chomsky 1981, 1982; Heim 1982; May 1985) and maybe also at S-structure. Berwick & Wexler (1982) argue that this requirement contributes to parsing efficiency and apply it to a model of on-line sentence processing. In particular they argue that the c-command restriction narrows the search space for the antecedents for bound pronouns. Given the assumption that taking scope over some constituent involves c-commanding that constituent at some level of representation, the examples involving relational readings are intriguing since the requirement that the antecedent c-command the dependent phrase is met neither at S-structure nor at LF. Still it seems to be possible to interpret a sentence initial *wh*-phrase relative to the interpretation of other NPs in the sentence. The relevant restriction seems to be that the sentence internal NP must c-command the gap position associated with the initial *wh*-phrase. If this is correct we wouldn't expect relational answers to be available when the position of the gap c-commands the position of the quantifier. This seems to be correct as shown by the following examples.

(7) [Which man]$_i$ [e$_i$ loves no woman?]
    a. John
    b. *Her son-in-law

Here, as predicted, an individual answer is fine, but not a relational answer.[6]

We have thus seen that a sentence initial interrogative phrase may be interpreted relative to the interpretation of some NP in the body of the sentence. It's straightforward to show that more than one NP inside the sentence may be relevant for determining the exact interpretation of the initial wh-phrase. Consider the dialogue in (8).

(8) Which letters does *every woman* ask **her lover** to return to her?
    The ones where *she* promises **him** to be faithful for ever

(8) shows that potentially any number of NP interpretations in the immediate syntactic context may interact with the interpretation of a single NP given certain syntactic restrictions. In the next section, we will look at how factors from the discourse setting enter into the picture.

2.2 Relational readings of other NPs

So far we have used direct questions and their possible answers as a means of bringing out relational readings. The phenomenon of relational readings isn't limited to interrogative quantifiers, however. As we will see in this section, giving a NP a relational interpretation seems to be an option that is available for most types of NPs, although it clearly varies with the context of utterance. Consider first the interpretation of **pronouns** in so-called paycheck sentences as in the following example taken from Cooper (1979).[7]

(9) John gave his paycheck to his mistress
    Everyone else put *it* in the bank

On the most plausible reading of (9), *it* in the second sentence does not refer to any particular paycheck. Rather, *it* seems to pick out, for any person distinct from John, that person's paycheck. Using the terminology in this chapter, we can say that *it* in this context is interpreted relative both to *everyone* and to *his paycheck* in the preceding sentence. Cooper accounts for this by interpreting pronouns as definite NPs but with a free property variable which in most cases will be determined by the context. In the case of (9), *it* may be interpreted as 'the unique thing that has the property of being u's paycheck', where u is an individual variable. When u gets bound by the quantifier *everyone*, we get the relational interpretation, which seems most natural given the preceding context.

Relational readings also arise in sentences with **demonstrative expressions** as in (10).

(10) John gave his first paycheck to his mother
     Everyone else spent *that paycheck/that one* on his mistress

It might be revealing to ask what is being demonstrated in (10). On the most plausible reading, it is certainly not a specific paycheck, nor the property of being the first paycheck. Given any person besides John, *that paycheck* or *that one* picks out that person's first paycheck. The case is thus very similar to personal pronouns as discussed with respect to example (9).

We now turn to some examples involving definite NPs, which in the philosophical literature are traditionally known as **definite descriptions**. As the example in (11) shows, these also allow for relational readings quite straightforwardly.

(11)   John gave his paycheck to his mother and lived off his savings
       Everyone else lived off *the paycheck* and didn't touch *the savings*

It is possible to make the relational reading even more explicit by using an inherently relational common noun such as *relative*. One illustration is given in (12).

(12)   When we looked through the medical records, it turned out that
       every patient had problems with *the same relative*, namely *the father*

If we disregard the situation where all the patients are related and hence where the very same person could be the source of everyone's troubles, the most plausible interpretation is the one where *the same relative* in (12) picks out, for each patient, the person who stands in a particular relation to him/her.

We next turn to **indefinite descriptions** to see if they also may be interpreted in a relational manner. Consider the statement in (13) and the way the various continuations may be interpreted. Since indefinite descriptions rarely are used anaphorically, contrary to definite descriptions and demonstratives, we will have to modify our procedure somewhat. We will introduce an indefinite description in a lead-in sentence and then evaluate the interpretation possibilities of various continuations to see whether they show any evidence that the indefinite NP is interpreted relationally, i.e. as varying in a systematic way with the interpretation of other NPs in the context. We will first consider the readings available when the indefinite phrase is unstressed.

(13)   John has problems with *a relative*
       a. Everyone else has problems with *a relative*
       b. So does everyone else

The most natural interpretation of (13a) seems to be the one where it's synonymous with the VP deletion example in (13b). Both these continuations express that everyone else has relative problems without requiring that they have problems with the same relative, *mutatis mutandis*, that John has. Presumably what the VP-deletion ranges over is something like 'having problems with a relative' and the indefinite phrase is free to pick out different relatives for different persons. We can, however, make the relational reading more salient by replacing the unstressed indefinite article *a* with the stressed form *one*, or by modifying the indefinite phrase as in (14).

(14)   John has problems with *a certain relative*
    a. Everyone else has problems with *a certain relative*
    b. So does everyone else

For many speakers, the discourse in (14) can be used to describe two different situations. In one situation, we know only that everyone has problems with one of their relatives, regardless which. The second situation would be one where each person, x has problems with the person who stands in the same relation to x as John's problematic relative does to him. The question arises whether this means that a sentence like (14a) or (14b) in the context given in (14) is ambiguous, i.e. whether the two readings are truth conditionally different. I don't think they are, but what is interesting is that people still might want to say that they describe different situations. In the next section, I will illustrate how these two situations can be associated with one and the same discourse within the framework of Situation Semantics.

We saw in (13) that a mere unstressed indefinite NP does not easily give rise to relational interpretations. Why should the addition of *certain* or heavy stress make a relational reading of an indefinite NP more available? Suppose the use of an indefinite NP means that the choice of individual is basically free. Then the reason we don't get a systematic relational interpretation for the continuations in (13a,b) is understandable. If we are free to pick any relative, there is no salient relation which determines how we are supposed to pick out problematic relatives. Stressing the indefinite phrase, replacing *a* with *one*, or adding *certain*, may be taken as signals that the choice of individual is not free and consequently the situation where for each person you pick out problematic relatives in the same way is readily available. There is certainly a lot more to be said about the interpretation possibilities for indefinite NPs but that would take me beyond the scope of this chapter.[8] I just note that the behaviour of indefinites provides additional ground on which to study what factors make relational readings salient.

3   A Situation Semantics account for relational interpretations

We have seen that relational readings arise not only with interrogative quantifiers like *who* and *which* but also with pronouns, demonstrative NPs like *that one*, and definite and indefinite descriptions like *the paycheck* and *a (certain) relative*. We now turn to the question of how these readings can be accounted for in a semantic theory. In earlier work (Engdahl 1986), I have worked out one account for relational interpretations within the framework of Montague grammar, using a PTQ-style translation into intensional logic as a means for representing the interpretations. In retrospect I think this is a convenient and explicit way to express the relevant readings, but it doesn't say anything about how and why these readings arise, nor about how people actually construct these interpretations. The interesting issue, as I see it, is rather what implications a semantic theory of natural language should draw from the fact that the interpretation of various NPs depends both on the interpretation of quantifiers in the same sentence and on facts established through the interpretation of previous discourse. In the context of this volume I would like to outline how relational interpretations can be handled in Situation Semantics. One reason for investigating how relational readings could be expressed in Situation Semantics is that this theory provides the means of accounting for how the context of the utterance as well as the speaker's and the hearer's background assumptions may enter into the understanding of a sentence.

In Barwise & Perry (1983), meaning is understood to be a relation between situations, viz. an utterance situation, a described situation, and various resource situations. I believe this theory provides a natural way of handling the various interpretational dependencies that we have seen arise in the examples discussed.

3.1 Basic notions

Let us think of situations simply as sets of facts. We assume that facts have some internal structure which we can represent as follows:[9]

$$\langle\langle \text{loc}, \text{rel}_n, \text{arg}_1, \ldots, \text{arg}_n; \text{polarity} \rangle\rangle$$

A fact consists of a location, an n-place relation, n arguments and a polarity value. An example of a fact is given in (15).

(15) $\langle\langle \text{loc}_d, \text{kiss}, \text{John}, \text{Mary}; 1 \rangle\rangle$

Suppose loc_d picks out the discourse location, (15) then represents the fact of John kissing Mary here and now. We will say that a sentence like *John is kissing Mary* **describes** a situation if the fact in (15) is a member of that situation. The relation, abbreviated rel, clearly plays an important role in determining the structure of a fact. It's the relation, in this case the verb, that provides information about how many arguments there must be as well as of what type these must be, i.e. whether the arguments must be individuals, locations, properties or situations. We will assume that this information is part of the lexical content of a word. Given that we know the lexical content of *kiss*, we know that it provides fact structures of the type illustrated in (16).

(16) $\langle\langle \textbf{loc}, \text{kiss}, \textbf{a}, \textbf{b}; 1 \rangle\rangle$

(16) is not a fact since we don't know where the kissing takes place, nor who is involved. We will refer to structures such as (16) as **parameterised facts**. Once the values for the parameters **loc**, **a**, and **b** in (16) are set, it becomes a fact.[10] (16) represents a rather uninformative parametrised fact. All we know is that there is some kissing going on somewhere. The parametrised fact in (17) on the other hand

(17) $\langle\langle \text{loc}_d, \text{kiss}, \textbf{a}, \text{Mary}; 1 \rangle\rangle$

represents the fact that Mary is being kissed here and now without specifying who does the kissing. In order to determine whether (17) corresponds to a fact in an actual situation, we must see if there is any way of setting the value of the parameter to some individual in the context and then find out whether that individual is in fact kissing Mary. Since setting of location parameters won't play any role in the present discussion, I will just leave them out from now on. The setting of individual parameters, however, will turn out to be important. In fact, the setting of the value of an individual parameter is precisely what is involved when we interpret a sentence with a personal pronoun. Consider the following sentence.

(18) John kisses *her*

In order to interpret this sentence fully and to determine whether it describes an actual situation, we must decide to whom *her* refers. This is in some sense analogous to setting the individual parameter **b** in the parametrised fact in (19).[11]

(19) $\langle\!\langle$ kiss, John, **b**; 1 $\rangle\!\rangle$

Consequently we will get different interpretations depending on whom the value of the parameter **b** gets set to. The same options are available in the following example.

(20) a. Mary dreamt that she was sailing
　　 b. $\langle\!\langle$ dream, Mary, [s | s | $\langle\!\langle$ sail, **a**; 1 $\rangle\!\rangle$]; 1 $\rangle\!\rangle$

I am assuming that a verb like *dream* may take as its second argument a situation, or more precisely a **property** (represented by [. . .]) of situations. Thus (20a) describes a situation where Mary stands in the dream relation to a property of situations. A situation *s* will have this property if there is some way of setting the parameter **a** in $\langle\!\langle$ sail, **a**; 1 $\rangle\!\rangle$ so that the resulting fact is in *s*. There are basically two ways we can set the value of the parameter **a**; either we can set it to some salient person in the context, in which case we get the deictic interpretation of the pronoun, or we can set it to Mary which gives us what is sometimes called the bound interpretation of the pronoun.

In order to illustrate how relational interpretations arise in this theory, we first need to look at how quantifier phrases are interpreted. We recall that relational readings appear when there is some interaction between a NP and some quantifier. Quantifiers enter into the composition of facts in Situation Semantics in two ways. The first way is illustrated by the example in (21), which on its most straightforward interpretation describes just one situation.

(21) A dog barked

A situation is described by (21), which contains an individual which is a dog and which barked at some location in the past. The second way quantifiers contribute to the structure of facts can be illustrated by considering examples like (22).

(22) A dog barks

In addition to the reading where (22) describes a situation in which some dog is barking at the utterance time, this sentence also has the so-called generic reading on which it doesn't describe any particular situation. According to this reading, it doesn't say anything about a particular dog, rather it says something about dogs in general, namely that whenever you have a situation with a dog in it, that dog barks. We can thus think of the interpretation of the quantifier *a dog* as restricting the described situation to be of a certain type, namely one containing certain types of facts. To pursue this second way of looking at quantifiers, let us consider an example with a universal quantifier as in (23).

(23) a.   Every man whistles
     b. $\langle\!\langle$ man, **a**; 1 $\rangle\!\rangle$
     c. $\langle\!\langle$ whistle, **a**; 1 $\rangle\!\rangle$

A sentence such as (23a) will describe those situations which, for any setting of the parameter **a**, if they contain the fact resulting from (23b), will also contain the fact resulting from (23c).[12]

In a similar way, *no man whistles* can only describe a certain kind of situation, viz. those situations that have in common that whenever there is some whistling going on, the individual who is whistling is not a man.

Let us return briefly to example (21).

(21)   A dog barked

The reason (21) tends to be interpreted as describing just one situation presumably has to do with the presence of the past tense verb *barked*. The location parameter thus has to be set to some time preceding the present and in the absence of further contextual information, we tend to pick out just one specific time in the past. Notice, however, that there is nothing that prevents (21) from being understood in the second way mentioned above, i.e. as constraining the type of situation described by the sentence. We can make this reading salient by providing some context as in (24).

(24)   Every time I rang the doorbell, a dog barked

Here the most natural interpretation is one where the interpretation of *a dog barked* constrains the type of situation described by (24). One might still wonder why this kind of reading is so easy to get with sentences in the present tense, whereas sentences in the past seem to require some extra setting to be interpreted in this way. Put otherwise, why is there a simple generic present but no simple generic past? R. Cooper has suggested to me that there is in fact something like the generic past, but it doesn't show up in examples like (21) for the simple reason that dogs still exist and it would be more appropriate to use (22). But if we turn to extinct species, a sentence like (21) becomes perfectly natural on a generic interpretation, as for instance in (25).

(25)   A dinosaur didn't bark

(I use a negated predicate here simply because I don't know what sounds dinosaurs made.) (25) may be used about a particular dinosaur in a particular situation, or it may be understood as being about dinosaurs in general and restricting the situation to be of a certain type, viz. the type of past situation such that whenever it contains a dinosaur, that dinosaur doesn't bark.

3.2 Relational interpretations and parameter setting

We now have the necessary notions to look at sentences with several NPs where the interpretation of one NP may depend on another as in (26).

(26) a. Every man loves his mother
      b. ⟪man, **a**; 1⟫
      c. ⟪love, **a**, **b**'s mother; 1⟫

Given what I have said about how *every* restricts the described situation to be of a certain type, we know that (26a) describes a situation which contains the parametrised facts in (26b) and (26c) once the values of the parameters **a** and **b** have been set to some individual or individuals. The parameter **b** can be set in different ways. One way is to set its value to one particular individual, let's say Bill. In this case we get the deictic reading of (26a) where every man loves Bill's mother. The other way would be to set the value of **b** to the value of **a** which will give us the bound reading: Every man loves his own mother. The two interpretations of (26a) thus depend on how the parameter corresponding to *his* gets set: whether it gets set to one specific individual or whether it gets set to some individual whose identity depends on the setting of some other parameter in the parametrised fact.

Essentially the same approach will now give us relational readings of pronouns in cases where the setting of some parameter might be determined by the interpretation of a previous sentence as in the following variation on the paycheck example.

(27) a. John gave his paycheck to his mistress
      b. Every woman put *it* in the bank

(27b) describes the type of situation which contains the parametrised facts in (28).

(28) a. ⟪woman, **a**, 1⟫
      b. ⟪put, **a**, **b**, in the bank; 1⟫

Just as in the previous example, we can set the value of **b** to a specific individual in which case we get the unlikely deictic interpretation of *it*. To set the value of **b** to be the value of **a** wouldn't make much sense in this example, but there is nothing to prevent us from setting it to some individual whose identity covaries with the value of **a**. Given the preceding context which mentions *John* and *his paycheck*, setting the value of **b** to be the paycheck of whichever individual the parameter **a** is set to seems to be a plausible step in the interpretation of (28a). Assuming that definite descriptions like *the paycheck* and demonstratives like *that paycheck* also involve the setting of parameters, relational readings of sentences with such expressions will arise in parallel fashion.

Let us now return to where we started from, relational readings of questions as in (1), repeated here as (29).

(29) a. Which book did every author recommend?
      b. ⟪author, **a**; 1⟫
      c. ⟪recommend, **a**, **wh**; 1⟫

I will assume that *wh*-phrases involve a particular kind of parameter, and that in asking a direct question, the speaker requests the addressee to provide the setting for this *wh* parameter. On these assumptions, (29)(a) will contain at least the two parameterised facts in (29)(b,c). Answering a question will amount to providing a value for the *wh* parameter, given settings for any other parameters there might be.

The addressee might provide a value either by pointing or referring to an individual, in which case we get the individual reading. The addressee might also run through each way of setting the **a** parameter and suggest a value for **wh**. This would correspond to what we have referred to as the pair-list reading. The third way of answering the question – the one which brings out the relational interpretation, naturally arises in a case where the addressee doesn't know who all the authors are but knows that there is some way you can correlate authors and books recommended by them. In that case the addressee specifies what type of individual the **wh** parameter could be set to through a constraint on situations. In the context of the question in (29)(a), an answer like *his latest book* then could be understood as specifying a condition on the setting of the **wh** parameter in (29)(c). Essentially what we are doing then is adding the parametrised fact in (29)(d),

     (29) d.   《**a**'s latest book, **b**: 1》

and requiring that the described situation contain all the facts (29)(b–d) once their parameters have been set in such a way that the **wh** parameter in (c) is set to the value of the parameter **b** in (d).

Given that the interpretation of noun phrases by the approach suggested here will always involve the setting of parameters, relational readings will arise as soon as the setting of one parameter interacts with the setting of another parameter. I see it as one advantage of Situation Semantics that no special mechanism needs to be invoked in order to account for relational interpretations of noun phrases.

3.3 Constraints on parameter setting

From the point of view of a linguist interested in both the availability of certain readings and the systematic non-availability of other readings, it does not suffice to show that relational readings can be captured in some particular framework. We also need to account for certain systematic restrictions on relational interpretations. In terms of Situation Semantics, this question becomes one of accounting for when the setting of one parameter cannot involve the setting of another parameter. For instance we need to account for the contrast, noted above in connection with example (7), between (30) where the setting of the parameter in the interpretation of the *wh*-phrase may be related to the setting of parameters in the interpretation of *no man*, whereas this is not possible in (31).

     (30)   Who does *no man* love?
           His mother-in-law

(31)   Who loves *no man?*

   *His mother-in-law

Presumably the S-structures of (30) and (31) would be as in (32) and (33), disregarding subject–auxiliary inversion.

(32)   [who$_i$] [no man loves e_i]

(33)   [who$_i$] [e_i loves no man]

In the Government-Binding framework, the contrast between (30) and (31) would presumably be related to the fact that *no man* c-commands and thus can bind a pronoun in the gap position in structures corresponding to (34), but not in structures corresponding to (35).

(34)   *No man* loves *his* mother-in-law

(35)   **His* mother-in-law loves *no man*

Since I haven't discussed how relational readings could be accounted for on a Government-Binding approach,[13] it won't be possible here to consider how restrictions on relational readings could be accounted for in any detail. I will just make the observation that there are presumably two places in which these restrictions could be stated. One could build into the *wh*-interpretation rule which maps structures like (32)–(33) into LF representations some proviso which ensures that the interpretation of an initial *wh*-phrase can be relativised to the interpretation of some quantifier only if that quantifier c-commands the empty category which is coindexed with the *wh*-phrase. Alternatively one would have to encode the same information in the LF representation in some way so that the interpretation rules which map LF representations into interpretations make the correct distinctions. In both cases one would presumably need both syntactic information (relative positions at S-structure of quantifiers and gaps) and semantic information (identifying quantifiers and their scopal properties).

Let us now consider how the systematic nonavailability of relational interpretations for examples like (31) can be accounted for in terms of setting parameters.[14] First we need to look a bit closer at the interpretation of *wh*-phrases. As mentioned briefly above, I assume that their interpretation involves a particular kind of **wh** parameter which differs from other parameters in that the setting of this parameter is left to the addressee in case of direct questions. Furthermore I will assume that the interpretation of a *wh*-phrase such as *who* or *which book* is essentially of the same type as the interpretation of NPs such as *everyone* and *some book*. There are several reasons for making this assumption. As we have seen earlier, such quantifier NPs can be used to answer questions by providing conditions on the setting of the **wh** parameter, as illustrated further in (36).

(36)   Who is coming to dinner?

   a.   Nobody

   b.   Someone I met in Windsor Great Park

   c.   Two linguists

   d.   Most of the girls in my class

Following Barwise & Cooper (1983) and Cooper (1987, in preparation), I will assume that such NPs should be interpreted as involving a relation between properties of individuals (cf. note 12) where the determiner of the NP specifies the relation. The structure of an NP interpretation will be as in (37).

(37) $\langle\langle \text{rel}, P_1, P_2; 1 \rangle\rangle$

The arguments to the relation are properties, here represented as P_1 and P_2. The value of P_1 will be set by the interpretation of the common noun and the value of P_2 will be supplied by the VP interpretation. The interpretation of an NP like *every woman* will thus be as in (38).

(38) $\langle\langle \text{every}, [\mathbf{a} \mid \langle\langle \text{woman}, \mathbf{a}; 1 \rangle\rangle], \mathbf{P_2}; 1 \rangle\rangle$

According to (38), the every relation holds between the property of being a woman and some other property which remains to be specified. In parallel fashion, the interpretation of *who* will be as in (39).

(39) $\langle\langle \mathbf{whr}, \mathbf{whP}, \mathbf{P_2}; 1 \rangle\rangle$

We assume that the interpretation of a *wh*-phrase, contrary to ordinary NPs, is parametrised with respect to the relation involved and the noun property in addition to the property supplied by the VP. The interpretation of a direct question like (36) can then be represented as in (40).

(40) $\langle\langle \mathbf{whr}, \mathbf{whP}, [\mathbf{a} \mid \langle\langle \text{coming-to-dinner}, \mathbf{a}; 1 \rangle\rangle]; 1 \rangle\rangle$

The task of the addressee now is to specify values for both the relation parameter and the noun property parameter. The sample of answers given in (36) gives an illustration of how this can be done. For example (36c) will correspond to the fact in (41).

(41) $\langle\langle \text{two}, [\mathbf{a} \mid \langle\langle \text{linguist}, \mathbf{a}; 1 \rangle\rangle], [\mathbf{a} \mid \langle\langle \text{coming-to-dinner}, \mathbf{a}; 1 \rangle\rangle]; 1 \rangle\rangle$

We can now turn to an example where a relational interpretation arises as in (30).

(30) Who does *no man* love?
      His mother-in-law

This question corresponds to the parametrised fact in (42).

(42) $\langle\langle \text{no}, [\mathbf{a} \mid \langle\langle \text{man}, \mathbf{a}; 1 \rangle\rangle], [\mathbf{a} \mid \langle\langle \text{love}, \mathbf{a}, [\text{s} \mid \text{s} \models$
      $\langle\langle \mathbf{whr}, \mathbf{whP}, \mathbf{P_2}; 1 \rangle\rangle]; 1 \rangle\rangle]; 1 \rangle\rangle$

A few comments about how we get this interpretation might be in place. I am assuming that the syntax generates a structure with an initial *wh*-phrase and an empty NP position as in (43).

(43) $[[_{\text{Comp}}\text{who}] [_{\text{s}}\text{no man loves } [_{\text{NP}}e]]]$

The interpretation rule for such structures will unify the information provided by the initial *wh*-phrase with the information provided by the interpretation of the gap and the result will be something along the lines of (42). What we have there is a situation where the *no* relation holds between the property of being a man and some NP interpretation where both the *wh*-relation and the *wh*-property remain to be specified. Notice that in figuring out who has the property of being a man, we must set an individual parameter, represented as **a**. When we come to determine the *wh*-property, we again need to set an individual parameter. The setting of this parameter can then be systematically related to the setting of **a**, as we saw earlier in discussing (29). One way of characterising the type of individual whom no man loves would be as in (44).

(44) $\langle\!\langle$no, [**a** | $\langle\!\langle$man, **a**; $1\rangle\!\rangle$], [**a** | $\langle\!\langle$love, **a**, [s | s $\models$
        $\langle\!\langle$**b**'s mother-in-law, c; $1\rangle\!\rangle$]; $1\rangle\!\rangle$]; $1\rangle\!\rangle$

There are several parameters over individuals that need to be set in (44). The relational readings arise just in those cases when these parameters are set to the same value or to values which are systematically related. It seems that once the setting of a parameter has been actualised while we figure out what the facts in the situation are, then this setting may influence further choices of parameter settings.

Let us now contrast the interpretation of (42) with that of (31) which does not allow for relational readings. The interpretation of (31) is given in (45).

(31)   Who loves *no man?*
       *His mother-in-law

(45) $\langle\!\langle$**whr, whP**, [**a** | $\langle\!\langle$love, **a**, [s | s $\models$
        $\langle\!\langle$no, [**b** | $\langle\!\langle$man, **b**; $1\rangle\!\rangle$], **P2**; $1\rangle\!\rangle$]; $1\rangle\!\rangle$]; $1\rangle\!\rangle$

The main relation of the fact in (45) is the *wh*-relation. In order to set this relation we need to set the *wh*-property, which amounts to figuring out which individuals have this property. At this point no other parameter settings have been actualised. It's not until we determine the interpretation of the VP *loves no man* that some individuals are actualised through parameter setting. Consequently it seems as if the failure to get relational readings for questions like (32) follows from the fact that when we determine the *wh*-relation, no individuals have been actualised through parameter setting.

Stepping back somewhat from the technicalities, it appears that these results follow from the assumption that it's the subject NP which determines the main relation of the fact described by a sentence. If in the setting of this parameter we introduce some individuals, then these are available in the setting of other parameters, e.g. in the interpretation of the object NP. But the setting of the subject relation cannot (systematically) correlate with the setting of parameters in the object NP interpretation unless this takes wide scope. In some sense I have imported the structural asymmetry between subjects and objects into the interpretation. Consequently relational readings will always be available when the quantifier occurs in subject position. When the quantifier occurs in object position a whole set of factors seem to interact in determining whether a relational interpretation is possible or not. One such factor is whether the quantifier in object position is of the type that easily takes wide scope, such as *each*, or inherently prefers narrow scope as in the case of *no*. On the present approach this means that the determiner relation of the interpretation of the quantifier will matter. Hence we would expect relational interpretations to be possible when we replace *no* in (31) with *each* as in (46).

(46) Who loves *each man?*
His mother-in-law

A second contributing factor seems to be the choice of common noun in the object NP. As pointed out to me by Lyn Frazier, relational answers are possible in the following types of questions.

(47) Which man loves *no mother-in-law?*
a. *Her* son-in-law
b. The son-in-law

(48) Which man loves *every first born male* most?
a. *His* grandfather
b. The grandfather

The definite descriptions in the (b) answers clearly tend to receive a relational interpretation, just like the (a) versions with explicit bound pronouns, despite the fact that the object NP doesn't take scope over the subject NP. It seems that what makes the difference is the presence of either an overt relational noun in the sentence (like *mother-in-law*) or an expression which conjures up a relational scenario (like *first born male*). In the absence of such overt relational expressions, such readings are very hard to get. Compare (49).

(49) Which man recommends *no book?*
*Its author

A third contributing factor is the nature of the embedding verb. For instance, experiencer verbs tend to shift the perspective so that an object NP more easily takes scope over the subject (cf. note 6).

What emerges from this rapid overview is the impression that there is an asymmetry between subject and object position. In order for a quantifier in object position to take wide scope and give rise to relational interpretations, several conditions have to be met whereas this is not required for quantifiers in subject position. Whether this asymmetry is a consequence of the syntactic structure or is a semantic fact pertaining to the predication relation between subject and predicate is still an open and interesting question but one that would take us beyond the scope of this chapter.[15]

3.4 Parameters and mental representations

In the preceding section I have discussed the role that parameter setting plays in the interpretation of sentences. In this section I want to make some more general points about parameters. It might be revealing to draw a parallel with the use of parameters in theoretical discussions of language acquisition. Within the Chomskian tradition it is commonly held that the child arrives at the specific grammar of the language spoken around her/him partly by setting a number of parameters whose values are left unspecified by

Universal Grammar. For instance, one parameter that needs to be set is whether the language is head final or head initial. We can think of the child as starting out with very general hypotheses about language and subsequently narrowing these down through parameter setting to a set which characterises a specific language. The role of parameters in the interpretation of sentences and discourse is quite similar. Any expression of the language, be it a word, a phrase, or a sentence, taken out of context, is open to a large number of interpretations. Another way to say this is to say that it is underdetermined with respect to a variety of possible interpretations, where underdeterminacy can be linked to the presence of parameters. Each parameter then represents a way in which the interpretation can vary. For instance, a common noun like *book* will be interpreted as a one-place relation or property with a parameter for individuals. In order to figure out whether some particular individual has this property, we need to set the value of the parameter to be that individual. Similarly, the interpretation of an NP like *every woman* involves a parameter over properties, etc. Once these linguistic expressions are used in a particular context, some of the indeterminacy will be resolved, but other aspects of indeterminacy will remain and it won't be until we have full information about place and time of utterance and the speaker's intentions that we can set the parameters associated with the location, occurrences of pronouns and deictic adverbials and eventually arrive at a completely specific interpretation of the sentence in its context. It's presumably for this reason that Barwise & Perry emphasise that meaning in Situation Semantics is a relation between an utterance situation, a described situation, and various background or resource situations. To return to our analogue with acquisition: just as the child progresses towards a more specific grammar by setting parameters, so the interpretation of a sentence might be seen as a sequence of settings of parameters, each of which will tie down the interpretation a little more. Parameter setting in the course of interpreting linguistic expressions is thus a way of getting from a very general, underspecified situation to a specific, fully determined situation.

In the examples we have been looking at in this chapter, parameter settings have been influenced by parameter settings in the interpretation of other constituents in the same sentence or in previous discourse. We have seen that questions like (1), repeated here as (50)

(50)   Which book did *every author* recommend?
        a. War and Peace
        b. *His* most recent book

can be understood as asking the addressee to provide a value for the parameter associated with the interpretation of *which book*. There are two ways in which this could be done; either with respect to a specific situation, in which case the addressee can name or point to a specific book as in the answer in (50a), or by providing a characterisation of the type of book by suggesting a restriction on the parameter setting as in (50b).

The Situation Semantics approach outlined here handles the various readings of the sentence types discussed directly by the semantics, i.e. by the interpretation rules for lexical items, phrases, and sentences, in particular by the ways parameters can be set. Parameters, then, are not syntactic objects; rather they are means of identifying various aspects of indeterminacy of the interpretation of linguistic expressions, indeterminacy that will be resolved by syntactic context, discourse context, and speaker intentions. This approach apparently contrasts with other approaches which annotate syntactic representations such as LF with semantic features such as $+/-$ REFERENTIAL, $+/-$ QUANTIFICATIONAL. However, the contrast might be only superficial. Actually spelling out what it means for some constituent to be marked with a feature like [+REFERENTIAL] when the LF representation is interpreted could conceivably amount to something along the lines I have sketched here in terms of Situation Semantics. The real contrast then would amount to whether one believes that annotating a syntactic representation is necessary to account for the readings that arise. As should have become clear from my arguments in this paper, I don't think so. I believe we can get the desired results by looking at the interaction between syntactic configurations and interpretation rules without also annotating syntactic representations with semantic features. In Situation Semantics, understanding a sentence involves figuring out what the facts in a situation described by a given sentence may or must be. Certain sentences will involve only facts pertaining to a particular situation, others will describe types of situations as we have seen. Which way a sentence tends to be interpreted presumably depends on its context but also to what extent the situations the listener has to construct reflect standard assumptions about the way the world is and how individuals are related. For instance, provided with the information that someone is an author, it seems natural to refer to some book written by her/him. It is standard associations like this that seem to account for the relative availability of relational interpretations. On the Situation Semantics approach we can say that relational readings in such contexts reflect one aspect of our ability to perceive uniformities across situations.

NOTES

1 An earlier version of this chapter was presented at a workshop on Interrogative Quantification in Groningen. I am grateful to Lars Hellan, Alice ter Meulen, Almerindo Ojeda, and Barbara Partee for their comments on that version. For the present version I have benefited from discussions with Robin Cooper and Lyn Frazier and comments from Sheila Dooley Collberg as well as very helpful suggestions from Ruth Kempson.

2 Cf. Groenendijk & Stokhof (1983) who make a similar three-way distinction and who also argue that the readings are distinct.

3 For a fuller presentation of the arguments, the reader is referred to Engdahl (1986, chapter 2).

4 In the Scandinavian languages, the possessive pronoun in the interrogative

quantifier would be a reflexive pronoun, hence clearly a bound anaphor. See Engdahl (1986) for examples and discussion of their implications.

5 Reinhart (1976) and later works defines c-command as in (i):

(i) α c-commands β iff α does not dominate β and the first branching node dominating α also dominates β.

6 As Lyn Frazier has pointed out to me, the requirement that the NP c-command the gap position must be qualified to account for cases involving experiencer verbs as in (i).

(i) [Which letters]$_i$ [e_i impress *every woman* most?]
     Her first love letters

Here the NP in object position doesn't c-command the gap in subject position but it still can take scope over it, as is also shown by the declarative counterpart in (ii).

(ii) *Her* first love letters impress *every woman* most

7 This example retains the relevant features from Karttunen's original example (i), but avoids the additional problem with the comparative construction.

(i) The man who gave his paycheck to his wife was wiser than the man who gave *it* to his mistress. (Karttunen 1969)

8 Cf. Heim (1982) for some important considerations. Groenendijk & Stokhof (1983) argue that we need to assume relational readings for indefinites in general and that these are truth conditionally distinct from non-relational readings. Their argument is based on examples such as (i).

(i) There is *a woman* whom every man loves
     a. Mary   (individual continuation)
     b. *John loves Mary,
          Bill loves Suzy . . .   (pairwise continuation)
     c. *His* mother   (functional continuation)

Noting that a pair-list continuation does not result in a well-formed interpretable discourse, whereas the functional (what we here call relational) continuation does, Groenendijk & Stokhof conclude that the functional interpretation arising from indefinite NPs is not merely an abbreviation for, for example, the pair-list interpretation. Since it is normally assumed that *there* insertion sentences are truth-conditionally equivalent to the corresponding simple sentences, in this case (ii), this claim needs to be investigated seriously.

(ii) Every man loves a woman

9 I here just give a simplified account of some basic notions in Situation Semantics. The notation I use is similar to the one introduced in Cooper (1984a,b and this volume). For further details concerning the situation theoretical basis for Situation Semantics, see Cooper (in preparation). Cooper & Engdahl (in preparation) contains applications of this theory to a number of constructions in English, including questions and relational interpretations of NPs.

10 I am using parameters here in a slightly wider sense than what is common in current Government-Binding theory, but a sense that agrees with the use of parameter in science in general. Note that the value of a parameter is not just + or −. The values will be objects of different types corresponding to the types of arguments the relation requires.

11 Actually, given that there is more than one person named John, we must also set the value of some parameter associated with the use of *John* in a particular sentence to some specific individual named John.

12 In more precise terms, I take *every* to be a relation that holds between properties.

(I have followed the approach taken in Cooper (1984a, 1987).) What this relation is, is spelled out in the structural constraint in (i) where [...] represents a property. $\models$, pronounced **supports**, holds between a situation and a fact if that fact is in the situation.

(i)   If s $\models \langle\!\langle$every, [**a** | $\langle\!\langle$r, . . ., **a**, . . .; i$\rangle\!\rangle$], [**a** | $\langle\!\langle$r′, . . ., **a**, . . .; i′$\rangle\!\rangle$]; 1 $\rangle\!\rangle$
       then if s $\models \langle\!\langle$r, . . ., **a**, . . .; i$\rangle\!\rangle$, then s $\models \langle\!\langle$r′, . . ., **a**, . . .; i′$\rangle\!\rangle$.

According to (i), if the *every* relation holds between two properties, then any individual who has the first property will also have the second property.

13 See Engdahl (1986, chapter 5) for some discussion of this.

14 The following section is a condensed version of parts of Cooper & Engdahl (in preparation). The reader is referred to that paper for details, regarding both the syntactic structures and the interpretation rules assumed.

15 Besides examples having to do with relational readings, we also need to account for certain restrictions on the interpretation of pronouns. For instance we need to account for why the value of the parameter in the interpretation of *he* in (i) cannot be the same as the value of the parameter in *him*, whereas this is necessary in the case of *himself* in (ii).

    (i)   He loves him
    (ii)   He loves himself

Within the Government-Binding framework, such facts are handled by the Binding Theory which uses a partitioning of NPs into three distinct types, each subject to a special binding principle. Using a Situation Semantics approach, we would have to constrain the setting of parameters in the same fact. Some ideas on how this could be done are outlined in Engdahl (1984). See also Cooper (1984b) for suggestions about how to handle reflexives in Situation Semantics.

REFERENCES

Barwise, J. & Cooper, R. 1981. Generalised quantifiers and natural language. *Linguistics and Philosophy* 4: 159–219.

Barwise, J. & Perry, J. 1983. *Situations and attitudes*. Cambridge, Mass.: MIT Press.

Berwick, R. & Wexler, K. 1982. Parsing efficiency, binding, and c-command. In D. Flickinger, N. Macken & N. Wiegand (eds.) *Proceedings of the First West Coast Conference on Formal Linguistics*, Stanford.

Chomsky, N. 1981. *Lectures on government and binding*. Dordrecht: Foris.

Chomsky, N. 1982. *Some concepts and consequences of the theory of government and binding*. Cambridge, Mass.: MIT Press.

Cooper, R. 1979. The interpretation of pronouns. In F. Heny & H. Schnelle (eds.) *Syntax and semantics*, vol. 10, New York: Academic Press, 61–92.

Cooper, R. 1984a. Sentence negation in situation semantics. *Proceedings of the Twentieth Annual Meeting of the Chicago Linguistic Society*, Chicago.

Cooper, R. 1984b. Lectures on preliminary ELIUSS. Ms, Center for the Study of Language and Information, Stanford.

Cooper, R. 1987. Preliminaries to the treatment of generalized quantifiers in Situation Semantics. In P. Gärdenfors (ed.) *Generalized quantifiers: linguistic and logical approaches*. Dordrecht: Reidel.

Cooper, R. In preparation. Introduction to Situation Semantics. Ms., University of Edinburgh.

Cooper, R. & Engdahl, E. in preparation. Situation Semantics for long distance dependencies. Ms., University of Edinburgh.

Engdahl, E. 1984. Anaphors, gaps, and questions in Situation Semantics. Ms., Center for the Study of Language and Information, Stanford.

Engdahl, E. 1986. *Constituent questions*. Dordrecht: Reidel.

Groenendijk, J. & Stokhof, M. 1983. Interrogative quantifiers and Skolem functions. In K. Ehlich & H. van Riemsdijk (eds.) *Connectedness in sentence, discourse, and text.* Tilburg University.

Heim, I. 1982. The semantics of definite and indefinite noun phrases. Ph.D thesis, University of Massachusetts.

Karttunen, L. 1969. Pronouns and variables. *Proceedings of the Fifth Annual Meeting of the Chicago Linguistic Society*, Chicago.

May, R. 1985. *Logical form; its structure and derivation*, Cambridge, Mass.: MIT Press.

Reinhart, T. 1976. The syntactic domain of anaphora. Ph.D thesis, Massachusetts Institute of Technology.

III

On the syntactic base for interpretation

4

Bound variable anaphora

ROBERT MAY

1 Are there bound variable pronouns?

For an element α to qualify as an occurrence of a bound variable it must satisfy two conditions, one necessary, the other sufficient, relative to a coindexed operator β:

Necessary Condition: α is c-commanded by β.

Sufficient Condition: α is locally Ā-bound by β.

I presume that because of well-known arguments as to the generality of bound variable anaphora, these conditions apply at LF, at which both *wh* and quantified phrases occur in Ā-positions.

When these conditions are applied to bound variable anaphora, that is, the occurrence of pronouns as bound variables, it turns out that the cases standardly used to illustrate the phenomenon do not satisfy them both. For example consider *Everyone/who saw his mother* under the syntactic analysis in (1):

(1) everyone$_i$/who$_i$ [e$_i$ saw his$_i$ mother]

The occurrence of the pronoun here is not, strictly speaking from the syntactic point of view, a bound variable at all, since it is *not* Ā-bound. Rather it inherits, so to speak, its status as a bound variable, in the semantic sense, from being A-bound by a trace, which itself is a bound variable, satisfying both the Necessary and Sufficient Conditions. I will henceforth refer to this type of case as a pseudo-variable construction. In fact, under virtually all current theories of bound variable anaphora, cases like (1) are taken as paradigmatic; the common thread which runs through them is that they come to affirm in various ways the following proposition:

Proposition: There are no syntactic occurrences of pronouns as bound variables

That is, the shared notion is that there are no well-formed occurrences of pronouns as true bound variables, i.e. where they are locally Ā-bound, so that if the Proposition seems paradoxical, it is because it entails the rejection of the Sufficient Condition on bound variable anaphora. The primary reason for maintaining the Proposition is well known. It is to account for weak crossover, the absence of a bound variable interpretation in *His mother saw everyone/Who did his mother see*:

(2) everyone$_i$/who$_i$ [his$_i$ mother saw e$_i$]

Here since the pronoun is locally Ā-bound it cannot be a bound variable. Bound variable anaphora requires the intermediation of another bound element.

In this chapter I will argue, counter to current approaches, that the Proposition is false and that the Sufficient Condition holds for bound variable anaphora. Rather than banning outright the occurrence of local Ā-binding, as those do who subscribe to the Proposition, I will propose that this is a perfectly legitimate and attested form of binding. The constraints we observe on this kind of binding will be seen to follow from constraints inherent in the system of Ā-binding itself, and will attempt to reduce the possibilities of bound variable anaphora to constraints on Ā-binding.

2   Some contemporary theories

Before proceeding, I wish to outline briefly some theories of bound variable anaphora, so that it can be seen just how they come to affirm the Proposition.

2.1   Chomsky/Higginbotham

This treatment, first presented informally in Chomsky (1976) and in considerable detail in Higginbotham (1980), incorporates the idea that pronouns must have an occurrence of an antecedent in an A-position to their left in order to qualify as bound variables. Thus, the pseudo-variable case, *Everyone/who saw his mother*, where the pronoun will have a trace as antecedent, allows of bound variable anaphora, but weak crossover is excluded, as the pronoun has its antecedent trace to its right. Clearly since this theory stipulates that a bound variable pronoun must have an antecedent in an A-position it affirms the Proposition, as, given the structural configurations of English, any pronoun which is locally Ā-bound will necessarily lack an antecedent of the appropriate type.

While this approach, particularly as presented by Higginbotham, covers a great range of detail, I think it might be criticised for a certain lack of naturalness, as it is unclear why constraints holding of LF should be stated in terms of linear string precedence – why should leftness, as opposed to rightness be the appropriate predicate in which to state the constraint? Rather, it seems more appropriate that conditions on LF, if anything, should be stated in structural terms; the next theory we turn to in fact has just this property.

2.2   Koopman & Sportiche

This analysis, developed in Koopman & Sportiche (1982) introduces the Bijection Principle. The idea here is that there must be a one-to-one correspondence between Ā-binders and bindees. A point in favour of this analysis, given the comment of the previous paragraph, is that it is stated strictly in structural hierarchical terms. It straightforwardly distinguishes the pseudo-variable from the weak crossover cases. The former is well-formed because the *wh*-phrase or quantifier locally Ā-binds only one element, its trace, while the latter is excluded, since both the trace and the pronoun are locally Ā-bound. Obviously this theory also has the Proposition as a theorem, since (leaving resumptive pronouns to the side), in virtue of trace theory, a *wh* or quantifier will already Ā-bind one category, and to bind another, such as a pronoun, would contravene the constraint.

It is known that the Bijection Principle as stated by Koopman & Sportiche is too strong, as it excludes well-formed across-the-board and parasitic gap constructions, in which a single operator Ā-binds multiple empty categories. We may thus prefer a version of this principle due to Safir (1984), which allows multiple Ā-binding, so long as all of the bound elements are of the same type; viz. all traces or all pronouns. This allows as well-formed the constructions just mentioned, but treats the pseudo-variable and weak crossover cases as under the Koopman & Sportiche constraint. For our purposes, then, these approaches will be considered equivalent.

2.3 Reinhart

Brief mention should also be made of proposals of Reinhart (1983). In her view all anaphoric connections are between *A-positions*, and bound variable pronouns are just those which have c-commanding A-antecedents (regardless of whether these antecedents are quantificational or not). The pseudo-variable construction is allowed, as either the trace of the *wh*-phrase or the quantified phrase, in its surface position, licenses the pronoun as a bound variable, while weak crossover is excluded because neither of these elements c-commands the pronoun at S-Structure. Consequently, the Proposition is affirmed in the strongest possible sense, thus Reinhart denies the relevancy of Ā-binding for bound variable anaphora.

2.4 Partee & Bach

All of the proposals discussed thus far share basic presuppositions on linguistic theory falling under the rubric of extended standard theory. A different approach, falling within extended Montague grammar is explored by Bach & Partee (1980) and Partee & Bach (1984). The idea here centres around developments of NP-storage, as introduced by Cooper; see Cooper (1983), as well as May (1987) for some commentary. Partee & Bach propose that a rule of grammar is an *n*-tuple of the following form (leaving aside certain parts irrelevant to the discussion):

⟨PS rule, semantic rule, LPST, QST, conditions⟩

The first member of such *n*-tuples will be a phrase structure rule, and the second will normally be function application. My interest here, however, is in the last three members, as it is they which give rise to the anaphora constraints. The LPST – the local pronoun store – is a set of indices, while the QST – the quantifier store – is a set of pairs of quantifier meanings and indices. The conditions allow for stores either to be composed, disjoined or identified. A sample of the relevant phrase structure rules, along with some of the conditions on the LPST and the QST which they introduce, is provided in (3):

(3) a. $S \rightarrow NP\ VP$, LPST(NP) $\cap$ LPST(VP)$=\varnothing$, LPST(S)$=$ $QST_I(S)$

b. $NP \rightarrow DET\ N$, LPST(DET) $\cap$ LPST(N)$=\varnothing$, LPST(NP)$=$ $QST_I(NP)$

c. $VP \rightarrow V\ NP$, LPST(VP)$=$LPST(V) $\cup$ LPST(NP)

By rule (c), LPST(VP), the composition under set union of the pronoun stores of the verb and the object noun phrase, contains the index of the object NP. By rule (a), the LPST of the subject must be disjoint from that of VP – hence the standard 'disjoint reference' effects. QST_I is the set of indices of the quantifier store. By rule (b) this set will also be the LPST of the NP, so that the disjointness effect is extended to crossover cases such as (4):

(4) He saw [$_{NP_i}$ everyone$_j$'s mother]

Here, by rule (b), LPST(NP) will contain the index of the quantifier embedded in it, since this is stored for later quantifying. This index is in turn passed up to the VP, as specified by rule (c), but by rule (a), the LPST(VP) must be disjoint from that of the subject NP. Hence the subject NP cannot be indexed j, and thus cannot be a bound variable, as it cannot bear an occurrence of the same index as the quantifier phrase, (which itself will be assigned broad scope through the functioning of the quantifier store). The pseudo-variable case, on the other hand, will be accounted for by virtue of the first condition of rule (b). Consider the structure (5):

(5) Everyone saw [$_{NP_i}$ his$_j$ mother]

By rule (b), j is excluded from LPST(NP) by the disjointness condition on the pronoun stores of the determiner and the noun. Since the pronoun store of VP will not contain j either, there is nothing blocking *everyone* bearing this index as well, since even if it bears this index, the disjointness condition will be satisfied. Thus the pronoun can be a bound variable in this structure.

While it comes to do so for rather different reasons, and states matters in rather different terms, it is plain that Partee & Bach's approach equally well has the consequence of affirming the Proposition, as it excludes (4) and allows (5). Their analysis, however, does face a difficulty not afflicting the other approaches considered (as Partee & Bach themselves note). This has to do with weak crossover:

(6) [$_{NP_i}$ His$_j$ mother] saw everyone$_j$

As in the example just discussed, LPST(NP), that is the pronoun store of the subject, does not contain j, the index of the pronoun. Hence, the disjointness condition imposed by rule (a) is satisfied with the pronoun and the quantifier phrase co-indexed, and with the quantifier phrase having broad scope (by the functioning of the quantifier store). But this prediction is clearly counterfactual. A possible recourse would be to join the LPST of DET with that of the NP, but that would have the undesirable effect of barring anaphoric connections for the pseudo-variable case and sentences such as *His mother loves him*. The problem here is that the difference in anaphoric possibilities for (6), as compared with (5), apparently is a function of asymmetric relations between the subject and object positions. But the storage system, as developed by Partee & Bach and unlike the other approaches considered, is fundamentally symmetrical, so that (6) is treated in precisely the same way as (5), leading to the inadequacies in the treatment of crossover just noted.

While all of these approaches have something to recommend them, and while each may perhaps be criticised for some conceptual and/or empirical shortcoming, my central objection to them centres rather around their affirmation of the Proposition, which I believe to be fundamentally incorrect. Where the mistake lies is in viewing the possibility of bound variable anaphora as in some way derivative from the possibilities of relations between argument positions. What we need to recognise is that what is significant are in fact Ā-binding relations. In the next section I will turn to the empirical reasons showing why we need to look at matters in this way.

3 The problem

The problem for all of the aforementioned theories can be garnered by contemplation of the following example, the importance of which was initially discussed in May (1977), to which the reader is referred for many more examples of this type:

(7) Somebody from every city despises it/its architecture

The observation about this sentence is that the pronoun, whether it be the object of the verb or contained within the object, can be understood as a bound variable. And not only that – when the pronoun is understood in this way the quantifier phrase which binds it, *every city*, must correspondingly be understood with broadest scope. To loosely paraphrase its meaning: for every city, there is somebody from that city such that they despise that city/ that city's architecture. To my mind giving a proper account of this correlation of properties – the inverse linking of quantifier scope along with bound variable anaphora – is the key to a proper theory of bound variable anaphora.

Now, why is this a problem for the theories above? For a theory such as Reinhart's matters are straightforward: the quantified phrase simply does not c-command the pronoun, and hence it cannot be a bound variable. Also it is not clear how the scope interactions are to be obtained on her theory. For the LF-theories of Chomsky/Higginbotham and Koopman & Sportiche, which follow the ideas of May (1977) regarding scope, the scope properties can be captured by movement of *every city* to give something roughly like (8):

(8) every city$_i$ [somebody from e_i]$_j$ [e_j despises it$_i$]]

But this representation, unfortunately is not well-formed on either of those theories, since on the one hand it_i is to the right of its antecedent e_i, and on the other *every city* Ā-binds these two categories. The difficulty for Partee & Bach is that the LPST of the subject NP will include the indices of the QST, and hence the index of *every city*; but the LPST of the subject must be disjoint from that of the object. Consequently the pronoun cannot be a bound variable. This problem while it has not gone totally unnoticed – both Higginbotham (1980) and Safir (1984) provide *ad hoc* conditions to cover these specific cases – is, in fact, endemic to all of the approaches to bound variable anaphora sketched above.

The type of bound variable anaphora displayed by (7) is, I assert, true bound variable anaphora; it is the impossibility of this sort of anaphora to which theories which maintain the Proposition are committed. That is, it is a case in which bound variable anaphora is possible just in virtue of Ā-binding. It is not an isolated case, although it is, because of the correlated interactive scope effects, probably the most interesting. The same type of true bound variable anaphora can be found in the following examples; their *wh*-counterparts, which display the same anaphora properties, are also provided, along with that of inverse linking.

(9) a. Everyone's mother loves him/his sister
     b. They told every boy's parents that he should take the exam
(10) a. John read every book before filing it
     b. They criticised every artist after he/his patron had left the room
(11) a. Which people from which city despise it/its architecture
     b. Whose mother loves him/his sister
     c. Which book did John read without filing it

In (9) the quantifier is embedded, as in (7), in a noun phrase while in (10) it occurs as object. In none of the examples does it c-command, at S-structure, the pronoun, which nevertheless is understood anaphorically – in fact, as a bound variable.

Now one might question my assertion that the pronouns in these cases are bound variable pronouns. For instance, Reinhart (1983) simply attempts to deny the data, claiming that examples like (7) do not show bound variable anaphora, although she agrees that the quantifiers are inversely linked. For the particular examples she cites, I simply disagree with the judgements; all appear to me to allow bound variable anaphora:

(12) a. People from each of the small western cities hate it
     b. Gossip about every businessman harmed his career
     c. The neighbours of each of the pianists hate him

Partee & Bach (1984), on the other hand, don't deny the anaphoric linkage; rather they think it is of a different kind, suggesting that they are donkey pronouns. But I doubt that this could be right, since singular donkey pronouns cannot have *every*-phrases for their antecedents; rather such phrases can only occur in donkey-contexts with plural pronouns.

(13)   The person who owns every donkey beats *it/them

But in (7) we readily observe that there is an *every*-phrase which binds a singular pronoun.

Such scepticism can perhaps be laid to rest by noting the results of a positive test for bound variable anaphora, which shows quite conclusively that the examples above are in fact of this variety. Lasnik (1976) and Reinhart (1983) point out that if a pronoun can be understood with sloppy identity relative to a deletion context, then it is in a position in which it can occur relative to the position of its antecedent, as a bound variable. Thus consider (14):

(14)   Nobody from New York rides its subways, but everybody from Tokyo does

Clearly this sentence is ambiguous; in particular it allows of a sloppy construal in which Tokyoites ride Tokyo's subways. But then *it* is in a position relative to the embedded complement position, in which it can be a bound variable. And this is exactly the configuration which we observe to hold between the quantifier phrase and the pronoun in (7). Notice that this diagnostic establishes the pronoun as a bound variable relative to some structural position. Thus while we might find some particular sentences of the relevant form which don't show bound variable anaphora, this would not in and of itself show that bound variable anaphora is proscribed in this syntactic configuration. Rather I would maintain that any such cases would always be found in correlation with a lack of inverse linking of the quantifiers. But then the lack of bound variable anaphora would follow directly, since at LF the quantifier phrase would not Ā-bind the pronoun. In this case there would be failure of the Necessary Condition on bound variables.

I take it as established then that there are genuine instances of bound variable anaphora, in which the pronoun is locally Ā-bound, and which stand in contradistinction to the pseudo-bound variables, in which there is local A-binding. As such these cases counterexemplify the various contemporary theories of bound variable anaphora, as outlined above. It is therefore time to proceed to a theory which can properly characterise the constraints on true bound variable anaphora, and hence can distinguish, among its consequences, weak crossover from inverse linking.

4   A theory of bound variable anaphora

4.1   Some theoretical assumptions

I will approach bound variable anaphora within the context of the theory of LF-representation developed in May (1985). That theory is based on the *Theory of Adjunction*, which can be formulated as in (15):

(15)   Theory of Adjunction

(i)   A Category $C = \{n_1, \ldots, n_n\}$

(ii) C dominates $\alpha =_{df} \forall n \; \varepsilon \; C$ (n dominates α)

That is categories are sets of nodes, and to be dominated by a category is to be dominated by every member node. The following is the primary theorem:

(16)   Adjuncts are not dominated by the categories to which they are adjoined.

When the Theory of Adjunction is joined to the definition of c-command offered by Aoun & Sportiche (1983):

(17) α c-commands $\beta =_{df}$ every maximal projection dominating α dominates β, and α does not dominate β,

the following theorem is derived:

(18)   The c-command domain of adjuncts is demarcated by the maximal projection immediately dominating the category to which they are adjoined.

So, for instance, the c-command domain of an S-adjunct would be S', of a VP-adjunct S, and so on. The *Theory of Scope* is as follows, where as usual the coincidence of scope and c-command domain is assumed:

(19)   Theory of Scope

    (i)   A quantifier may have arbitrary scope

    (ii) A Σ-sequence is freely interpreted.

The intent of clause (i) is that QR may adjoin a phrase to any node, so long as it can be properly interpreted in that position. I presume that since the semantic clauses are formalised relative to the notions sentence and sentential function, this will amount to adjunction to any node in which the quantifier has clausal scope. By the theory of adjunction, note, these nodes will include VP, as VP-adjuncts have S as their c-command domains. The intent of clause (ii) is that sequences of quantifiers in a particular structural configuration may take on any relative scope dependency, including being scopally independent. The configuration is defined as follows:

(20) σ is a Σ-sequence $=_{df} \forall \; O_i, \; O_j \; \varepsilon \; \sigma$, O_i c-commands O_j, and O_j c-commands O_i.

The precise semantic details for the Theory of Scope are provided in May (1988).

We are in need of one further piece of theoretical apparatus, the *Theory of Paths*, as developed in Pesetsky (1982):

(21)   Theory of Paths

$$\forall \; p,q \; \varepsilon \; S \; (p \cap q \rightarrow (p \subseteq q \lor q \subseteq p))$$

(21) expresses Pesetsky's *Path Containment Condition* (PCC). A *path* is a set of successively immediately dominating nodes (N.B. not categories) leading from a bindee to a c-commanding Ā-binder. Each contiguous pair of nodes in a path is a *path segment*, and a path is just a set of such segments. The set of paths associated with a representation is a *path structure*. Where S is a path structure, and p and q are path segments, the PCC states that if paths intersect, one must wholly contain the other. Any structure whose paths intersect and merely overlap is ill-formed. Note that paths intersect only if

they share at least one path segment, so that paths sharing a single node do not intersect, and that paths are nondirectional, so that the path segment defined by $\{\alpha, \beta\}$ is identical to that defined by $\{\beta, \alpha\}$.

We can now state the *Theory of Bound Variable Anaphora*:

(22) Theory of Bound Variable Anaphora

Bound variable pronouns must satisfy the Path Containment Condition

As Pesetsky conceives the Path Containment Condition, it is a constraint which regulates Ā-binding of empty categories. The Theory of Bound Variable Anaphora, then, is simply a generalisation to all cases of Ā-binding, regardless of whether the bindee is empty or not. We are now in a position to consider the various cases of bound variable anaphora, relative to this nexus of assumption about LF.

4.2 The cases

4.2.1 Weak crossover
The analysis of weak crossover is as follows. Take the structure in (23), the paradigmatic weak crossover configuration:

(23)

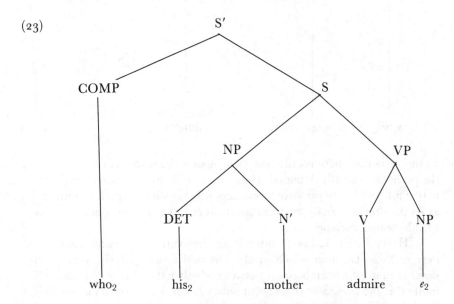

Under our assumptions, as this structure contains two locally Ā-bound elements, the trace of *wh* and the pronoun, it generates two paths, as indicated:

$$\text{path}(his_2) = \{NP, \quad\quad S, S'\}$$
$$\text{path}(e_2) = \quad\quad \{VP, S, S'\}$$

The paths have an intersection, the segment defined by the pair of nodes $\{S, S'\}$, but neither path properly embeds within the other. Since there is only an overlap of paths, (23) violates the path condition, and is ill-formed. Weak crossover follows directly.

What about pseudo crossover – that is, the possibility of anaphora in *Who admires his mother* as opposed to *Who does his mother admire?* The structure here is (24):

(24)

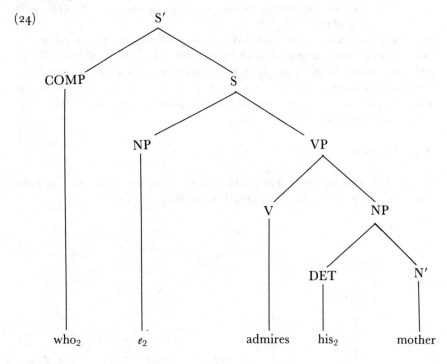

In this structure there is only one path, as only the trace is locally Ā-bound; the pronoun is locally A-bound. Hence there is no intersection of paths to be had at all, and hence the structures vacuously satisfies the path condition. So as on the previous analyses, this case turns out to be just as much a case of a pseudo bound variable.

Harry Leder makes an interesting observation regarding weak cross-over in Swiss-German which nicely falls under the analysis. What Leder notes is that (25) is ambiguous between whether the phrase *syni Meuter* 'his mother' is the subject or object, but only when it is understood as the object can it be understood as a bound variable:

(25)   Syni Meuter het jedes Chind garn
       his mother AUX every child love
       'His mother loves every child / Every child loves his mother'

What is curious about this observation is that, because of verb second phenomena, in either case *syni Meuter* is topicalised, so that if we assume that the quantified phrase *jedes Chind* is adjoined to S at LF, the relation of these two phrases is the same in either case. The relevant structures are as in (26):

(26) a. $[_{S'}$ syni$_i$ Meuter$_j$ het $[_S$ jedes Chind$_i$ $[_S$ e_j $[_{VP}$ e_i garn]]]]

   b. $[_{S'}$ syni$_i$ Meuter$_j$ het $[_S$ jedes Chind$_i$ $[_S$ e_i $[_{VP}$ e_j garn]]]]

It should be apparent that both of these structures satisfy the Necessary
Condition, since in each case the quantified phrase c-commands, and hence
has within its scope, the pronoun. This is because the quantified phrase is
adjoined to S, so that its c-command domain is adjudged relative to the next
maximal projection up, which is S', and which dominates the pronoun *syni*.
But is sufficiency also attained by these structures, by their manifesting
proper path structures? In these structures there are now three paths, as
shown:

(27) a.   path $(syni_i)$ $=$ $\{S, S'\}$
          path (e_i) $= \{VP, S, S\}$
          path (e_j) $=$ $\{S, S, S'\}$

   b.   path $(syni_i)$ $=$ $\{S, S'\}$
          path (e_i) $=$ $\{S, S\}$
          path (e_j) $= \{VP, S, S, S'\}$

(Notice that the path of the pronoun is a 'backwards' path, but a path
nonetheless, since it leads from the pronoun to its c-commanding Ā-binder.
That this should be possible just follows from the characteristics of adjunction.) Here the paths to consider are those of the traces, as while the path of
the pronoun does intersect that of e_j, it properly embeds in its path. But since
in (27a) there is overlap but no embedding, (26a) is ill-formed, but (26b) is
well-formed, as in its path structure there is proper embedding. It thus
follows that bound variable anaphora is possible only where the topicalised
phrase containing the pronoun is the object, comparable to English *Every
child loves his mother.*

We have, it turns out, in fact derived too strong a result; as Leder
points out the problem with the topicalised subject case, as with weak crossover generally, is just that the pronoun cannot be understood as a bound
variable. But as it is here the relevant structure, (26a), is marked as completely ill-formed on the basis of the relationship of the two Ā-bound traces,
and changing the index of the pronoun would not ameliorate this situation. It
turns out, however, that this is not the only possible structure for this sentence; alternatively, the quantified phrase can be adjoined to VP:

(28) $[_{S'}$ syni$_i$ Meuter$_j$ het $[_S$ e_j $[_{VP}$ jedes Chind$_i$ $[_{VP}$ e_i garn]]]]

Its path structure is well-formed, as none of the paths overlap:

   path $(syni_i)$ $=$ $\{S, S'\}$
   path (e_i) $= \{VP, VP\}$
   path (e_j) $=$ $\{S, S, S'\}$

The question then is: Can the pronoun be a bound variable in this structure?
No, since the pronoun is a VP-adjunct, its c-command domain is S; but S
does not dominate the pronoun contained in the topicalised constituent.

Thus this structure does not satisfy the Necessary Condition, preventing a
bound variable interpretation, regardless of the index of the pronoun. We
thus obtain the desired contrast.

4.2.2 Inverse linking Having observed the adequacy of the proposed
account for weak crossover, what of its treatment of inverse linking, that
bugaboo of other theories? Before that can be answered we need to examine
another aspect of these cases. It is this. If in *Somebody from every city despises its
architecture* the quantifier *every city* is to c-command the pronoun, then presumably it must be extracted from the NP which contains it at S-Structure. But,
as is well known, such NPs are extraction islands, witness the ungrammaticality of **Which city does everybody from despise its architecture.* How can these
aspects of this construction – islandhood and inverse scope – be reconciled?

The answer lies in assigning the structure in (29), where the phrase
superficially embedded in NP has been adjoined not to S, but to the NP itself:

(29)

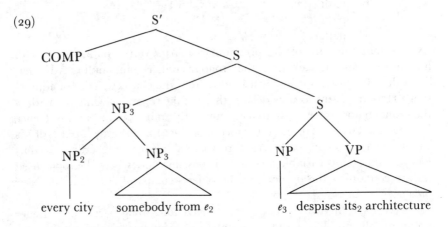

What are the properties of this structure? First, is NP a possible adjunction
site? Yes, since adjunction at LF can be freely to any node. Second, is it an
island violation? No, the phrase *every city* is not extracted from NP, but rather
is adjoined to it. Does it have clausal scope? Yes. It is not dominated by NP_3
so its c-command domain rises up to the next maximal projection dominating it, which will be S' (not S, only one node of which dominates it – note that
the containing phrase, which is also quantificational, has been adjoined to
S). Does it c-command the pronoun? Yes, since it is contained within the NP-
adjoined phrase's c-command domain. Finally, does it have a well-formed
path structure? Again, yes, as can be discerned by examination; (the ellipsis
just denotes irrelevant nodes within NP):

$$\text{path } (e_2) \quad = \quad \{\ldots NP_3, NP_3\}$$
$$\text{path } (it_2) \quad = \{VP, S, S, NP_3\}$$
$$\text{path } (e_3) \quad = \quad \{S, S\}$$

Here the only intersection of path segments is found in those for it_2 and e_3, but they properly embed. Given our assumptions, (29) precisely represents all of the relevant properties of inverse linking constructions.

Inversely linking, it turns out, also displays crossover effects, so that the pronoun cannot be construed as a bound variable in (30):

(30)   It/Its architecture is despised by somebody from every city

The relevant structure is (31), with the path structure as indicated, where for illustration I consider only the weak crossover case:

(31)

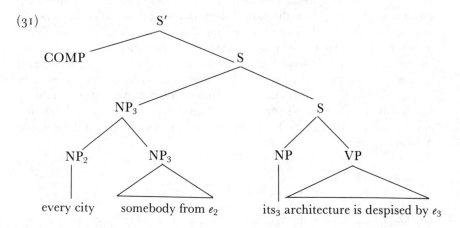

$$\text{path } (e_2) \quad = \quad \{\ldots NP_3, NP_3\}$$
$$\text{path } (it_2) \quad = \quad \{S, S, NP_3\}$$
$$\text{path } (e_3) \quad = \{\ldots VP, S, S\}$$

From the standpoint of c-command and binding, and of island violations, this structure has exactly the same properties as that above. What differs is its path properties; here the path of the pronoun and of e_3, intersect but no longer embed. Rather they display the illicit overlap, so that this structure is now taken as well-formed. If the pronoun, note, were to bear some index different from that of the trace, then the structure would be well-formed, as the pronoun would then generate no path at all.

4.2.3 Scope and bound variables One of the cases that initially was employed to motivate the Necessary Condition on bound variable anaphora was the interaction with scope found in examples like (32):

(32)   Every pilot hit some Mig that chased him

The observation here is that if *every pilot* has broader scope, then bound variable anaphora is possible, but that bound variable anaphora is excluded if this phrase has narrower scope. The structure it will be assigned, assuming that both quantified phrases are adjoined to S, is as in (33), again given with its associated paths – recall that such a structure will itself be ambiguous between the two scopal interpretations, as the adjoined phrases mutually c-command and form a Σ-sequence:

(33) $[_S[_{NP}$ some Mig that chased $him_2]_3$ $[_S[_{NP}$ every $pilot_2$ $[_S$ e_2 hit $e_3]]]]$

$$\text{path } (e_2) \quad = \quad \{S, S\}$$
$$\text{path } (him_2) = \{\ldots NP, S, S\}$$
$$\text{path } (e_3) \quad = \quad \{VP, \quad S, S, S\}$$

The problem here is that when the pronoun is taken as a bound variable, and thus coindexed with the universal phrase, the result runs afoul of the path condition. This is because the path of the pronoun and that of e_3 intersect and improperly overlap. How can this circumstance be rectified? One possibility would be to attach the quantified phrases in the other order, but as the reader can verify this would just lead to another path condition violation between the paths of the traces. The other alternative is to take the tack employed above, and attach the object phrase to VP, as suggested initially by Koopman & Sportiche (1982). (If we had a representation such as that above it would also violate the Bijection Principle, as a single operator would Ā-bind two variables.) This gives (34):

(34) $[_S[_{NP}$ every $pilot_2$ $[_S$ e_2 $[_{VP}[_{NP}$ some Mig that chased $him_2]_3$ $[_{VP}$ hit $e_3]]]]]$

$$\text{path } (e_2) \quad = \{S, S\}$$
$$\text{path } (e_3) \quad = \quad \{VP, CP\}$$

The difference here is that the pronoun is no longer Ā-bound; that is, this case has turned from one of true bound variable anaphora to one of pseudo bound variable anaphora. Under this analysis it is perfectly well-formed, with the indicated path structure, which now only has paths of the traces. But they have no intersection at all, so the path condition is vacuously satisfied. Scope in this structure, by the way, will be fixed with *every city* having broader scope. This is because there is no Σ-sequence, as S dominates the VP-adjoined phrase but not the S-adjoined phrase. Scope therefore just follows the hierarchical order of the constituents. In contrast, (33) above, relative to which scope can freely vary, will be well formed just in case the pronoun has no anaphoric interpretation.

The scope related effects of bound variable anaphora disappear if we flip the subject and object NPs and create a weak crossover environment:

(35) Some Mig that chased him hit every pilot

Here there is no alternative but to adjoin both quantified phrases to S if there is to be any possibility of bound variable anaphora:

(36) $[_S[_{NP}$ every $pilot_3$ $[_S[_{NP}$ some Mig that chased $him_3]_2$ $[_S$ e_2 hit $e_3]]]]$

$$\text{path } (e_2) \quad = \quad \{S, S\}$$
$$\text{path } (him_2) = \{\ldots NP, S, S\}$$
$$\text{path } (e_3) \quad = \quad \{VP, \quad S, S, S\}$$

At this point we can see that, from the standpoint of paths, this is just a garden variety crossover violation; it is, for all intents and purposes no different from (33), and is ruled out, as is (33), because of the illicit relation of the paths of the pronoun and one of the traces of LF-movement. And as should be apparent at this point, if the pronoun bears some other index, distinct from those of the empty categories, then the resulting structure is well-formed, but with a non-anaphoric construal.

4.2.4 **Reconstruction** The examples in (37) exemplify what I have in mind which falls under this rubric:

(37) a. Whose mother loves him
     b. Whose mother does he love

(37a), as discussed in section 3, is of a piece with inverse linking. Even though the binding operator, in this case the *wh*-phrase, does not c-command it in S-structure, the pronoun can still be understood as a bound variable. In (37b), on the other hand, which displays the same S-Structure c-command properties *vis-à-vis* the *wh*-phrase and the pronoun, bound variable anaphora is not possible. This has led to the suggestion that this latter case undergoes 'reconstruction', to give something like: *Who$_i$ [he$_i$ loves e$_i$'s mother]*.

The reason for this manoeuvre is to reduce the impossibility of bound variable anaphora to be reduced to a violation of Principle C of the Binding Theory, and hence to view it comparably to the strong crossover violation *Who does he love*. I am dubious of any such approach, however, since it has never been made particularly clear in what sort of formal operation reconstruction consists, and moreover, reconstruction does not provide any insight as to why bound variable anaphora is possible in (37a). But I am most dubious because there is a straightforward account of the contrast in (37) along the lines we are discussing.

As mentioned, (37a) is strongly reminiscent of the inverse linking cases, and the approach to it is similar in also involving adjunction to NP. The only difference is that the NP which is adjoined to already resides in COMP, so that we have the following structures:

(38) [s'[who$_2$ [e$_2$'s mother]]$_3$ [e$_3$ admires him$_2$]]
     path (e$_2$)   =   {NP$_3$, NP$_3$}
     path (him$_2$) = {VP, S, S', NP$_3$}
     path (e$_3$)   =   {S, S'}

(39) [s'[who$_2$ [e$_2$'s mother]]$_3$ [he$_2$ admires e$_3$]]
     path (e$_2$)   =   {NP$_3$, NP$_3$}
     path (he$_2$) =   {S, S', NP$_3$}
     path (e$_3$)   = {VP, S, S'}

As before, c-command relations are properly encoded; since the *wh*-phrase is adjoined to NP, S' is the first dominating maximal projection, so that the *wh*-phrases c-command the pronouns. The path structures are as indicated – observe that in that of (38) the path of e$_3$ embeds in that of the pronoun, but overlaps with it in the path structure of (39). Consequently, we account for the well-formedness of bound variable anaphora in *Whose mother saw him*, in contrast to its absence in *Whose mother did he see*.

The analysis of these cases is based directly on their LF-representation, and clearly obviates the need for any sort of overt reconstruction of phrases occurring in COMP. In doing so it denies the validity of the generalisation from 'reconstruction' to 'strong crossover', that is, that the lack of anaphora in *Who does he admire* and *Whose mother does he admire* are of a piece, and due to restrictions on binding from A-positions. Rather the analysis here embeds the claim that the appropriate generalisation is from 'weak crossover' to 'reconstruction', that is, there is a lack of anaphora in *Who does his mother admire* and *Whose mother does he admire* because of restrictions on binding from Ā-positions. In this regard I am in agreement with the spirit, if not the letter, of both Higginbotham (1980) and Safir (1984). The treatment also shows that reconstruction should not be considered a unified phenomenon, as there are cases of a different sort to which the present analysis is simply not relevant. (40) is an instance:

(40)   Which picture of himself do you think John likes best

Here there is a problem because at S-Structure this is an apparent violation of Principle A of the Binding Theory; what is problematic here has nothing at all to do with Ā-binding, but rather with A-binding of the reflexive. These cases thus simply do not fall under the proposed analysis, which in so far as it is correct, indicates that any proper consideration of so-called reconstruction must bifurcate it into at least two quite distinct phenomena, only one of which falls under constraints on bound variable anaphora.

4.2.5 Crossed binding All the examples considered thus far have involved one pronoun, although we have examined what happens when there are multiple quantifiers which can vary in scope. But what if there are in addition to the multiple quantifiers also multiple pronouns? The most well-known case of this sort are the crossed binding, Bach–Peters sentences:

(41)   Every pilot who shot at it hit some Mig that chased him

The point about these examples is that regardless of the scope order of the quantifiers the pronouns can be simultaneously understood as bound variables. In Higginbotham & May (1981) a syntactic and semantic approach to such cases was developed. From the syntactic perspective what was important was that a structure of symmetrical scope was derived in which each quantified phrase c-commanded the appropriate pronoun. In the theory of May (1985), which I am assuming here, scope is in general represented symmetrically, so that Absorption, as the rule was called in Higginbotham & May, is subsumed as but a special case of QR. Now I have assumed thus far that the symmetrical configuration, in which there is mutual c-command, involves adjunctions to S; for (41) this will give (42):

(42) [$_S$[some Mig that chased him$_2$]$_3$ [$_S$[every pilot that shot at it$_3$]$_2$
      [$_S$ e_2 hit e_3]]]

There is a problem here, however, with path structure; that associated with
(42) is ill-formed:

path (e_2)   =   {S, S}
path (e_3)   =   {VP, S, S, NP$_2$}
path (him_2) = {... NP$_3$, S, S}
path (it_3) = {... NP$_2$, S, S}

The problem with the lack of embedding among the paths of the two pronouns and that of e_3 are apparent.

It turns out, however, that there is another possible LF-representation
for crossed binding sentences which encodes precisely the same c-command
relations as (42) but a different path structure. The derivation here trades
upon an assumption already employed in the analysis of inverse linking,
namely that there can be adjunction to NP. The idea is that one of the
quantified noun phrases is adjoined to S, and then subsequent adjunctions
are to that NP. This gives rise for the crossed binding case to a structure
which I give schematically in (43):

(43)

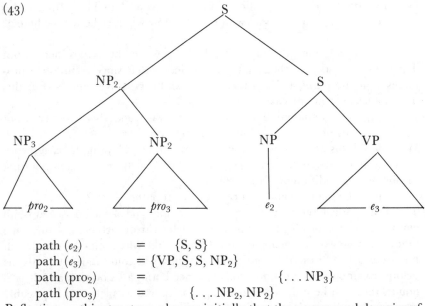

path (e_2)   =   {S, S}
path (e_3)   = {VP, S, S, NP$_2$}
path (pro$_2$) =   {... NP$_3$}
path (pro$_3$) =   {... NP$_2$, NP$_2$}

Reflecting on this structure, observe initially that the c-command domains of
NP$_2$ and NP$_3$ are identical; for both phrases it is demarcated as S. For the
latter phrase this is so because it is not dominated by NP$_2$, to which it is
adjoined. Consequently, each of these phrases c-commands both the trace
and the pronoun with which it is coindexed, as desired. (Note that NP$_2$

category as a whole does not dominate *pro*$_2$, but only part of it; hence this is a legitimate case of c-command.) Turning to the path structures, it is clear that there is no overlap of paths; in fact the only ones which intersect, namely those of the traces, properly embed. Neither of the pronominal paths intersect with any other paths. Thus here the simultaneous anaphoric interpretation of the pronouns is perfectly permissible, representing the characteristic crossed binding pattern of these sentences.

4.2.6 Type identical variables Assuming then that all Ā-bound categories, be they empty or lexical, generate paths, allows us to give a straightforward explanation of the central properties of bound variable anaphora, without recourse to any special principles or constraints. Rather the observations regarding crossover, inverse linking, 'reconstruction', crossed binding and the like simply follow from the general theory of Ā-binding. There is, however, one issue which merits consideration before concluding discussion. Many languages allow the use of resumptive pronouns as a device for Ā-binding into positions in which Ā-binding of empty categories is proscribed. This is even so in English in examples such as (44a), which sharply contrasts with its counterpart in (44b), in which the pronoun is absent; (see Pesetsky (1982) for discussion of ECP effects in the context of Path Theory):

>   (44) a. ?John's the guy who I don't know whether he will be here or not
>   b. *John's the guy who I don't know whether will be here or not

The approach just sketched makes a prediction that since resumptive pronouns generate paths at LF, they should exhibit crossover effects. But this does not seem to be the case:

>   (45) Every student about whom Mary was wondering whether or not his professor failed him is sitting over there

Why should this be so? The answer, I believe, lies in adapting to path theory the underlying idea of Safir's (1984) parallelism constraint, by incorporating the following condition on path structures:

>   (46) Union all coindexed type-identical paths

That is all paths having their origins in the same type of category, that is, all empty categories or all pronouns, and which bear occurrences of the same index are unioned into a single path. Other paths which may be coindexed, but are projected from different category types, will count independently, as before. Examples like (45) now follow. Since both paths originate with pronouns, they will be unioned into a single path, and as such cannot possibly come into conflict with the path condition on path consistency, in contrast to (47), which is a crossover violation:

>   (47) Every student about whom Mary was wondering who his professor failed is sitting over there

The contrast in crossover is also found in other languages in which the use of resumptive pronouns is less marked than in English. Thus in the following examples, from Hebrew and Modern Irish respectively, the pronoun cannot be construed as a bound variable in the (a) cases, in which there has been movement, but can in the (b) cases, in which a resumptive pronoun is employed. (The former examples were brought to my attention by H. Borer; the latter examples are due to J. McCloskey.)

(48) a. Miriám raatá et haíš se   imó   ahavá *e*
         saw   man that mother-his loved

     b. Miriám raatá et haíš se   imó   ahavá otó
         saw   man that mother-his loved   him
         'Miriam saw the man that his mother loved *e*/him'

(49) a. Cén   fear a   sábháil a   mháithair *e*
         which man that saved   his mother

     b. Cén   fear a   sábháil a   mháithair e
         which man that saved   his mother   him
         'Which man did his mother save *e*/him'

Thus it appears that the constraint given as (46) above is of quite general application when we find multiple occurrences of pronouns occurring as bound variables.

5   Closing remark

In this paper I have been looking at an approach to bound variable anaphora which embeds what I believe is the correct generalisation, namely that the Proposition is false and that there are true bound variable pronouns, that is, pronouns which are locally Ā-bound. The perspective I have taken on these cases, a perspective I share with other approaches, is relational, in the sense that the possibility of true bound variable anaphora is a function of how the binding of this element relates to the binding of other elements in the structure. The constraints on this relation are regulated by Path Theory, as this is embedded in the nexus of assumptions made regarding the syntax of Logical Form. Moreover the constraints on bound variable anaphora have been seen to be nothing special, in the sense that they just fall out from more general conditions governing Ā-binding of any type of category. In this sense the theory here views both pronouns and empty categories as on a par, not only in their semantic function, but also in their syntactic role. To the extent that the analysis is correct, it would thus express the optimal analysis of bound variable anaphora in natural language.

REFERENCES

Aoun, J. & Sportiche, D. 1983. On the formal theory of government. *The Linguistic Review* 2: 211–36.
Bach, E. & Partee, B. 1980. Anaphora and semantic structure. In J. Kreiman & A. Ojeda (eds.) *Papers from the Parasession on Pronouns and Anaphora*. Chicago, Illinois: Chicago Linguistic Society, The University of Chicago.

Chomsky, N. 1976. Conditions on rules of grammar. In N. Chomsky, *Essays on form and interpretation*. New York: North-Holland, 1977.

Chomsky, N. 1982. *Some concepts and consequences of the theory of government and binding*. Cambridge, Mass.: MIT Press.

Cooper, R. 1983. *Quantification and syntactic theory*. Dordrecht: Reidel.

Higginbotham, J. 1980. Pronouns and bound variables. *Linguistic Inquiry* 11: 679–708.

Higginbotham, J. & May, R. 1981. Questions, quantifiers and crossing. *The Linguistic Review* 1: 41–79.

Koopman, H. & Sportiche, D. 1982. Variables and the bijection principle. *The Linguistic Review* 2: 139–61.

Lasnik, H. 1976. Remarks on coreference. *Linguistic Analysis* 2: 1–22.

May, R. 1977. The grammar of quantification. Ph.D thesis, MIT, Cambridge, Mass. (Distributed by Indiana University Linguistics Club.)

May, R. 1985. *Logical form: its structure and derivation*. Cambridge, Mass.: MIT Press.

May, R. 1987. Review of R. Cooper *Quantification and syntactic theory*. *Language* 62: 902–8.

May, R. 1988. Interpreting logical form, ms., University of California, Irvine, Irvine, Calif. To appear in *Linguistics and Philosophy*.

Partee, B. & Bach, E. 1984. Quantification pronouns and VP anaphora. In J. Groenendijk, T.M.V. Janssen & M. Stokhof (eds.) *Truth, interpretation and information*. Dordrecht: Foris.

Pesetsky, D. 1982. Paths and categories. Ph.D thesis, MIT, Cambridge, Mass.

Reinhart, T. 1983. *Anaphora and semantic interpretation*. London: Croom Helm.

Safir, K. 1984. Multiple variable binding. *Linguistic Inquiry* 15: 603–38.

5

On implicit arguments

MICHAEL BRODY AND M. RITA MANZINI

Consider sentences of the type of (1) or (2):
  (1) Mary was saying to leave
  (2) The book was being written to make money
These sentences are interpreted roughly as in (3) and (4) respectively:
  (3) ($\exists x$) Mary was saying to x [x to leave]
  (4) ($\exists x$) The book was being written by x (for) x to make money
Within the theory of Government and Binding, which will provide the framework for our discussion, the understood subject of the infinitival sentence is the empty category PRO (Chomsky 1981, 1986). The nature of the understood dative in (1) and of the understood agent in (2) is, however, an open question. In particular, within the framework that we assume, they cannot correspond to empty categories, as we will argue below. Understood elements that are realised neither lexically nor as empty categories are generally known as implicit arguments. It is with implicit arguments that this chapter is mainly concerned.

Our discussion so far is compatible with a number of characterisations for implicit arguments, including in particular a pragmatic characterisation. The assumption that they exist is based so far on the interpretation of sentences like (1) and (2). For such interpretive properties a pragmatic account is in principle available. In this chapter, however, we will argue that implicit arguments are grammatically defined entities, and that they interact in crucial ways with a number of subcomponents of grammar.

Examples of the type of (1) and (2) were first pointed out in Manzini (1983), in the context of a proposal for unifying control with binding theory. In section 1, we will provide a brief summary of this theory, taking into account also the proposals in Brody (1985). We will argue that this version of the theory necessitates the presence of implicit arguments in sentences of the type of (1) and (2), to bind the PRO in the subject position of the infinitival.

In section 2, following ideas in Chomsky (1986), Rizzi (1986), and Roeper (1987) we identify implicit arguments with theta-roles not projected to syntactic positions, and we examine some of their properties in detail. One of our major conclusions will be that implicit arguments can correspond to both agents and datives, as in our original examples (1) and (2), but cannot correspond, at least in English, to direct objects.

In section 3, we examine implicit arguments in the light of the projection principle. This principle requires that all theta-roles subcategorised for must be projected to syntactic positions; implicit datives seem then to represent a straightforward counterexample to it. To explain the distribution of implicit arguments, we will propose a radical modification of the projection principle. Assuming, as in Brody (1985), that S-structure is the fundamental level of representation, our version of the projection principle will say that structural Cases must be projected to syntactic positions. Thus the inherent Case dative with its associated theta-role is allowed not to project, creating an implicit argument. Such a modification of the projection principle has wide ranging consequences, for some of which we will try to account systematically. In particular we will discuss why in general nonsubject theta-roles must be projected, the main content of the standard projection principle.

In section 4, finally, we consider the null direct objects of Italian discussed in Rizzi (1986). We will argue that Italian null objects are in chains headed by a zero clitic corresponding to an implicit argument. As we will show, this conception falls naturally within our theory of implicit arguments. The historical evidence from English presented in Rizzi (1986) in this connection will also be considered.

1   Binding theory and control

According to Chomsky (1981), anaphors and pronominals are subject to conditions A and B of binding theory respectively, as in (5):

(5)   A   An anaphor must be bound in its governing category

B   A pronominal must be free in its governing category

In the core cases, the governing category for an element α can be defined as the minimal category that contains α, a governor for α and a subject; a more complete definition of the notion requires that the subject be accessible to α, as in (6):

(6) γ is the governing category for α iff

γ is the minimal category that dominates α, a governor for α and a subject accessible to α

In turn, a subject is said to be accessible to α if there is an indexing under which it binds α and which does not violate the i-within-i condition. The i-within-i condition states that the following configuration is excluded: $[_i \ldots i \ldots]$.

Under the definition of governing category in (6), binding theory does not account for the choice of antecedents of PRO. According to Chomsky (1981), PRO is a pronominal anaphor. If it is governed and has a governing category, it is subject both to binding condition A, requiring it to be bound in its governing category, and to binding condition B, requiring it to be free in it. It follows that PRO must be ungoverned and cannot have a governing category. But if so, binding theory cannot account for its choice of antecedents.

In this chapter, we adopt the theory of empty categories in Brody (1985). Under this theory PRO is a pure anaphor. The ungoverned status of PRO follows from a condition on chains which requires heads of chains to be Case linked. An element is Case linked if it is governed and has Case, or if it is not governed and does not have Case. Given the assumption that lexical NPs, but not empty categories have Case, the first option corresponds to lexical NPs, the second to PRO.

Following Manzini (1983) and Brody (1985) we then assume that the notion of governing category can be extended to apply to PROs. In particular, following Brody (1985) we assume a notion of g-governor, defined as in (7):

(7) β g-governs α iff
β governs α, or β governs the c-domain of α

(The *c-domain* of α is the domain that contains all and only the nodes that α c-commands – that is, the first maximal projection that dominates α.)

Given (7), the definition of governing category in Chomsky (1981) can be modified as in (8), where the notion of governor is substituted by the notion of g-governor:

(8) γ is a governing category for α iff
γ is the minimal category that dominates α, a g-governor for α, and a subject accessible to α

Under the definition of governing category in (8) binding theory now subsumes control. Consider for example a control sentence embedded in object position, as in (9):

(9) John believed that Mary wanted [PRO to behave well]

In (9) PRO is g-governed by the verb, *want*, that governs the control sentence. The sentence S that immediately contains the control sentence is the governing category for PRO, since S dominates the g-governor for PRO and a subject, *Mary*, that is accessible to PRO. It follows that PRO is required to be bound in S, hence it must be bound by *Mary*. It cannot remain free, and receive arbitrary interpretation; nor can it be long-distance bound, for example by *John*.

Under the definition of governing category in Chomsky (1981), or the modified version of it in (8), the search for a governing category goes on until an accessible subject is found. In Manzini (1983) an alternative way of considering the accessibility requirement is suggested. Under this conception, the search for a governing category stops when the first subject is found, but at this point the subject is checked for accessibility. If the subject is accessible then the notion of governing category is properly defined; if not, no governing category is defined at all. Following this conception of accessibility the notion of governing category is then formulated as in (10):

(10) γ is a governing category for α iff

   (i) γ is the minimal category that dominates α, a g-governor
         for α and a subject β; and

   (ii) β is accessible to α

The empirical consequences of this move can be seen when control sentences embedded in subject position are taken into account. Consider for example (11):

(11)   John believed that [PRO to behave well] Agr could be useful to
       Mary

In (11) the g-governor of PRO is Agr. As in (9) the sentence S that immediately contains the control sentence is the minimal category that dominates a g-governor for PRO and a subject. However, the subject is not accessible to PRO, since coindexing of the PRO with the subject that dominates it would create an i-within-i configuration. Under the definition of governing category in (10), then, PRO in (11) does not have a governing category. But this means that binding theory does not apply to it. Hence we expect PRO to be able to have a long-distance binder, for example *John* in (11); to be able to have an antecedent that does not c-command it, as *Mary* in (11); and to be able not to have an antecedent at all, and to be arbitrary in reference. These predictions seem to be correct.

The predictions of the present theory of binding for lexical anaphors in the subject position of object and subject nominals are essentially the same as for PROs in the subject position of subject and object control sentences respectively. Consider for example (12) and (13). In (12) the anaphor in the object nominal is predicted to be bound in the first sentence that contains it; in (13) the anaphor in the subject nominal is predicted not to have a governing category, hence in particular to be able to be long-distance bound by the matrix subject or to have an antecedent that does not c-command it, like the embedded object:

(12)   They liked each other's pictures

(13)   The boys thought that each other's pictures pleased the girls

However, lexical anaphors lacking a governing category seem, contrary to PROs, to need an antecedent in all cases. So in particular in (13) *each other* cannot be assigned arbitrary interpretation. That lexical anaphors must have antecedents will then have to be introduced into the grammar as an independent assumption.

Consider now the example in (14):

(14)   Mary heard that John was saying [PRO to leave]

The PRO in (14) is essentially in the same position as the PRO in (9), and their governing category is in both cases the sentence that immediately contains the control sentence. By binding condition A, PRO is then predicted to be bound within this sentence. But the PRO in (14), contrary to the PRO in (9), does not seem to be bound at all; rather, it seems to be free and interpreted as arbitrary in reference. Examples of the type of (14), however, differ from examples of the type of (9) in at least one other respect. In (9) all of the complements of the verb that selects the control sentence are realised. In (14) there is one complement, roughly corresponding to the dative Case, that seems to remain unrealised. Suppose we say that this dative in fact binds the PRO. If so, the structure ceases to be a violation of the theory of control.

On the other hand if our theory of control holds and PRO must be bound in the sentence that immediately contains the control sentence, it also follows that it cannot be long-distance bound, hence in particular in (14) it cannot be bound by the matrix subject *Mary*. This seems to be correct. Furthermore, if the PRO in (14) is bound by the dative we correctly predict that the dative will be interpreted as the antecedent of PRO. In short, there is evidence that the apparently unrealised dative in sentences of the type of (14) nevertheless controls the PRO. Adopting current terminology we will henceforth refer to elements like the dative in (14) as implicit arguments.

Consider now a sentence of the type of (15):

(15)   Mary thought that [PRO to behave well] could be useful

(15) reproduces the configuration in (11); PRO does not have a governing category, it is not subject to binding theory and does not require a controller. In (15), however, as in (14), one of the arguments seems to remain unrealised, again a dative/benefactive; this then should be able to control the PRO. So we predict that (15) admits the interpretation '. . . for x to behave well could be useful to x', though, as in (11), and unlike in (14), PRO can also be bound by *Mary* or be free.

Examples of the type of (16) and (17), on the other hand, have quite different properties from examples of the type of (11) and (15):

(16)   Mary thought that [PRO to behave well] would be easy for Peter

(17)   Mary thought that [PRO to behave well] would be easy

Though (16) and (17) prima facie replicate the configurations in (11) and (15), the behaviour of the PRO is similar to that found in (9) or (14). In (16) in particular PRO is controlled by *Peter*; correspondingly in (17) PRO is controlled by the implicit dative/benefactive, yielding the interpretation '. . . for x to behave well would be easy for x'. In both cases long-distance control by *Mary* is impossible, as is free interpretation. Given the theory of control presented here, we expect structural differences to underlie this contrast between (11) and (16).

A possible hypothesis is that the control sentence in (16) is not in subject position, but in some sentence initial Ā position. From this position, it is 'reconstructed' into its D-structure position, which we can assume is the object position. It follows that PRO must be bound in the sentence immediately superordinate to the control sentence; where in turn it can be bound by the benefactive if the control sentence is in its 'reconstructed' position. As for the control sentence in (11), we can assume either that it is in subject position proper, or that it is in sentence initial Ā position and is 'reconstructed' in subject position; in both cases the predictions concerning control remain unchanged. In fact, the adjectives that pattern like *easy* in (16) as opposed to *useful* in (11) seem to overlap with the adjectives allowing *tough* movement. If a precondition for *tough* movement is that the infinitival sentence moved from is in a subcategorised position, then the different structures postulated for (16) and (11) could be independently motivated.

On the basis of examples such as (17), Epstein (1984) and Borer (1986) conclude that all PROs associated with arbitrary interpretation are in fact bound, by what in our terms is an implicit argument; similarly, through the implicit argument, all apparently long-distance bound PROs are locally bound. The potential counterexamples quoted are of the type of (18) or (19); in (18) or (19) all argument positions in the matrix sentence are filled, thus leaving no room for an implicit argument, but arbitrary interpretation of the PRO seems to be possible:

(18)   The waiter knows what to order

(19)   To misbehave in public could irritate the police

According to Borer (1986), however, examples of the type of (18) have altogether special properties, while examples of the type of (19) are marginal with arbitrary interpretation of the PRO.

This disregards examples of the type of (11). The contrast between the two classes of adjectives involved in (11) and (15) and (16)–(17) is particularly striking in examples of the type of (20)–(21):

(20)   To teach *them* maths is useful to *the children*

(21)   *To teach *them* maths is easy for *the children*

The reading under which *them* is coreferential with *the children* makes the free reading of PRO obligatory; as before, there is no unfilled position in the matrix sentence that could correspond to an implicit argument. (21), which is a configuration of obligatory control, is then ill-formed; (20), which is not, is perfectly well-formed, and not marginal.

Finally, the examples considered so far argue for the existence of implicit datives/benefactives. However there is a well-known class of control facts that argues for the existence of at least a second class of implicit arguments, corresponding roughly to agent theta-roles. Consider purposive sentences. In general, a PRO subject of a purposive sentence must be bound in the first sentence that contains the control sentence, as in (22):

(22)   Mary said that [John wrote the book [PRO to help Peter]]

In (22), where the control sentence is taken to be attached under the embedded sentence, PRO cannot have arbitrary control, and it cannot be long-distance bound, as for example by *Mary*. In fact, the only possible controller for PRO is *John*.

Consider then the example in (23):

(23)   Mary said that [the book was written [PRO to help Peter]]

In (23) long distance control of the PRO by the subject of the matrix sentence *Mary* is impossible. However PRO seems to be free and associated with arbitrary interpretation rather than bound within the embedded sentence. But again the exception disappears if we assume that in (23) the apparently unrealised agent in the embedded sentence controls the PRO. This in turn yields the intuitively correct interpretation '. . . the book was written by x for x to help Peter'. Hence examples of the type of (23) provide evidence in favour of the existence of implicit agents parallel to the implicit datives/benefactives of the examples in (14), (17) and (15).

2 What is an implicit argument?

Our next question concerns the nature of implicit arguments. A possible hypothesis is that they correspond to some type of empty category. However, they cannot be NP-traces, since in the examples that we have considered no movement can have taken place from the A-position corresponding to the implicit argument to any other position. Similarly, they cannot be PROs; for at least implicit datives clearly correspond to positions selected by a head, hence governed by it.

This still leaves two possibilities open. The first possibility is that the implicit argument is a variable. Of course it can only be a variable if it is bound by some operator. But while no overt operator is present in any of the examples considered, one can always postulate the existence of an empty operator. Furthermore, if the correct interpretation for the sentences under consideration is to be obtained, the empty operator/variable pair must have arbitrary reference. This again is possible if the empty operator is not itself bound. The problem with this analysis is not its feasibility, but the arbitrariness of the restriction of these empty operator/variable pairs to precisely the implicit arguments contexts. In fact, the variable analysis is explicitly adopted for what we have termed implicit datives or benefactives in Borer (1986); as far as we can see, the restriction of the empty operator/variable pairs to datives or benefactives is stipulated.

Finally, the last type of empty category that implicit arguments could correspond to is pro. If we assume that pros can be licensed and identified only by the strong Agr of languages like Italian, essentially as in Chomsky (1982), then implicit datives and agents cannot correspond to pros. This does not mean that the licensing conditions for pros cannot be extended; in fact, the pro analysis is explicitly adopted for datives/benefactives in Epstein (1984). As before, then, the problem with this analysis is not its feasibility, but its lack of explanatory power.

If on the other hand implicit arguments are not empty categories, what are they? According to Chomsky (1986), an implicit argument is lexically, rather than syntactically, represented, and is a constituent of a V head. According to Roeper (1987), an implicit argument is a theta-role that does not license a category though it can license one. According to Rizzi (1986), an implicit argument is a theta-role that is not projected to a position. All these proposals follow essentially the same line of thought, and it is this that we will pursue here.

Consider the projection principle. In the formulation of Chomsky (1986) the projection principle requires every theta-role selected by a head to be categorically represented. Given a verb V associated with a theta-role θ, the syntactic representation corresponding to it is as in (24), where '—' denotes the syntactic category, or position, associated with the theta-role:

(24)   V+θ —

In the case of an implicit argument, V can be associated with the representation in (25), where the theta-role does not project to a syntactic category or position; if so, an implicit argument can be identified with an unprojected theta-role:

(25)   V+θ

The existence of implicit arguments seems then to require a reconsideration of the projection principle.

At the same time, not all theta-roles selected by a head can correspond to an implicit argument; while we have found evidence of implicit arguments corresponding to datives, there are no direct object implicit arguments, as in (26):

(26)   *Mary persuaded [PRO to leave]

Hence while a relaxation of the projection principle seems to be in order to allow for an unprojected dative, some version of it still seems to be needed to exclude the occurrence of any unprojected direct object. Any explanatory theory of implicit arguments will have to account for this dative/direct object split.

In Chomsky (1986), where only implicit agents, i.e. external theta-roles, are dealt with, no problem concerning the projection principle arises. The projection principle does not force external theta-roles to be categorically represented; rather the presence of a subject, not necessarily a theta-position, is enforced by the extended projection principle. Hence the standard version of the projection principle predicts that implicit arguments can correspond to agents.

The problem of datives is discussed in Roeper (1987) and Rizzi (1986). Roeper (1987) takes into account the distinction between datives or agents and direct objects by stipulating that implicit arguments correspond to theta-roles that otherwise license PPs. Rizzi (1986), on the other hand, assumes that the difference between direct object theta-roles and other internal theta-roles is that the former are directly associated with a head, while the latter are associated with a head through autonomous theta-markers, typically prepositions. The idea is that theta-roles directly associated with a head are obligatorily projected to a position. However, the selection of an autonomous theta-marker is optional; if it is selected, then again the theta-role with which it is directly associated must be projected. An implicit argument corresponds to the case when the autonomous theta-marker is not selected.

In the next section we shall return to the question of the proper formulation of the projection principle. For the moment let us turn to the other properties of implicit arguments. Let us consider the derivation of the control examples involving implicit arguments. A more complete representation of the relevant portion of, say, (14) at S-structure is as in (27):

(27)   . . . John was saying$+\theta$ [PRO to leave]

By the theory of binding and control PRO must as before be bound in the superordinate sentence in (27). If the implicit argument θ binds the PRO, the requirement of the theory is satisfied.

In order for the implicit argument to bind the PRO in (27) it is of course necessary that c-command holds between the two. However, it is not difficult to define c-command for implicit arguments in such a way as to obtain the desired result. In particular, we can define implicit arguments to c-command exactly those positions that are c-commanded by the category of which they are implicit arguments, as in Williams (1985) and here in (28):

(28)   An implicit argument α c-commands β iff

the category γ of which α is an implicit argument c-commands β

Under the definition in (28) the implicit argument in (27) c-commands the PRO and can bind it, as desired.

Similarly, we can assume that a more complete representation of the relevant portion of (23) is as in (29), where we assume that the purposive sentence is attached under a sentential node:

(29)   . . . the book [$_{VP+\theta}$ was written t] [PRO to help Peter]

Assuming that agent theta-roles are assigned by the VP, in (29) the implicit argument θ c-commands the PRO. Hence it can bind PRO, satisfying the requirements of the theory of binding and control.

Now, given that an implicit argument can control a PRO, the question naturally arises whether it can enter into other binding relations. Given our theory, if an implicit argument controls a PRO, we expect that it can bind lexical anaphors as well. Consider first implicit agents. Unfortunately, the data are not clear-cut; however, it seems that an implicit agent can in fact bind a reflexive, as in (30), from Chomsky (1986):

(30)   Damaging testimony is sometimes given about oneself

Notice that independently of implicit arguments we have assumed that PROs and lexical anaphors differ with respect to their requirements on antecedents. In particular, lexical anaphors need an antecedent in all cases, while PROs can be antecedentless. According to Chomsky (1986), reciprocals, contrary to reflexives, cannot be bound by implicit agents, as in (31); in a similar vein, the explanation suggested is that reciprocals require specific antecedents, which implicit arguments are not:

(31)   *Damaging testimony is sometimes given about each other

Consider then implicit datives. Binding of reflexives by implicit non benefactive datives is impossible according to Rizzi (1986). However, there are comparatively few examples that are potentially relevant, and some of them seem to us to be quite possibly acceptable, for instance (32):

(32)   An analyst can put difficult questions about oneself

Whatever the situation with nonbenefactive datives, on the other hand, it seems that benefactives can serve as the antecedents of lexical anaphors. Consider for example (33), quoted by Lasnik (1984) in a context antagonistic to our present conclusions:

(33)   Books about oneself make interesting reading

The interpretation of (33) is roughly '(y's) books about x make interesting reading for x'. There is no question that *oneself* is bound by the subject of the nominal; the only available antecedent is then the implicit benefactive. Thus the situation with datives/benefactives seems to be comparable to the situation with agents.

Let us consider now some possible alternatives to the theory of implicit arguments that we have presented so far. According to Jaeggli (1986) the agent theta-role in a passive is assigned to the *-en* suffix, though the *-en* suffix can in turn transmit it to a *by* phrase; the representation of a passive then is as in (34), and implicit arguments coincide with theta-roles assigned to *-en* suffixes:

(34)   . . . the book [was write+en t . . .
                                  θ

Obviously if not only agents but also datives can be implicit arguments, then this analysis is not general enough.

Jaeggli also argues that though implicit arguments can control PROs in adjunct sentences, as in (23), they cannot control PROs in object sentences, as in (35); this contrast is then used to argue that two different control relations are involved, thematic control and argument control respectively:

(35)   *John was promised [PRO to leave]

However implicit agents can control a PRO in an object sentence in examples of the type of (36); hence, whatever the explanation for (35), Jaeggli's conclusion seems incorrect:

(36)   It was decided to leave

In Borer (1986), the grouping together of agents and datives (benefactives) as implicit arguments is explicitly called into question. The elements that in our terms are implicit datives are identified in Borer with a variable bound by an empty operator, while the implicit argument analysis is accepted for agents. The argument that implicit datives correspond to empty operator/variable pairs is based on examples of the type of (37), where the two PROs must be interpreted as coreferential:

(37)   [PRO crossing the Rockies], [PRO to behave well] is easy/useful

According to Borer in (37) the empty operator that binds the dative variable takes scope over both PROs. Both PROs furthermore must be bound by the empty operator, because of the assumption that control is always obligatory. Hence the correct interpretation follows.

We have questioned Borer's assumption that control is obligatory in all cases; in (37) control is obligatory with *easy*, but not with *useful*. Hence one crucial link in Borer's argument is missing. Furthermore, as pointed out in Lebeaux (1984), a coreference effect holds between the two PROs in examples of the type of (38):

(38)   To know her is to like her

But in (38) there is no position in the matrix sentence that could be filled by a variable bound by an empty operator; hence Borer's analysis cannot apply to this case.

Notice that while we reject Borer's idea that implicit datives correspond to empty operator/variable pairs at S-structure, we have been assuming all along that they are quantifier-like in their interpretation. In this respect we agree with Epstein (1984), though we reject Epstein's idea that implicit datives are pros at S-structure. Following Lebeaux (1984), furthermore, we can assume that arbitrary PROs are also quantifier-like at LF, or, in general, that all arbitrarily interpreted elements are. Suppose then we assume that if in (38) both PROs have the same scope, they are obligatorily identified. This not only explains (38), but the same schema of explanation can be applied to (37) as well.

Borer on the other hand uses gerund sentences of the type in (37) to argue not only for the variable analysis of implicit datives, but also for a different analysis for implicit datives and agents. According to Borer, while implicit datives can bind the PRO subject of the gerund sentence, implicit agents cannot. Here, however, we disagree with Borer's facts. An example like (39) seems to us to be well-informed with control of the gerund by the implicit agent, and the usual coreference effect of the two PROs:

(39)   Taking into account the convict's good behaviour, it was decided
         to reduce his term of imprisonment

The proposals in Williams (1985) call into question the existence of implicit agents, and in general of implicit arguments, by an alternative analysis of control into result sentences. Consider first a sentence of the type of (40):

(40)   Grass is green to promote photosynthesis

According to Williams the matrix subject *grass* cannot control the PRO in (40) because it could not be the subject of the embedded predicate *to promote photosynthesis*. The whole matrix sentence or the event it expresses, 'the being green of the grass', must then control the PRO. Williams's idea is that cases of control by implicit agents into result sentences can also be reanalysed as involving event control. Let us consider whether in fact sentences of the type of (40) provide evidence in favour of event control. To begin with, an example of the type of (41) seems to be perfectly well formed:

(41)   Grass promotes photosynthesis by being green

But in (41) *grass* is the overt subject of a predicate *promotes photosynthesis*; hence control of the PRO by *grass* cannot be ruled out in (40) on Williams's grounds.

More evidence in favour of event control is provided according to Williams by sentences of the type of (42):

(42)   John went to New York to annoy Mary

(42) admits of two interpretations. One possible interpretation is roughly equivalent to 'John went to New York so that (being in New York) he could annoy Mary'. The other interpretation is roughly equivalent to 'John went to New York so that by his very going to New York, he could annoy Mary'. Williams equates the first interpretation with control of the result sentence by *John*; the second interpretation is equated with event control. Consider, however, a sentence of the type of (43):

(43)   John went to New York to amuse himself

(43) is ambiguous in exactly the same way as (42). However, binding condition A requires *himself* to be bound by PRO, and an event bound PRO presumably could not bind *himself*. Hence examples of the type of (43) seem to argue against taking the ambiguity in (42), or indeed (43), as an ambiguity between event and non event control.

On the other hand, there is no doubt that (42) and (43) are ambiguous. We propose that this ambiguity is independent of control and that the event reading is a byproduct of the result sentence being a sentential scope adverbial. Consider for example a sentence like (44):

(44)   John hired Mary to do the job

In (44) PRO can be controlled by either *Mary* or *John*; we can furthermore assume that the possibility for *Mary* to bind the PRO depends upon the result sentence being attached under VP. The event reading is possible in (44) with subject control, but not with object control.

Finally, the case of implicit arguments, i.e. theta-roles not associated with a position, must be distinguished from the case of theta-roles never projected to the syntax. The latter case can correspond, as pointed out in Rizzi (1986a) to the intransitive use of verbs that also have a transitive subcategorisation frame. Thus there are two ways in which a theta-role can be 'optional'; either it is optionally projected to a position (the case of implicit arguments), or it is optionally selected in the lexicon (the case of transitive/intransitive pairs). In the case of verbal passives the possibility of non selection of the agent theta-role in the lexicon does not arise; hence, unless the agent theta-role is projected to a position it will always be an implicit argument.

3   Theta and case theory

Consider now again the projection principle, which requires lexical thematic structure to be represented categorially, at every syntactic level of analysis.

As Chomsky (1986) points out, 'A consequence of the projection principle is, to put it informally, that if some element is "understood" in a particular position, then it is *there* in syntactic representation, either as an overt category that is phonetically realized or as an empty category assigned no phonetic form . . .' As we have seen, agent theta-roles need not be categorially represented – they can produce implicit arguments. The existence of such syntactically active unprojected agent theta-roles is allowed for by the assumption that 'The projection principle requires that complements of heads must be syntactically represented at every level . . . but it says nothing about subjects. Thus it distinguishes between, what Edwin Williams calls "internal" and "external" arguments, specifically, object and subject. The projection principle requires that the former be syntactically realized, but not the latter . . .' (Chomsky 1986).

In the previous section we have arrived at the generalisation that not only agents but also theta-roles expressed by datives can correspond to implicit arguments. In other words, agents and dative θ-roles contrast with theta-roles expressed by direct objects in that only the latter need be projected to a categorial representation. If the observation that not all complement theta-roles need to be categorially represented is correct then clearly the projection principle cannot be maintained in the above form. Suppose that our generalisation that contrasts subjects and datives with direct object is correct. The obvious question to ask is then the following: why are dative and subject theta-roles exceptions to the projection principle? We shall suggest below that this way of formulating the problem is not the productive way of approaching it.

Before we delve deeper into this question, let us turn to a more general conceptual issue having to do with the status of Case and θ-theory. As has often been noted there is a lot of potential redundancy between Case and θ-theoretic requirements. Thus if Case assignment is obligatory, in the sense that all Cases need to be assigned to some category, as proposed in Vergnaud (1982) or Manzini (1983b), there will be two reasons that make it obligatory for a transitive verb to have a categorially represented object. One is that the relevant theta-role needs to be projected; the other is that the Case assigned must be taken up by some syntactically represented element. One way of approaching this problem and at the same time giving an account of the function of Cases in the grammar can be found in Chomsky (1981, 1986). He assumes that Case assignment is optional and that a category needs to have Case in order to be visible for theta-role assignment – i.e. theta-roles can only be assigned to Case-marked elements. What is not explained by this approach is why it is precisely Case that makes a category visible and not some other property, such as being governed, lexical, etc. To this extent we then have no explanation why there should be such entities as Cases, and Case theory in the grammar. Of course there may be no explanation.

Let us, however, try to construct one. Suppose that Cases are to syntax what theta-roles are to the lexicon. We assume in other words that while theta-roles create lexical structures, syntactic structures are created by Cases: syntactic structures are not projections of theta-frames of heads, but projections of their Case-frames. According to this theory, Cases are necessary in syntax, since without them there would be no syntactic representations, only lexical ones created by θ-frames. Or to state the point in a different way, we immediately explain why there must be such nonsemantic features assigned by heads of constructions as Cases, if we assume that syntactic structures are not created by the projection of θ-structure.

In the remainder of this section we shall first discuss how this way of looking at the matter handles the empirical problem concerning the distribution of implicit arguments and then go on to develop the theory based on this alternative version of the projection principle so that it can account for the basic cases handled by GB theory.

In the context of our theory of the projection principle as a condition that requires all Cases to be syntactically represented, it is clear that the question of why agents and theta-roles expressed by datives need not be categorially represented should be turned upside down. No theta-roles are necessarily categorially represented – at least the projection principle carries no such requirement. So the right question is the opposite: what makes it necessary for certain theta-roles, for example those expressed by direct objects or subjects of non passive sentences to be projected to the syntax? But this question does not now concern the effects of the projection principle. With respect to this principle the question that arises is this: why is it that nominative and accusative Cases but in general not datives need to be categorially represented?

Consider the last question first. The difference between dative Case and either accusative or nominative Case is essentially the difference between structural and inherent Case. According to Chomsky (1986) 'we distinguish the "structural Cases" objective and nominative, assigned in terms of S-structure position, from the "inherent Cases" assigned at D-structure . . . We assume that inherent Case is assigned by α to NP iff α θ-marks NP, while structural Case is assigned independently of θ-marking.' Suppose we accept a distinction between inherent and structural Case formulated in these terms. Suppose furthermore that we formulate our revised projection principle as in (45):

(45) Cases are categorially represented in the syntax

We shall assume along the lines of Brody (1985) that S-structure is the fundamental level of representation, from which D-structure is derived. If so (45) can be taken to refer to only those Cases that are not assigned together with their corresponding theta-roles at D-structure, i.e. the structural Cases, nominative and accusative. As for the inherent Cases they may or may not be projected to a position, and no projection requirement holds of the related theta-roles, as is the case for theta-roles in general. Hence inherent Cases like dative can correspond to implicit arguments.

So far then the projection principle (45) has enabled us to account for the possibility of implicit arguments corresponding to inherent Cases. But how does (45) allow for implicit agents? By (45) nominative Case obligatorily projects a subject position; however, though a theta-role may be available for assignment to the nominative position, nothing in (45) itself forces this theta-role to be assigned. If nothing else in the grammar forces the assignment, then the theta-role which could in principle be assigned in the nominative position can be an implicit argument. Clearly nothing else forces theta-role assignment to subject in the case of passive; in fact passivisation depends on the theta-role available for the nominative position not being assigned; whence implicit agents.

Suppose then that we are correct in our account of how (45) in the absence of independent constraints allows for both implicit datives and agents. Still, in requiring nominative and accusative to be projected to syntactic positions, (45) does not account for the obligatory presence of subjects where nominative Case is not available – i.e. in the case of PRO. For this case it seems to be necessary to postulate very much as in Chomsky (1981) an extended version of the principle which ensures that clauses have subjects. One possible form that this extension of the projection principle may take is (46):

(46)   Infl must project a position that it governs

Let us now return to the first of the two questions we asked above. Under the standard version of the projection principle implicit arguments, i.e. theta-roles that are not categorially represented, are an anomaly. Under our alternative view, which is based on the Case-projection principle in (45), the problem is the opposite: why is it that certain theta-roles are necessarily categorially represented? The case of theta-roles associated with inherent Cases is clear: since these are associated – i.e. assigned together – the theta-role will have to be projected whenever the inherent Case is. This leaves the necessity of categorial representation of theta-roles assigned to subjects of active sentences and to objects to be explained.

Consider then the simple sentence in (47):

(47)   John kissed Mary

Since *John* and *Mary* are arguments, if the subject or object theta-roles were not categorially represented by having created theta-positions then the theta-criterion would be violated; there could not be a one-to-one correspondence between theta-positions and arguments. Is it always possible to attribute the obligatory nature of the categorial representation of these theta-roles to the theta-criterion? Suppose for concreteness that we state the theta-criterion as in (48) – see Chomsky (1986), Brody (1985, 1987); (48) holds at D-structure:

(48)   a.   Each argument is in a theta-position
        b.   Each theta-position contains an argument

Let us now examine subjects first. If the subject position contains an argument then this argument must be in a theta-position at D-structure. If there has been no movement, as in (47), and the argument is in the same position throughout the derivation then the subject position must be a theta-position; the theta-role therefore is not available to create an implicit argument. Suppose the argument has moved to this subject position from a D-structure theta-position. This is the case of the passive considered above: nothing prevents the nonassignment of the subject theta-role and correctly so since it can act as an implicit argument.

What is going to prevent nonassignment of the subject theta-role in nonpassive sentences where an argument moved to subject position, e.g. as in (49)?

(49)   *John kissed e

We shall assume, adopting the position in Chomsky (1986) (or e.g. Sportiche 1983), that NP-traces cannot occur in Case-marked positions, and more generally that only heads of (A-)chains may be Case-marked. This will ensure the correct distinction between (49) and the passive. Incidentally, this should not be taken to imply that we wish to take Case absorption as the defining property of the passive. Thus the existence in some languages of impersonal passives, i.e. structures like (50),

(50)   Es wurde getanzt (=It was danced)

where we have passive morphology with a nontransitive verb, suggests in our terms that passive morphology is contingent on the nonprojection of the subject theta-role and not on the absorption of accusative Case.

Now suppose that the subject position contains a nonargument. This may be an NP-trace or an expletive heading a chain. Assuming that all NPs are in some chain, expletives such as *there* or *it*, or their empty correspondents in null subject languages are necessarily in some chain. Following Brody (1984, 1985, 1986) and Chomsky (1986) we assume that all chains must have a theta-role, more precisely that they must all contain some theta-position, and furthermore that this theta-position is always the root (most deeply embedded) position of the chain. (For various ways of deriving these results see the works quoted). The expletive in subject position that heads a chain then must head a chain whose root is a theta-position. This theta-position must contain an argument at D-structure by the theta-criterion, hence all expletives must be in a chain that also contains an argument. So there cannot be an unlinked expletive in a subject position with the agent theta-role unprojected, e.g. (51) with the meaning 'One kissed Mary'

(51)   *It/There kissed Mary

Since only the head of the chain may be in Case-marked position, parallel to (49) we exclude the case of an expletive-argument chain where the argument is in a Case position, e.g. (51) when *It/There* and *Mary* are taken to be members of the same chain.

If the argument is not in a Case-marked position, then the expletive-argument chain can be formed as in (52).

(52)   There is a man in the garden

If the expletive is related to the argument through the intermediary of one or more NP-traces as in (53), then exactly the same comments apply, with the further proviso that this NP-trace must occupy a Caseless non-thematic position (as it is neither the head nor the root of the chain):

(53)   There seems (e to appear) e to be a man in the garden

Let us turn to the remaining case: the subject position is occupied by an NP-trace. If the head of the chain is an expletive we have the situation exemplified in (53). Suppose that the NP-trace is in a chain headed by an argument. The NP-trace then may be the D-structure position of the argument as in (54) or it may be an intermediate trace as the subject of *appear* in (55):

(54)   John seems e to like Mary

(55)   John seems e to appear e to like Mary

Since the root position of the chain must be a theta-position, the theta-role of the embedded subject in (54) must be projected. In (55) there is no theta-role to create the intermediate trace position. Would it be possible then to have an intermediate NP-trace in a potential theta-position, where the theta-role is not projected but remains an implicit argument? This case in fact reduces to that of the example in (49). Thus consider (56):

(56)   a.   John seems e to have been hit e
       b.   *John seems e to have hit e

The theta-role available for the position of the intermediate NP-trace in these examples may fail to get projected, and indeed we have the implicit argument in the passive Case. (56b) is excluded for independent reasons – just as in (49) the nonhead of the chain is Case-marked.

Let us now turn to the question of why the theta-role corresponding to the accusative always has to project to the categorial representation of the object. As we have seen, if the object position contains an unmoved argument as in (47), the relevant theta-role has to be projected in order for the theta-criterion to be satisfied. Suppose that the argument in object position has moved there from a theta-position as in (57):

(57)   a.   John considered Bill [e to like Mary]
       b.   John PERSUADED Bill [e to like Mary]

(57a) is a 'subject to object raising' structure that is not excluded by the theory as we have developed it so far. (57b) contains the nonexistent verb PERSUADE, which differs from 'persuade' only in that the former governs the embedded position. So (57b) with the subject to object raising derivation would mean roughly: 'John persuaded one that Bill should like Mary'. Clearly at least (57b) should be excluded.

Suppose that reanalysis is triggered obligatorily by S' deletion. This process will create structures like (58), where the embedded subject becomes the object of the reanalysed predicate (on reanalysis see Manzini 1986):

(58)   a.   John considered-to-like-Mary Bill–
       b.   John PERSUADED-to-like-Mary Bill

It is natural to assume that the reanalysed predicate projects just one object position; if so, the presence of *Bill* excludes in (58) the presence of a trace. Hence in general raising-to-object is not a viable option if reanalysis is obligatory in these constructions. Note we have now excluded all possibilities of movement to object position, since the only possible launching position for this is the embedded subject.

Consider the flat analysis in (59):

(59) a. John considered [Bill] [to like Mary]
      b. John persuaded [Bill] [to like Mary]

This would be excluded by the extended projection principle (46) which requires the Infl of the embedded S to project a subject position. How about an inflectionless predicate as in (60)?

(60) a. John considered [Bill] [clever]
      b. John persuaded [Bill] [clever]

Suppose that we allowed the structure in (60a) as proposed in Williams (1983). This would not violate our assumptions – the accusative position in this case would be allowed to receive a theta-role from an element, the embedded predicate, that is different from the one that Case-projected the position (the matrix verb *consider*). Moreover, given our assumptions, we could not account straightforwardly for the impossibility of a structure like (60b) interpreted as 'John persuaded one that Bill is clever'. In other words we need to explain why the object theta-role of *persuade* must be assigned to the object position and cannot remain an implicit argument leaving the nonthematic object position free to be filled by an argument that receives a theta-role from elsewhere.

We can assimilate the impossibility of this construction to that of (61):

(61)   *John [seems that it is late] [angry]

Here *John* in a position that is not θ-marked by the main verb could receive a theta-role from another predicate, *angry*. Chomsky (1986) suggests that the ungrammaticality of this structure is due to his Uniformity Condition. This requires an element that is θ-governed by more than one category to be θ-marked either by all or none of these categories (where α is θ-governed by β iff α and β are in a configuration that would allow β to θ-mark α). (61) violates the Uniformity Condition since *John* is θ-governed both by the VP, *seem that S*, and by *angry*, but it is θ-marked only by the latter. Similarly (60) would violate this condition, since *consider* and by hypothesis *persuade* assign no theta-role to *Bill*, a category they θ-govern. But this category receives a theta-role from its other θ-governor, the embedded predicate. One consequence of our assumptions is then that flat structure analyses are excluded in general, and we need an ECM analysis also for small clause cases like (60a). Notice that the problem of what excludes (60b) when both *persuade* and *clever* assign a theta-role to *Bill* is not pertinent to our present concerns – it arises in any grammar where the theta-criterion requires one-to-one correspondence between arguments and theta-positions (and not theta-roles).

For *consider*, then, we can only have the standard ECM analysis, as in
(62):

(62) a.   John considers [Bill to be clever]
     b.   John considers [Bill clever]

Our last problem with this constructions is what prevents a similar structure
for *persuade*:

(63) a.   John PERSUADED [Bill to be clever]
     b.   John PERSUADED [Bill clever]

where again (63) is interpreted as 'John persuaded one that Bill should be/is
clever, i.e. with an implicit argument corresponding to the object theta-role.
We shall assume that *persuade*-type verbs have two Cases; the structural
accusative and an inherent Case associated with the theta-role of the post-
accusative complement. There are then two possibilities. Either (63) violates
the Case-projection principle – the accusative Case has not been projected.
Alternatively, we may take the postverbal S to be in the position created by
the accusative; however, the theta-role that *persuade* can assign to its object
requires a +human recipient, a requirement that a clausal argument cannot
fulfil.

Finally, consider the case of an expletive in object position. Since there
are no unlinked expletives, the object position could only contain expletives
that are part of a chain involving an argument/theta position. Now in general
the object position cannot contain the head of an expletive argument chain
for the following reasons. There are no expletive argument chains across a
clause boundary, hence the argument linked to the expletive in object position would have to be a complement of the verb. But the Case assigned to
nonaccusative complements is inherent Case, which is always associated
with a theta-role. We assume the implicational relationship holds in both
directions; the theta-role assigned to these elements is always tied to a(n)
inherent) Case. Hence an expletive argument chain headed from the object
position would always violate the condition that only the head of a chain may
be Case-marked. Suppose then that the object position contains an NP-trace.
This trace must be that of an argument, by the considerations just reviewed.
Since, as we have seen, there can be no movement to object position the trace
must correspond to the D-structure position of the argument. Therefore the
corresponding theta-role must be projected to avoid the violation of the theta
criterion. Notice that if the object position is not Case-marked as in the case
of passive, the presence of a categorial representation for the theta-role is
ensured by the assumption that this is necessary for the moved element to be
related (through a chain) to the object theta-role; i.e. chain formation can
involve only syntactic categories – implicit arguments cannot be members of
chains.

4 Italian null objects

Implicit arguments appear to behave as pronominal elements with respect to binding theory. Rizzi (1986a) notices that the 'null objects' of Italian, that he does not consider to be implicit arguments, have pronominal properties. The same seems to be true of English implicit agents and datives. In particular, implicit arguments can be bound by an element with an arbitrary interpretation. For example, the agent and dative theta-role of the most deeply embedded verb in (64) and (65) can be taken to be coreferential or disjoint in reference with the arbitrary PRO subject of *believe*:

(64) PRO to believe that an article can be written-θ without effort is preposterous

(65) PRO to believe that it would be easy-θ to write the article was ridiculous

According to Chomsky (1986) implicit arguments (agents) cannot be bound; this is true in Chomsky's examples (see (69) and (70) below), but only because the available antecedents are specific. Furthermore, a binder for an implicit argument has to be outside its governing category, as is shown in (66) and (67), when the implicit benefactive or agent cannot be bound by the subject of the same sentence:

(66) PRO to be kissed-θ is easy ($\neq$ PRO to kiss oneself is easy)

(67) PRO to shout-θ PRO to leave is difficult
($\neq$ PRO to shout to oneself PRO to leave is difficult)

On the basis of examples like (66) and (67) we must then conclude that a theta-role not assigned to a category is a pronominal for the purposes of the binding theory.

As is evident, arbitrary interpretation is a property of both implicit arguments and PROs. Indeed this is what made the examples in (64) and (65) possible, since implicit arguments can be controlled only by an element with arbitrary interpretation. Suppose that arbitrary interpretation is a default case for theta-roles. We are then in a position to explain why antecedentless PRO has arbitrary interpretation: this follows as the default case if a theta-role (projected or unprojected) is associated with no features that ensure specific reference.

There are two ways in which a theta-role may become associated with lexical features that make nonarbitrary interpretation possible. First, it may be assigned to a lexical category. However, a lexical category will not necessarily have specific interpretation; rather it will be taken as arbitrary if it has no features that conflict with the default interpretation. This seems to be the case with *si* in Italian and *one* in English. Secondly, the theta-role may be assigned to an empty category which inherits features from some lexical antecedent, as in (68):

(68) a.   John tried PRO to go

    b.   Who did John see t

    c.   The man e John saw t

Note that we assume that an empty category can inherit features that make nonarbitrary interpretation possible from a (lexical) quantifier phrase. Thus it is the lexical nature, rather than the referentiality of the antecedent that seems to be relevant. Alternatively we may assume that the possibility of nonarbitrary interpretation of variables is due to their being associated with Case features.

We assume then that in the default case theta-roles have arbitrary interpretation. Similarly we may take it that it is the default case for theta-roles to be pronominal. The default case is fully realised with implicit arguments. Note that implicit arguments cannot inherit features from an antecedent that would make specific reference possible; hence the impossibility of (69) and (70) in the relevant coreferential interpretation:

(69)   John believes that an article can be easily written-θ

      ($\neq$John believes that an article can be easily written by him)

(70)   John believes that it is easy-θ to write an article

      ($\neq$John believes that it is easy for him to write an article)

As illustrated in (68a) a categorially represented theta-role behaves differently: it can inherit referential properties. When no such inheritance takes place as in the case of antecedentless PRO the empty category shows only one of the default properties, that of arbitrary interpretation; it does not show the other default property – it is not a pronominal but an anaphoric element. In the context of the theory of empty categories adopted here, where all of them are anaphors, our assumption has to be that the anaphoric nature of empty categories overrides the default pronominal specification of the theta-role assigned to them, just like the referential properties of the antecedent may override the default arbitrary interpretation of PROs.

Let us now return to the question of obligatory theta-role projection to direct object positions. As we have seen in section 3, chain-theoretical principles ensure that this position cannot contain an element that heads a chain with more than one member. There can be no expletive argument chain headed from object position and there can be no movement to this position either. If there is only a one-member chain in that position this must contain an argument, which must be associated with a theta-position, hence the object theta-role must be projected. If the object position is Case marked, it cannot be a nonhead member of an A-chain.

Consider now Ā-chains. In English, if the object position contains a nonhead of an Ā-chain this can only be a variable, i.e. an argument, so this reduces to the previous case; the theta-role must be assigned to satisfy the theta-criterion. But now suppose that a language allows Ā-chains to be headed in an Ā-position which does not make it necessary for the associated category in Ā-position to be a variable. We may think of chains headed by

clitics as instantiating this situation. Suppose furthermore that the requirement that each Ā-chain must have a theta-position is relaxed so that such an
Ā-chain can also satisfy it. Under such circumstances our prediction would
be that the object theta-role does not have to be projected to the object
position as long as the Ā-position is a theta-position.

Now suppose that in some language an implicit argument can participate in Ā-chain formation, in particular it can head Ā-chains. We predict
that in such a language an implicit argument can form a chain with the Case-
projected object position and no theta-role needs to be assigned to this
position. (This must be an Ā-chain because nonhead members of Ā-chains
must not be Case-marked.) No such chains can be formed that involve
positions that have inherent Case since such Cases are associated with theta-
roles – if the Case is projected, so is the theta-role. Furthermore, we predict
that the interpretation of these implicit argument–expletive object chains will
be arbitrary, and that they will show pronominal properties, these being the
default properties of implicit arguments. Let us then see if this possibility is
realised.

Italian has implicit agents and datives exactly as English does.
However, as Rizzi (1986) points out, Italian also has a null object construction that does not exist in English. The null object of Italian can control, as in
(71), and bind a lexical anaphor, as in (72):

(71)   Questo induce a rivedere le proprie   opinioni
       this   induces to revise   one's own opinions
(72)   La musica riconcilia   con se stessi
       music   reconcilies with oneself

According to Rizzi, Italian null objects contrast in this respect with implicit
arguments, or at least implicit datives, since the latter are taken not to bind
lexical anaphors. If our discussion in section 2 is correct, no such distinction
holds. If so, the problem arises whether null objects can at all be told apart
from implicit arguments on empirical grounds. It may be that they can be
told apart on grounds other than binding properties. Here, however, we will
be satisfied with noting that implicit arguments (agents and datives) can
appear, in English, independently of null objects.

According to Rizzi, the null object of Italian can be bound by another
arbitrary element. If it is bound, however, it must be outside its governing
category, as in (73):

(73)   É un'illusione sperare che un buon pranzo possa riconciliare con
       se stessi
       it is an illusion to hope that a good meal may reconcile with
       oneself

In (73) the null objects of *riconciliare* and the PRO subject of the superordinate sentence can be given either a disjoint or a coreferential reading. Consider by contrast (74):

(74) In questo dipartimento é   difficile costringere a lavorare
       in this   department   it is difficult to force   to work

In (74) the null object of *costringere* and the PRO subject can only be taken to be disjoint in reference. In general, the null object cannot be bound by an (arbitrary) element within its governing category. This suggests that the null object has pronominal features.

What is then the nature of Italian null objects? We suggest that they correspond to the implicit argument-direct object chains postulated above. We have been implicitly assuming so far a relaxation of the definition of chains to allow implicit arguments to head chains. As we have seen they must not participate in chain formation in general – cf. the comments on the passive construction in the last paragraph of section 3. In effect they do not seem to participate in any kind of syntactic inheritance processes as the discussion of (69) and (70) suggests. Another way of looking at the problem may be the following. Nothing that we have said so far explains why the null object possibility exists in Italian but not in English. Suppose that the difference between Italian and English in having direct object implicit arguments is related to the fact that in general the option of a clitic chain is available in Italian, but not in English. A chain headed by an implicit argument is then just a special case of a clitic chain, a zero clitic chain. The implicit argument is now taken to be categorially represented, and we do not need to relax the condition that chain formation may only involve syntactic categories. We also have to say that the assumption that empty categories are necessarily anaphors holds only for empty categories in A-position, since as we have seen these implicit arguments are pronominals under the binding theory.

Consider now the theory of null objects proposed in Rizzi (1986). Rizzi argues for a revision and extension of the theory of pros in Chomsky (1982), under which Italian null objects are pros licensed by the V that governs them. Object pros are identified by the object theta-roles they are associated with, after these are assigned arbitrary features by the rule in (75):

(75) Assign *arb* to a direct object theta-role

According to Rizzi, this theory accounts not only for the examples considered so far, but also for an additional set of data, namely examples of the type of (76) and (77):

(76) Gianni ritiene   probabile che Mario venga
       Gianni believes likely   that Mario may come

(77) Ritengo piú   intelligente suo fratello
       I believe more intelligent his brother

Under Rizzi's theory a pro is licensed by the matrix verb *ritenere* in the subject position of the small clause. However, the pro is not associated with a theta-role, the arb assignment rule does not apply, hence the structure is predicted to be possible with the pro interpreted as an expletive.

Under the theory proposed here there is no analysis of (76) and (77) comparable to Rizzi's, since by definition a null object is bound by a theta-role, and cannot therefore be expletive. However, an altogether different analysis seems to be possible. Rizzi (1986b) argues that small clauses in Italian instantiate reanalysis of the type associated with Romance causative constructions. The crucial piece of evidence he presents is that a clitic selected by the head of the small clause can be associated with the verb selecting the small clause itself, as in (78):

(78) Chi ne   ritieni   capace
      Who of it you believe capable

Now consider the inverted subject example in (77). Under current theories of causative constructions, the presence of an inverted subject in Romance-type reanalysis structures depends either on the fronting of the predicate, as in Kayne (1975), or on the base generation of the subject in inverted position, as in Manzini (1983b). If so, a possible analysis for (77) has no empty category at all in the canonical subject position, but either predicate fronting or base generation of the inverted subject. Consider then (76), on the assumption that the embedded sentence is subcategorised by the adjective. If Burzio (1986) or Manzini (1983b) are correct, under Romance-type reanalysis nothing forces a predicate to have a subject position. If so, (76) has a possible analysis with no empty category in subject position either. Thus what we are suggesting is that the existence of sentences like (76) and (77) in Italian is independent of the existence of null objects, and depends on the separate properties of Romance-type reanalysis.

To support his argument Rizzi notices that in previous stages of English the existence of sentences of the type of (76) and (77) also correlated with the existence of null objects. Typical examples from Visser (1963–9) are in (79) and (80):

(79) a. I haue euer accompted my deuty to forbeare all suche maner
          of vnmannerly behauioure (St Thomas More, 1530)
      b. I see very clerely proved that it can be done none otherwise
          (St Thomas More, 1534)

(80) When he commaunded to receiue the man . . . into the church
      again, in which church commaunded he to receiue him? (St
      Thomas More, 1532–3)

The examples in (79) parallel Italian examples of the type of (76), as opposed to their modern English counterparts. The example in (80) shows that at the same stage of the development of English, and again in contrast with modern English, null objects were allowed. This correlation remains accidental under our theory, since the possibility of null object examples depends on the existence of implicit argument chains, and the existence of examples like (76) and (77) depends on the separate phenomenon of Romance-type reanalysis. To refute Rizzi's argument we will then ultimately have to show either that this correlation does not hold necessarily, and actually breaks down in some languages; or alternatively, that the true correlation is between the possibility or impossibility of implicit argument chains (in general clitic chains) and that of Romance-type reanalysis.

The major argument in favour of our theory of null objects is on the other hand that it relates identical properties of null objects and implicit arguments, relying on general principles of grammar to explain their complementary distribution. Rizzi's theory can in principle capture the correlation between arbitrary interpretation of null objects and of implicit arguments, since the arbitrary interpretation of a null object depends on assigning arbitrary features to the object theta-role. However, in Rizzi's theory the pronominal nature of null objects depends on the presence of an empty category with pronominal features, pro, in object position. Hence the fact that an implicit argument also has pronominal properties must remain a coincidence. Finally, it must be noticed that the existence of an empty category pro is a postulate of Rizzi's theory, that can be dispensed with under ours, allowing us to maintain that all empty categories are anaphoric. As for the occurrences of pros in the subject position of languages such as Italian, which account for pro-drop according to Chomsky (1982), we can dispense with them by going back to the original theory of pro-drop in Rizzi (1982), under which Italian-type Agr heads what can be taken to be a clitic chain which includes the empty subject. The specific features of Agr will override the arbitrary interpretation of the subject theta-role under the theory proposed here.

NOTE
Research for this article by M. Brody was funded by the Economic and Social Research Council (UK), grant reference number C 00 23 2201.

REFERENCES
Borer, H. 1986. Anaphoric Agr. Ms., University of California, Irvine.
Brody, M. 1984. On contextual definitions and the role of chains. *Linguistic Inquiry* 15: 355–80.
Brody, M. 1985. On the complementary distribution of empty categories. *Linguistic Inquiry* 16: 505–46.
Brody, M. 1987. On Chomsky's *Knowledge of Language*. *Mind and Language* 2: 165–77.
Burzio, L. 1986. *Italian syntax: a government-binding approach*. Dordrecht: Reidel.
Chomsky, N. 1981. *Lectures on government and binding*. Dordrecht: Foris.
Chomsky, N. 1982. *Some concepts and consequences of the theory of government and binding*. Cambridge, Mass.: MIT Press.
Chomsky, N. 1986. *Knowledge of language: its nature, origin and use*. New York: Praeger.
Epstein, S.D. 1984. Quantifier-pro and the LF representation of PRO$_{arb}$. *Linguistic Inquiry* 15: 499–504.
Jaeggli, O. 1986. Passive. *Linguistic Inquiry* 17: 587–622.

Kayne, R. 1975. *French syntax*. Cambridge, Mass.: MIT Press.

Lasnik, H. 1984. Some thoughts on implicit arguments. Ms., University of Connecticut, Storrs.

Lebeaux, D. 1984. Anaphoric binding and the definition of PRO. *North-Eastern Linguistics Society Proceedings* 14.

Manzini, M.R. 1983a. On control and control theory. *Linguistic Inquiry* 14: 421–46.

Manzini, M.R. 1983b. Restructuring and reanalysis. Ph.D dissertation, Massachusetts Institute of Technology.

Manzini, M.R. 1986. Phrase structure, extractions and binding. Ms., University College London.

Rizzi, L. 1982. *Issues in Italian syntax*. Dordrecht: Foris.

Rizzi, L. 1986. Null objects in Italian and the theory of *pro*. *Linguistic Inquiry* 17: 501–57.

Rizzi, L. 1986a. On chain formation. In H. Borer (ed.) *Syntax and semantics*, vol. 18. New York: Academic Press.

Roeper, T. 1987. Implicit arguments and the head-complement relation. *Linguistic Inquiry* 18: 267–310.

Sportiche, D. 1983. 'Structural invariance and symmetry in syntax'. Ph.D dissertation, Massachusetts Institute of Technology.

Vergnaud, J.-R. 1982. *Dependences et Niveaux de Représentation en Syntaxe*. Thèse de Doctorat d'Etat, Université de Paris VII.

Visser, F.T. 1963–9. *An historical syntax of the English language*, vols. 1 and 2. Leiden: Brill.

Williams, E. 1983. Against small clauses. *Linguistic Inquiry* 14: 287–308.

Williams, E. 1985. PRO and the subject of NP. *Natural Language and Linguistic Theory* 3: 297–315.

IV

*On internal representations and
natural language use*

6

Representation and relevance

DEIRDRE WILSON AND
DAN SPERBER

Utterances and thoughts are representations. What do they represent, and
how? The generally accepted answer is that they represent states of affairs.
Let us call this type of representation *descriptive*, and say that a thought or
utterance may *describe* a certain state of affairs.

This answer, though true, is incomplete. Utterances represent not only
states of affairs but also thoughts of the speaker; thoughts may be entertained
not only as descriptions of states of affairs but also as representations of
further thoughts. Let us call this type of representation *interpretive*, and say
that a thought or utterance may *interpret* a certain thought.

Whereas descriptive representation is relatively well understood, interpretive representation has not been seriously examined in modern semantics
and pragmatics. To the extent that the relation between utterances and
thoughts has been considered at all, it has been seen as involving strict
identity of propositional content; and the idea that a thought can be used to
represent another thought has not been pursued.

In this chapter, we discuss the notions of descriptive and interpretive
representation and the relations between them. We reject the idea that
interpretive representation is based on strict identity of propositional content; we show how an utterance may be used to represent a thought that
merely resembles it in propositional content, and a thought may be used to
represent another similar thought. We will illustrate the advantages of this
approach by applying it to three traditional semantic and pragmatic problems: the analyses of metaphor, irony, and interrogative utterances. Further
discussion may be found in Sperber (1985 chapter 2), Sperber & Wilson
(1986a chapter 4, sections 7–10), Sperber & Wilson (1986b) and Wilson &
Sperber (1988).

1 Description

Descriptive representation is truth-based. An utterance or thought describes
a state of affairs that makes it true. But which state of affairs is that?

Consider the exchange in (1):

    (1) a. *Mary*: You shouldn't
        b. *Peter*: Shouldn't I?

In the appropriate circumstances, Mary might use (1a) to tell Peter that he shouldn't smoke between courses, that he shouldn't smoke at table, that he shouldn't smoke in a restaurant, that he shouldn't smoke when she was present, that he shouldn't smoke before the loyal toast, or simply that he shouldn't smoke. Which state of affairs should Peter take her utterance to represent? Clearly, the state of affairs she *intended* it to represent. An adequate account of how utterances describe states of affairs must make reference to speakers' intentions.

One way of moving towards such an account would be to envisage an intermediate level of representation between utterances and the states of affairs they describe. Following Sperber & Wilson (1986a), let us call this the level of *propositional form*. The propositional form of an utterance is obtained by selecting a linguistically encoded logical form, completing it (if necessary) to the point where it represents a determinate state of affairs, and (if necessary) enriching it in various ways (see Carston this volume). Thus (1a) might have the propositional form in (2), which by hypothesis represents a determinate state of affairs:

(2)   Peter shouldn't smoke when Mary is present

According to this view, the relation between an utterance and the state of affairs it describes is analysable into three sub-relations: between an utterance and its linguistically encoded logical form, between the logical form of an utterance and its fully propositional form, and between the propositional form of an utterance and the state of affairs it describes; responsibility for analysing these sub-relations goes, respectively, to linguistic semantics, pragmatics, and the semantics of mental representations.

On current assumptions about the nature of mental representation, the relation between thoughts and the states of affairs they describe is less complex. Whereas the propositional content of an utterance may not be fully reflected in its linguistic form, it follows from the assumptions of methodological solipsism (see Fodor 1981) that every difference in propositional content must be reflected in the conceptual representation system, the language of thought. Thoughts, unlike utterances, are fully determinate as to the states of affairs they describe.

So far, pragmatic considerations, in the guise of speakers' intentions, have entered the picture at only one point: in determining the relation between the logical form of an utterance and its fully propositional form. If Mary says (1) intending it to have the propositional form in (2), her utterance will describe the state of affairs represented by (2), regardless of what her other intentions may be. Mary may, however, have a further intention in the matter, as can be brought out by comparing (1a) and (1b). These utterances have identical propositional forms, but are intended to be understood in different ways. We will say that they express different *propositional attitudes*, and analyse the relevant differences in attitude as differences in the way a propositional form is entertained: holding a belief about the actual world, for example, will be analysed as entertaining a propositional form as a true description of a state of affairs in the actual world.

The linguistic form of an utterance constrains the type of attitude it may be used to express. Declarative utterances are specialised for the expression of various types of belief or assumption: for example, the propositional form of (1a) may be entertained as a true description of the actual world, or of some alternative possible world that Mary and Peter are imagining. Which of these linguistically possible attitudes is expressed by (1a) is a matter for Mary to decide and Peter to discover by pragmatic means. An utterance may be linguistically indeterminate as to both propositional attitude and propositional form.

On the assumptions of methodological solipsism, distinctions among propositional attitude, like distinctions among propositional form, must be reflected in the conceptual representation system. We assume, therefore, that thoughts are fully determinate as to the propositional attitudes they express. A thought with the propositional form in (2) may be entertained as a true description of the actual world, a true description of some alternative possible world, and so on; the attitudes appropriate to interrogatives and imperatives will be discussed in section 6.

What thought does a given utterance represent? At this point, there is an obvious hypothesis: an utterance and the thought it represents have identical propositional forms, and express identical propositional attitudes. According to this hypothesis, if Mary says (1a) intending to express the propositional form in (2) as a true description of the actual world, then the thought her utterance represents has just the same propositional form, and expresses just the same attitude.

Some version of this hypothesis is more or less explicitly adopted in all recent work on pragmatic theory. In Gricean pragmatics, for example, there is a maxim of truthfulness whereby the speaker of a declarative utterance with propositional form P commits herself to the belief that P.[1] Obedience to such a maxim would guarantee that the propositional forms and propositional attitudes expressed by utterance and thought were identical; similar maxims might be developed for non-declarative utterances. The result would be a very tidy picture. At least where the maxims were in force, every utterance would simultaneously describe a certain state of affairs and express a certain attitude to it, and interpret a thought which described the same state of affairs and expressed the same attitude to it.

We will argue that this hypothesis is too strong. In the first place, an utterance does not always represent a thought with the identical propositional form: in loose talk and metaphor, the propositional forms of thought and utterance merely resemble each other to a certain degree. In the second place, the thought represented by an utterance is not always a description of a state of affairs: in irony and interrogative utterances, it is an interpretation of a further thought. A successful treatment of metaphor, irony and interrogatives depends on the realisation that interpretive representation is both a more complex and a more pervasive phenomenon than is generally recognised in modern semantics and pragmatics.

In the next section, we will discuss the role of resemblance in communication, and introduce a notion of interpretive representation based on resemblances in propositional form. In section 3, we will sketch a pragmatic theory which offers a general method of resolving linguistic indeterminacies. In the remainder of the chapter we will bring these ideas together to provide new analyses of metaphor, irony and interrogatives. We will end by contrasting the resulting picture with the more familiar descriptive approach.

2   Interpretation

In the appropriate circumstances, any object in the world can be used to represent any other object it resembles. A uniformed doll can be used to represent a soldier, an arrangement of cutlery and glasses can be used to represent a road accident, a set of vertical lines to represent the heights of members of a class. Such representations are used in communication for two main purposes: to inform an audience about the properties of an original, and for the expression of attitude. I may show you a uniformed doll so that you can recognise a soldier when you see one; I may communicate my attitude to soldiers by, say, kicking the doll.

Utterances, like other objects, enter into a variety of resemblance relations, which may be exploited in communication. Onomatopoeia is based on resemblances in sound, verbal mimicry on resemblances in phonetic and phonological form, direct quotation and parody on resemblances in syntactic and lexical form, translation on resemblances in logical form, and paraphrase and summary on resemblances in propositional form. Where verbal communication involves the exploitation of resemblances, the speaker does not necessarily commit herself to the existence of the state of affairs her utterance describes.

Consider the following exchange:

> (3) a.   *Counsel* (whispering to defendant): The money was never paid!
>   b.   *Defendant* (to Court): The money was never paid!

(3a) and (3b), though linguistically identical, are understood in very different ways. (3b) is straightforwardly analysable in terms of the maxim of truthfulness: the defendant guarantees the truth of the proposition expressed by his utterance. Let us say that this utterance is *descriptively used*. (3a), a direct quotation, is not descriptively used. The counsel does not guarantee to the defendant the truth of the proposition expressed: he uses (3a) to represent another utterance it resembles, namely, the utterance that he wants the defendant to produce.

Or consider the exchange in (4):

(4) a. *Child* (whining): Mummy, you KNOW I don't like cabbage
    b. *Mother* (whining exaggeratedly): Mummy, you KNOW I don't like cabbage

Again, (4a) and (4b) are linguistically identical. While (4a) is descriptively used, (4b), like (3a) above, must be understood as a direct quotation. It is used not to describe a state of affairs but to represent another utterance it resembles, namely, (4a).

These two exchanges illustrate the different purposes for which direct quotations may be used. (3a) is purely informative: it is used to inform the hearer of what he should say. (4b) is used for the expression of attitude: the mother caricatures the child's whining tone of voice in order to express her reaction to it.

Direct quotation presents problems for a framework with a maxim of truthfulness. The speaker does not observe the maxim of truthfulness; nor does she appear to be flouting it. Rather, her utterance seems to come with a different type of guarantee: a guarantee of faithfulness, not of truth. The speaker guarantees that her utterance is a faithful enough representation of the original: that is, resembles it closely enough in relevant respects.

It might be argued that direct quotations pose no serious threat to the maxim of truthfulness since they fall outside the domain of verbal communication proper. Verbal communication proper begins, and the maxim of truthfulness comes into play – or so a Gricean might argue – only when an utterance is chosen for its propositional form. Direct quotations are chosen not for their propositional form but for their superficial linguistic properties. However, many utterances present similar problems for the maxim of truthfulness, but fall squarely within the domain of verbal communication proper.

Consider the exchange in (5):

(5) a. *Child* (whining): Mummy, you KNOW I don't like cabbage
    b. *Mother* (whining exaggeratedly): Mummy, you KNOW cabbage makes me sick

(5b) is not a direct quotation; nor is it descriptively used. It differs from (4b) only in that it caricatures both the child's tone of voice and the content of what she said. It is used not only for its superficial linguistic properties but for its propositional form, and is a faithful enough representation of (5a) if it resembles (5a) closely enough in both respects. Where resemblances in propositional form are involved, we will talk of *interpretive resemblance* and *interpretive use*.

Under what conditions do utterances resemble each other in propositional form? We will say that two propositional forms resemble each other to the extent that they share analytic and contextual implications. The *analytic implications* of a propositional form P are non-trivial logical implications derivable from P by the application of inference rules requiring only a single premise as input. They are the implications that determine the propositional content of P in isolation from any context. However, propositional forms are entertained not in isolation but in a context of background assumptions. The *contextual implications* of P in the context C are propositions implied by neither C alone nor P alone, but by the union of C and P. We will say that two propositional forms P and Q (and, by extension, two thoughts or utterances with P and Q as their propositional forms) *interpretively resemble* one another in a context C to the extent that they share their analytic and contextual implications in the context C.

Interpretive resemblance is a comparative notion with two extremes: no resemblance at all (that is, no shared implications) at one end, and full propositional identity at the other. If two thoughts or utterances have the same propositional form, and hence share all their analytic implications, they also, of course, share all their contextual implications in every context. Let us say that when one thought or utterance is interpretively used to represent another, all of whose implications it shares, it is a *literal* interpretation of that other thought or utterance. On this account, literalness is just a special case of interpretive resemblance.

Let us illustrate these ideas with an example. Mary says to Peter:

    (6) a.   I met an agent last night
          b.   He can make me rich and famous

(6b) has two possible interpretations, (7a) and (7b):

    (7) a.   He can make me rich and famous, I believe
          b.   He can make me rich and famous, he says

On interpretation (7a), Mary's utterance is descriptively used: Mary commits herself to the existence of the state of affairs described. On interpretation (7b), her utterance is a case of free indirect speech. Free indirect speech does not commit the speaker to the existence of the state of affairs described: it is a case of interpretive representation. Mary's utterance represents another utterance that it resembles in propositional form.

Suppose that what the agent said was actually (8):

    (8)   I can make you rich and famous

Then Mary's utterance would be a literal interpretation of what the agent said: the two utterances would have identical propositional forms, and share all their analytic and contextual implications. Suppose that what the agent said was actually (9):

    (9)   I can do for you what Michael Caine's agent did for him

Then Mary's utterance would be a less than literal interpretation of what the agent said. However, in a context containing the assumption that Michael Caine's agent made him very, very rich and famous, the two utterances would share analytic and contextual implications, and hence resemble each other in propositional form.

Free indirect speech, like direct quotation, can be used for two main purposes: to inform an audience about the content of the original, or for the expression of attitude. By speaking in a manifestly smug, surprised, approving or sceptical tone, Mary may simultaneously inform Peter of what the agent told her, and express her reaction to what she has been told. Where interpretive representation involves such an expression of attitude, let us call the utterance *echoic*, and say that Mary *echoes* the agent's views.

The interpretive use of utterances, like the use of direct quotations, presents problems for a framework with a maxim of truthfulness. When Mary uses (6) to echo the agent's utterance, she does not commit herself to the existence of the state of affairs described; nor does she appear to flout the maxim of truthfulness. Rather, her utterance is accompanied by a different type of guarantee – a guarantee of faithfulness, not of truth. Mary guarantees that her utterance is a faithful enough representation of what the agent said. Moreover, since her utterance is chosen for its propositional form, this example cannot be dismissed as falling outside the domain of verbal communication proper.

Utterances, we have seen, can be interpretively used to represent other utterances. They are used in a similar way to interpret thoughts the speaker wants to attribute to someone else. For example, I may summarise the main tenets of the structuralists to recall them to a lecture audience; I may echo them in a smug, surprised, approving or sceptical tone to indicate my attitude to them. We will use this fact in section 5 as the basis for an account of irony. We want to argue, though, that in a more fundamental way, *every* utterance is interpretively used to represent a thought: the very thought the speaker wants to communicate.

If we are right, then every utterance comes with a guarantee of faithfulness, not of truth. The speaker guarantees that her utterance is a faithful enough interpretation of the thought she wants to communicate. An utterance may be used to represent a thought that merely resembles it in propositional form – identity being, of course, a special case of resemblance. According to this view, literal interpretation is only one possibility among many; for the modern pragmatic view, it is the only one. In a framework with a maxim of truthfulness, there is a guarantee of strict identity of propositional form between an utterance and the thought it represents. If we are right, the maxim of truthfulness must be abandoned.

At this stage someone might object that our approach introduces so many indeterminacies that it is hard to see how an utterance is ever understood. We have suggested that utterances are linguistically indeterminate as to the propositional form and propositional attitude they express; as to whether they are direct quotations, indirect quotations, or descriptions; and where interpretive resemblance is involved, as to how faithful a representation has been attempted. We have two answers to this objection. First, except for the idea that an utterance may be a less than literal interpretation of the speaker's thought, these are indeterminacies that exist and must be resolved on anyone's account. Secondly, we have available a pragmatic theory – relevance theory – which offers a general method of resolving

linguistic indeterminacies. In the next section we will briefly outline the
theory and its accompanying method of resolving indeterminacies, around
which our accounts of metaphor, irony and interrogative utterances will be
built.

3 Relevance

Human information processing requires some mental effort and achieves
some cognitive effect. Some effort of attention, memory and reasoning is
required. Some effect is achieved in terms of alterations to the individual's
beliefs: the addition of new beliefs, the cancellation of old beliefs, or merely a
change in his degree of confidence in old beliefs. We may characterise a
comparative notion of *relevance* in terms of effect and effort as follows:

Relevance
  a. Other things being equal, the greater the cognitive effect achieved by the
      processing of a given piece of information, the greater its relevance for the
      individual who processes it.
  b. Other things being equal, the greater the effort involved in the processing
      of a given piece of information, the smaller its relevance for the individual
      who processes it.

We claim that humans automatically aim at maximal relevance: that is,
maximal cognitive effect for minimal processing effort. This is the single
general factor which determines the course of human information processing.
It determines which information is attended to, which background assumptions are retrieved from memory and used as context, which inferences are
drawn.

To communicate is, among other things, to claim someone's attention,
and hence to demand some expenditure of effort. People will not pay attention unless they expect to obtain information that is rich enough in effects to
be relevant to them. Hence, to communicate is to imply that the stimulus
used (for example, the utterance) is worth the audience's attention. Any
utterance addressed to someone automatically conveys a presumption of its
own relevance. This fact, we call the *principle of relevance*.

The principle of relevance differs from every other principle, maxim,
convention or presumption proposed in modern pragmatics in that it is not
something that people have to know, let alone learn, in order to communicate
effectively; it is not something that they obey or might disobey: it is an
exceptionless generalisation about human communicative behaviour. What
people do have to know, and always do know when they recognise an
utterance as addressed to them, is that the speaker intends that particular
utterance to seem relevant enough to them to be worth their attention. In
other words, what people have to recognise is not the principle of relevance in
its general form, but the particular instantiations of it that they encounter.

Speakers may try hard or not at all to be relevant to their audience;

they may succeed or fail; they still convey a presumption of relevance: that is, they convey that they have done what was necessary to produce an adequately relevant utterance.

Relevance, we said, is a matter of cognitive effect and processing effort. On the effect side, it is in the interest of hearers that speakers offer the most relevant information they have. However, speakers have their own legitimate aims, and as a result may choose to offer some other information which is less than maximally relevant. Even so, to be worth the hearer's attention, this information must yield at least adequate effects, and the speaker manifestly intends the hearer to assume that this is so. On the effort side, there may be different ways of achieving the intended effects, all equally easy for the speaker to adopt, but requiring different amounts of processing effort from the hearer. Here, a rational speaker will choose the formulation that is easiest for the hearer to process, and manifestly intends the hearer to assume that this is so. In other words, the presumption of relevance has two parts: a presumption of adequate effect on the one hand, and a presumption of minimally necessary effort on the other.

As we have seen, the linguistic structure of an utterance grossly under-determines its interpretation. Various pragmatic theories appeal to complex sets of rules, maxims or conventions to explain how this linguistic indeterminacy is contextually overcome. We claim that the principle of relevance is enough on its own to explain how linguistic structure and back-ground knowledge interact to determine verbal comprehension.

In a nutshell, for an utterance to be understood, it must have one and only one interpretation consistent with the fact that the speaker intended it to seem relevant to the hearer – adequately relevant on the effect side and maximally relevant on the effort side. We will say that in this case the interpretation is *consistent with the principle of relevance*, meaning consistent with the particular instantiation of the principle. The speaker's task is to make sure that the interpretation she intends to convey is consistent with the principle of relevance; otherwise, she runs the risk of not being properly understood. The hearer's task is to find the interpretation which is consistent with the principle of relevance; otherwise, he runs the risk of misunderstand-ing the utterance or not understanding it at all.

To illustrate these ideas, consider how Peter might set about assigning a propositional form to (1a) above. The logical form of (1a) is incomplete: there are indefinitely many ways of developing it into a fully propositional form. However, not all these interpretations will be equally accessible to Peter. Imagine the following situation: Mary and Peter are alone in a restaurant; Peter is about to light a cigarette. Mary, who has never before objected to Peter's smoking, looks up at the 'No Smoking' sign and says, in a normal conversational tone, 'You shouldn't.' Manifestly, the first interpreta-tion to occur to Peter should be that Mary is saying he shouldn't smoke in the restaurant in question.

Is this interpretation consistent with the principle of relevance? Would it achieve adequate cognitive effects for the minimum necessary effort, in a way that Mary could manifestly have foreseen? It is easy to see how it might achieve adequate cognitive effects: for example, it might suggest how Peter should behave if he wanted to please Mary. As long as no other utterance would have achieved these effects more economically, this interpretation would also be satisfactory on the effort side, and therefore consistent with the principle of relevance.

Having found an interpretation consistent with the principle of relevance, Peter need look no further: there is never more than one. Although many interpretations may be adequate on the effect side, only one can be satisfactory on the effort side. Suppose that in the circumstances described, in which, by hypothesis, there is already one interpretation consistent with the principle of relevance, Mary in fact intended a different, less accessible interpretation: say, that Peter shouldn't eat meat. Could (1a), on this interpretation, be consistent with the principle of relevance?

Certainly, it might be adequate on the effect side: for example, it might suggest how Peter should behave if he wanted to please Mary. However, precisely because there is another, more accessible interpretation that is consistent with the principle of relevance, it could not be satisfactory on the effort side. No rational speaker would allow a hearer to waste his time on an unintended interpretation that he has no grounds for rejecting, since it is consistent with the only available criterion for evaluating interpretations, when by reformulating her utterance, she could have eliminated it entirely, or made the intended interpretation more accessible. It follows that the first interpretation tested and found consistent with the principle of relevance is the only interpretation consistent with the principle of relevance, and is the one the hearer should choose.

4 Loose talk and metaphor

An utterance represents a thought of the speaker. In a framework with a maxim of truthfulness, two further assumptions are made: that utterances are fully literal interpretations of thoughts of the speaker, and that the thought represented by a declarative utterance is entertained by the speaker as a true description of the actual world. In section 2, we suggested that both assumptions are false: on the one hand, an utterance may be a less than literal interpretation of the speaker's thought; on the other, that thought may itself be an interpretation of some further thought. In sections 5 and 6, we will show how the fact that thoughts may be interpretively used provides a natural explanation of ironical and interrogative utterances. In this section, we will show how the fact that utterances may be less than literal interpretations of thoughts of the speaker provides a natural explanation of loose talk and metaphor.

Mary says (10) to Peter, talking of Bill; her utterance has the propositional form in (11):

 (10)   He's an officer and a gentleman
 (11)   Bill is an officer and a gentleman

The maxim of truthfulness is designed to explain why Mary may use (10) to
indicate that she entertains (11) as a true description of the actual world,
thus conveying not only (11) but (12):

 (12)   Mary believes that Bill is an officer and a gentleman

We will show first how the same effect can be achieved without invoking a
maxim of truthfulness at all.

Utterances, we have said, are indeterminate as to how literally they
interpret the speaker's thought, as to whether that thought is entertained as a
description of a state of affairs or an interpretation of a further thought, and if
a description, as to whether it describes a state of affairs in the actual world
or in some alternative possible world. In section 3, we provided a general
method of resolving linguistic indeterminacies. Different resolutions yield
different understandings of (10). Suppose that (10) is understood as a literal
interpretation of a thought of Mary's, which is taken to be a true description
of the actual world. Then the effect would be the same as if a maxim of
truthfulness were in force.

Suppose now that Mary is merely talking loosely or metaphorically.
She does not want to communicate (11) or (12); she simply wants to convey
an impression of Bill as a certain type of man, with certain standards and
opinions and a certain outlook on life. In a framework with a maxim of
truthfulness, Mary's utterance, on this interpretation, would need special
treatment. According to Grice (1975), it would involve a flouting of the
maxim of truthfulness, with the resulting implicature that Bill is *like* an
officer and a gentleman. This analysis is itself problematic: for one thing, if
Mary merely wanted to communicate that Bill was like an officer and a
gentleman, she could have spared her hearer some effort by saying so
directly.

Instead of regarding loose or metaphorical utterances as deliberate
violations of a maxim of truthfulness, we will argue that they are simply the
result of choosing an utterance that is a less than literal interpretation of the
speaker's thought. The propositional forms of utterance and thought are not
identical; they merely share analytic and contextual implications.

Consider a concrete situation in which (10) might be loosely or
metaphorically understood. Peter has lent some money to Bill on the understanding that he will get it back later in the week. He wonders aloud to Mary
whether Bill will keep his word; Mary replies as in (10). Peter interprets her
utterance by computing its cognitive effects in a context based on his knowledge of the preceding discussion and his encyclopaedic understanding of
what it is to be an officer and a gentleman. Among these effects will be the
contextual implications that Bill is trustworthy, that he will repay the debt

by the appointed date, that he will not quarrel about how much he owes, that his cheque will not bounce, that Peter need not worry about getting his money back, and so on. Such effects will be highly accessible, in a way that Mary could manifestly have foreseen.

Is this interpretation consistent with the principle of relevance? It is adequate on the effect side: it answers Peter's question and provides evidence for the answer. It is satisfactory on the effort side: no other utterance would achieve the intended effect more economically. Hence this interpretation is consistent with the principle of relevance, and is, moreover, the *only* interpretation consistent with the principle of relevance. Although other, less accessible contexts might yield further contextual implications, by the criterion of consistency with the principle of relevance, these cannot be among the effects that Mary intended to achieve.

On this account, what makes Mary's utterance less than literal is that it communicates a subset of the analytic and contextual implications of (11) which does not imply, either analytically or contextually, the complementary subset. Therefore Mary's utterance (10) does not communicate (11) itself. On a literal interpretation, Mary's utterance would communicate a subset of the analytical and contextual implications of (11) which *does* imply its complement; in other words, Mary would be committing herself to the truth of all the implications of (11) – including, for example, the implication that Bill is a serving member of the armed forces – and therefore she would be communicating (11) itself. What is communicated by a loose or metaphorical interpretation is merely a sub-part of what is implied by a strictly literal one.

This account contrasts sharply with Grice's. In our view, all interpretations start loosely; some may then be tightened to the point of literalness. By the criterion of consistency with the principle of relevance, an utterance will be understood as loose or metaphorical unless nothing less than a fully literal interpretation will do. On the Gricean view, the order of events should be reversed. The hearer should start from the assumption that the utterance is fully literal, and reinterpret it as loose or metaphorical only if the initial hypothesis fails.

Here is some evidence that supports our account. How would you understand the following utterance?

(13)   I live 50 miles north of London

Is the speaker claiming that she lives exactly 50 miles due north of London? Though there is nothing patently absurd about this interpretation – some people do live exactly 50 miles due north of London – it is not the one you would choose. Indeed, it follows from the principle of relevance that, in most circumstances, someone who wanted to convey the information that she lived exactly 50 miles due north of London would not be able to do so by means of (13). In circumstances where a loose interpretation would be consistent with the principle of relevance, a literal interpretation would be inconsistent with the principle of relevance, and a speaker who wanted to convey the literal interpretation would have to find another way of doing so.

Utterances, then, are more or less literal interpretations of thoughts of the speaker. How literally they are understood is determined by the criterion of consistency with the principle of relevance. There is no need for a maxim of truthfulness, no need to analyse loose talk and metaphor as violations of pragmatic maxims or norms. This result should be welcome for another reason. Grice's maxims explicitly govern social, co-operative behaviour, and have no obvious analogues in thought. If there were a necessary connection between loose talk or metaphor and the flouting of co-operative maxims, it would be hard to explain why there is loose and metaphorical thought as well as talk. According to our account, the existence of loose and metaphorical thought is only to be expected. Thoughts, like utterances, can be descriptively or interpretively used: they can be entertained as true descriptions of states of affairs, or as more or less literal interpretations of other thoughts. Loose and metaphorical thought, loose and metaphorical talk, arise for exactly the same reasons, and are explained in exactly the same way.

5   Echoic utterances and irony

Consider the following exchange:

(14) a.   *Peter*: Ah, the old songs are still the best
      b.   *Mary* (fondly): Still the best

Both utterances have the propositional form in (15):

(15)   The old songs are still the best

Peter's utterance is descriptively used: Peter commits himself to the existence of the state of affairs described. In section 4, we argued that this effect, enforced in Gricean pragmatics by the maxim of truthfulness, is achieved when linguistic indeterminacies are resolved in a particular way, and the utterance is understood as a literal interpretation of a thought entertained by the speaker as a true description of the actual world.

In a framework with a maxim of truthfulness, Mary's utterance in (14b) would no doubt be analysed along the same lines as Peter's in (14a). In section 2 above, we suggested an alternative approach. Mary's utterance is echoic: that is, it indicates that she is entertaining the propositional form in (15), not as a true description of the actual world, but as a faithful representation of a thought she attributes to Bill, and to which she wants to express her reaction.

In this case, Mary's reaction is one of approval; from which it follows that Mary, like Peter, believes the old songs are best. Compare (16):

(16) a.   *Peter*: Ah, the old songs are still the best
      b.   *Mary* (contemptuously): Still the best!

Here, Mary's reaction to the thought she echoes is one of disapproval. She dissociates herself from it, perhaps indicating indirectly that she believes the old songs are *not* the best.

In ignoring the echoic nature of (14b) and (16b), the Gricean account does full justice to neither utterance. However, there is an added problem with (16b). Mary does not even indirectly commit herself to the existence of the state of affairs described: her utterance cannot possibly be analysed as obeying the maxim of truthfulness.

Ironical utterances, we would argue, fall into the same broad category as (16b). The speaker echoes a thought she attributes to someone else, while dissociating herself from it with ridicule or scorn. Returning to the scenario of section 4, let us suppose that after Mary has calmed Peter's doubts by assuring him, with glowing hyperbole, that Bill is an officer and a gentleman, Bill rudely denies all knowledge of his debt to Peter. After telling Mary what has happened, Peter remarks:

(17)   Truly, an officer and a gentleman

This utterance is clearly both ironical and echoic. Peter echoes Mary's earlier opinion in order to indicate how ridiculous and misleading it turned out to be. To understand (17) as ironical, all that is needed is a realisation that it is echoic, and a recognition of the particular type of attitude expressed.

Not all ironical echoes are as easily recognisable. The thought being echoed may not have been expressed in an utterance; it may not be attributable to any specific person, but merely to a type of person, or people in general; it may be merely a cultural aspiration or norm. For example, because the code of an officer and a gentleman is widely held up for admiration, a failure to live up to it is always open to ironical comment.

In the Gricean framework, irony is seen as involving a flouting of the maxim of truthfulness, with resulting implicature. (17), for example, would be seen as implicating that Bill is not an officer and a gentleman. One problem with this analysis is that it does not account for the important differences in stylistic effect between the ironical (17) and the ordinary assertion (18):

(18)   Bill is not an officer and a gentleman

On the Gricean account, the two utterances differ not in overall import but only in degree of explicitness: why, then, the marked difference in stylistic effect? On our analysis, these differences stem from the fact that one is an echoic interpretation, whereas the other is an ordinary assertion. To understand an echoic interpretation such as (17), the hearer has to recognise both the echoic allusion and the attitude being expressed. Neither is necessary for the comprehension of an ordinary assertion such as (18).

Another problem with the Gricean account of irony is the claim that what is implicated is invariably the opposite of what is said. I may dissociate myself from an opinion echoed without implicating the opposite. Many ironical understatements, exclamations and quotations illustrate this point. Take Mercutio's comment on his death wound:

(19)   No, 'tis not so deep as a well, nor so wide as a church door; but 'tis enough, 'twill serve

It is hard to see how this ironical understatement can be usefully analysed as implicating the opposite of what is said.

A Gricean persuaded by the echoic analysis of irony might try to incorporate it into his framework by claiming that although irony is echoic, an echoic utterance can only be recognised as such if it involves a flouting of the maxim of truthfulness. However, only a subset of echoic utterances would succumb to this treatment. Where the speaker endorses the opinion echoed, as in (14b) above, this approach would fail and the echoic nature of the utterance would go unperceived.

In our framework, the appeal to a maxim of truthfulness is unnecessary anyway, since there is already a criterion for distinguishing echoic from non-echoic utterances: the criterion of consistency with the principle of relevance. Sometimes, as with (14b) and (16b), the allusion may be so obvious that the echoic understanding is the first to be tested. At other times, the irony may be noticed only when a non-echoic understanding has been tried and has failed. In every case, the first interpretation tested and found consistent with the principle of relevance is the only interpretation consistent with the principle of relevance, and is the one the hearer should choose.

In the last two sections, we have suggested the following view of the representing relations between utterances, thoughts and states of affairs. An utterance is, in the first instance, a more or less literal interpretation of a thought of the speaker's, which may itself be entertained as a true description of a state of affairs, or as a more or less literal interpretation of an attributed thought. An ordinary assertion results when the utterance is a literal interpretation of a thought of the speaker's, which is itself descriptively entertained. Loose talk and metaphor result when the utterance is a less than literal interpretation of a thought of the speaker's. Irony results when the thought entertained by the speaker is a more or less literal interpretation of an attributed thought, and the speaker, moreover, dissociates herself from this thought with ridicule or scorn.

So far, we have said nothing about non-declarative utterances, which present their own traditional semantic and pragmatic problems. Here, we will look briefly at imperatives and interrogatives, and argue that while imperatives, like declaratives, may be descriptively used, interrogatives can be more fruitfully analysed as specialised for interpretive use.

6 Non-declaratives

In Wilson & Sperber (forthcoming) we survey a variety of approaches to the
semantics and pragmatics of imperatives and interrogatives, and conclude
that while existing descriptive approaches are in general empirically
inadequate, imperatives can be satisfactorily dealt with in recognisable descriptive terms, whereas interrogatives cannot.

To take just one example of a descriptive approach to imperatives,
Huntley (1984) suggests that the distinction between declaratives and
imperatives is a special case of a more general semantic distinction between
indicative and non-indicative mood. Semantically, he argues, indicatives
involve indexical reference to the actual world, whereas non-indicatives –
that is, imperatives, infinitival clauses and non-finite *that*-clauses – do not.
Non-indicatives 'represent a situation as being merely envisaged as a possibility, with no commitment as to whether it obtains, in past, present or
future, in *this* world' (Huntley 1984:122). In our terms, this amounts to the
claim that the propositional form of an indicative is entertained as a true
description of the actual world, whereas the propositional form of a non-
indicative is entertained as a true description merely of a possible world.

Huntley acknowledges – we feel with good reason – that this analysis of
imperatives may lay an inadequate semantic foundation for the prediction of
illocutionary force. It is hard to see why the hearer of an imperative utterance
should conclude, from the mere fact that the speaker is envisaging a certain
situation as a possibility, that he is being requested, advised, urged, etc. to
bring it about. Here there is a crucial difference between imperatives and
infinitival clauses. As Huntley predicts, the speaker of the infinitival
utterances (20a) and (20b) can envisage a certain state of affairs as a possibility without necessarily representing it as either achievable or desirable:

(20) a.   To spend all one's life in the same room. Imagine!

      b.   To meet the President of the United States. Hmm!

Hence, as one might expect, (20a) and (20b) can be seriously and literally
uttered without imperatival force (that is, without being intended or understood as orders, requests, advice, permission, or any of the other speech-acts
standardly performed by imperatives). By the same token, Huntley's
analysis predicts that imperatives can be seriously and literally uttered
without imperatival force. But of course, they can't.

We believe that the crucial semantic and pragmatic differences
between imperative and infinitival clauses are linked to differences in the
type of world they describe, and hence in the propositional attitudes they
express. As Huntley suggests, the propositional form of an infinitival clause is
entertained as a true description merely of a possible world. The propositional form of an imperative, by contrast, is entertained as a true description
of a world the speaker regards as both *potential* and *desirable*. A potential world

is one compatible with the individual's assumptions about the actual world, which may therefore be, or become, actual; a desirable world is one the individual regards as desirable from someone's point of view, not necessarily his own – another linguistic indeterminacy to be pragmatically resolved.

This semantic analysis of imperatives lays a stronger foundation than Huntley's for the prediction of illocutionary force. The very fact that I regard a certain state of affairs as achievable and desirable may give you a reason to try to bring it about. If I manifestly regard it as desirable from my point of view rather than yours, my utterance may have the force of a request; if I manifestly regard it as desirable from your point of view rather than mine, my utterance may have the force of a suggestion or a piece of advice. In Sperber & Wilson (forthcoming) we show how this basic semantic characterisation interacts with contextual factors and considerations of relevance to yield the full range of imperatival illocutionary forces.

The notions of potential and desirable world are not introduced *ad hoc* for the analysis of imperatives, but are useful in the analysis of other syntactic constructions. Hortatives, like imperatives, may be seen as describing worlds regarded as both potential and desirable, whereas optatives may be seen as describing worlds regarded as desirable but not necessarily potential: one can wish for, but not exhort someone to bring about, a state of affairs one knows to be unachievable.

On this approach, imperatives, optatives, hortatives, and declaratives are all recognisably truth-conditional: they all describe states of affairs that make them true. What distinguishes them is not their propositional form but their linguistically encoded propositional attitudes. These attitudes might themselves be called descriptive, since they determine the type of world the utterance describes. If interrogatives and exclamatives could be approached in similar terms, it would be reasonable to conclude that semantics was wholly concerned with descriptive representation, and that the notion of interpretive representation discussed in this chapter was of interest only to pragmatics. We will argue, however, that interrogatives and exclamatives are not analysable in purely descriptive terms.

In formal semantics, interrogatives have generally been seen as denoting either their sets of possible answers (Hamblin 1973) or their sets of true answers (Karttunen 1977). The main problem with this account is that it provides no obvious explanation of the pragmatic differences among positive questions such as (21), negative questions such as (22), and alternative questions such as (23):

(21)   Did you see Susan?

(22)   Didn't you see Susan?

(23)   Did you or did you not see Susan?

Each of (21)–(23) has the possible answers 'Yes' and 'No', and a true answer to any one is a true answer to all. For Hamblin and Karttunen, (21)–(23)

should thus be synonymous. Why is it, then, that while utterances of (21) are generally neutral in tone, the speaker of (22) suggests that she had expected the hearer to see Susan, and (23) sounds impatient or hectoring?

Bolinger (1978) develops this point at length, with a wealth of convincing examples. He goes on to argue that indirect questions introduced by 'if' are not synonymous with those introduced by 'whether': the former are embedded versions of yes–no questions such as (21) and (22), the latter are embedded versions of alternative questions such as (23). This indirectly supports the claim that yes–no questions are not synonymous with their alternative counterparts.

What we want to retain from the formal account is the idea that questions in some sense represent their answers. Formal semanticists call this relation 'denoting'. We think it is better described as interpretive representation. We regard interrogatives, like echoic utterances, as doubly interpretive: both represent a thought of the speaker's which itself interpretively represents another thought. The difference is that while echoic utterances are second-degree interpretations of attributed thoughts, interrogatives are second-degree interpretations of *desirable* thoughts.

According to this view, interrogatives are the interpretive counterpart of imperatives. Whereas imperatives describe desirable states of affairs, interrogatives interpretively represent desirable thoughts. What makes a thought desirable? In the framework of relevance theory, a thought is desirable only if it is relevant. Thus, interrogatives interpretively represent not possible answers, not true answers, but answers the speaker regards as *relevant*.

The pragmatic differences among (21)–(23) above can then be traced to their differences in propositional form. (21) expresses a positive proposition, (22) a negative proposition and (23) both a positive and a negative proposition. Assuming that a question is a fully literal interpretation of its answer, (21) should therefore indicate that a positive answer would be, if anything, more relevant than a negative answer, (22) that a negative answer would be, if anything, more relevant than a positive one, and (23) that a positive and a negative answer would be equally relevant.

Consider the implications of this account for the analysis of the negative question in (22). By asking 'Didn't you see Susan?' Mary indicates that a negative answer would be, if anything, more relevant than a positive one. Now of the three main types of cognitive effect, negative utterances quite regularly achieve relevance by contradicting existing positive assumptions. As has often been noted, the information that the President is not drunk today would normally only be relevant to someone who had thought he might be. By the same token, the information that Peter didn't see Susan would normally only be relevant to someone who had been expecting him to see her. This explains the overtones of surprise or reproach that often accompany negative questions.

If we are right, then although yes–no questions have fully propositional forms, and therefore describe determinate states of affairs, they are never descriptively used. The propositional attitudes encoded by interrogatives are not descriptive but interpretive: their propositional forms are entertained not as true descriptions of states of affairs, but as faithful enough interpretations of thoughts the speaker regards as desirable to someone (not necessarily herself). In Wilson & Sperber (forthcoming), we show how this semantic characterisation interacts with contextual factors and the principle of relevance to account for the various types of illocutionary force that yes–no questions can have.

Wh-questions fit straightforwardly into this framework. Although a wh-question has no fully propositional form (or only a very vague and general one), its linguistically encoded logical form may be entertained as a less than literal interpretation of a fully propositional form that the speaker regards as desirable to someone (not necessarily herself). In other words, wh-questions, like yes–no questions, are interpretively used to represent relevant answers.

One advantage of this approach is that it suggests a way of explaining the striking syntactic parallelisms between interrogative and exclamative sentences such as (24) and (25):

(24) How popular is Peter?

(25) How popular Peter is!

Formal semanticists rarely consider exclamatives. In traditional speech act terms, since interrogatives are requests for information and exclamatives are emphatic assertions, it is hard to account for the consistent cross-linguistic parallelisms between these two utterance types. We suggest that exclamatives, like interrogatives, are specialised for interpretive rather than descriptive use. Whereas a speaker who asks a question such as (24) indicates that some true completion of the incomplete thought represented by her utterance is relevant, a speaker who produces an exclamation such as (25) indicates that some relevant completion of the incomplete thought represented by her utterance is true. In other words, the speaker of (25) indicates that Peter is high enough on the scale of popularity for the fact to be worth noticing. Thus, the intuition that exclamatives are like emphatic assertions, and the striking parallelisms between exclamative and interrogative form, are simultaneously explained.

7 Conclusion

We began this chapter with the common assumption that thoughts and utterances describe states of affairs. We have shown that this assumption is true, at least for thoughts and utterances with fully propositional forms. However, we have argued that to concentrate exclusively on the states of affairs that thoughts and utterances describe would lead to inadequate semantic and pragmatic theories.

Thoughts and utterances express not only propositional forms but also propositional attitudes. Some attitudes are analysable in descriptive terms, as affecting not the state of affairs described but the type of world in which it is taken to obtain. Others, including those linguistically encoded by interrogatives and exclamatives, are not descriptive at all. Linguistic semantics cannot be approached in purely descriptive terms.

Modern pragmatics is based on the assumption that descriptive use of utterances is the norm. We have argued that this assumption has led to a neglect of many types of non-descriptive utterance (for example, direct and indirect quotations) which cannot reasonably be analysed as departures from a norm of truthfulness; and to a misanalysis of others (for example, loose talk and metaphor, echoic utterances and irony), which are now widely regarded as flagrant violations of communicative norms.

We have argued that better explanations result when utterances are treated as more or less faithful interpretations of thoughts of the speaker, which may themselves be entertained either as true descriptions of states of affairs or as more or less faithful interpretations of further thoughts (which may themselves be descriptive or interpretive). On this account, every utterance is, at the most basic level, interpretive, and only at the next level is it interpretively or descriptively used. If so, then a fundamental assumption of modern pragmatics is dead wrong. While the notion of a description – i.e. of a representation in virtue of truth-conditional properties – is the most fundamental one in semantics, the notion of an interpretation – i.e. of a representation in virtue of resemblance in content – is the most fundamental one in pragmatics.

NOTE

1 For ease of exposition, we will talk of a female communicator and a male addressee.

REFERENCES

Bolinger, D. 1978. Yes–no questions are not alternative questions. In H. Hiz (ed.) *Questions*. Dordrecht: Reidel, 87–105.

Fodor, J. 1981. Methodological solipsism considered as a research strategy in cognitive psychology. In J. Fodor *Representations*. Hassocks, Sussex: Harvester Press, 225–53.

Grice, H.P. 1975. Logic and conversation. In P. Cole & J. Morgan (eds.) *Syntax and semantics 3: Speech acts*. New York: Academic Press, 41–58.

Hamblin, C. 1973. Questions in Montague English. *Foundations of Language* 10: 41–53.

Huntley, M. 1984. The semantics of English imperatives. *Linguistics and Philosophy* 7: 103–33.

Karttunen, L. 1977. Syntax and semantics of questions. *Linguistics and Philosophy* 1: 3–44. Reprinted in H. Hiz (ed.) 1978. *Questions*. Dordrecht: Reidel, 165–210.

Sperber, D. 1985. *On anthropological knowledge*. Cambridge: Cambridge University Press.

Sperber, D. & Wilson, D. 1986a. *Relevance: communication and cognition*. Oxford: Blackwell; Cambridge, Mass.: Harvard University Press.

Sperber, D. & Wilson, D. 1986b. Loose talk. *Proceedings of the Aristotelian Society* 1985–6: 153–71.

Wilson, D. & Sperber, D. 1988. Mood and the analysis of non-declarative sentences. To appear in J. Dancy, J. Moravcsik & C. Taylor (eds.) *Human agency: language, duty and value*. California: Stanford University Press.

7

Implicature, explicature, and truth-theoretic semantics

ROBYN CARSTON

1 Introduction

Pragmatists have given much attention to what an utterance can convey implicitly since Grice brought it to their attention in his work on conversational implicature. Equally important, however, is the proposition explicitly expressed by the utterance of a linguistic expression, what is said, in Grice's terms, although this has been given only passing acknowledgement. Since what is said (the explicit) and what is implicated (the implicit) exhaust the (propositional) significance of the utterance, we are unlikely to have a coherent notion of the latter without consideration of the former.

In this chapter I consider the problem of distinguishing the proposition expressed (henceforth called the explicature[1]) from those implicated (implicatures). It might seem that there is no particular problem; after all, Grice and almost all those following him have assumed the explicature is the result of accessing the conventional sense of the linguistic form used plus assignment of referents to referring expressions and, occasionally, disambiguation of those words or phrases which have more than one sense. As an initial indication that matters might not be so straightforward let us consider B's utterance in (1):

(1) A: How is Jane feeling after her first year at university?

B: She didn't get enough units and can't continue

Let us suppose that (part at least of) A's interpretation of B's utterance is: 'Jane didn't pass enough university course units to qualify for admission to second year study, and, as a result, Jane cannot continue with university study. Jane is not feeling at all happy about this.' There are various vaguenesses and ambiguities left in this expression of the interpretation; this is inevitable in any natural language expression of an interpretation (which is itself a set of mental representations). I intend it merely to suggest the sort of interpretation A might reasonably give to this utterance. The question then is which aspects of this interpretation are explicitly expressed (that is, part of the explicature) and which are implicit (implicated)? The disambiguation of 'get' and 'units' and the referent assignment to 'she' are surely part of the explicit content, while the assumption that Jane isn't feeling happy is surely implicit. But what about 'to qualify for admission to second year study', and 'with university study' which enrich and complete the two clauses of the conjunction, and the 'as a result', linking the two conjuncts. Are these part of what is explicated or part of what is implicated? Since they are not given linguistically, one might think they must be implicated, but then what is the explicature of the utterance? It must be 'Jane didn't pass enough university course units and Jane cannot continue (something ??)'. It's not clear that this constitutes a propositional form,[2] that is, it isn't possible to specify what conditions in the world must obtain for it to be true. The same difficulty applies to the implicated bits of meaning – they are nonpropositional on their own and need to be embedded in some other representation in order to be truth evaluable. What could this representation be? The best candidate would seem to be the complete form 'Jane didn't pass enough university course units to qualify for second year study', etc. But, if so, either the utterance has no explicature at all or the explicit content is duplicated by or contained within an implicature of the utterance.

I try to establish criteria for distinguishing explicature and implicature so that such apparent enigmas as the above may be resolved. On the one hand, I suggest a criterion of functional independence of explicatures, which ensures that what counts as an explicature isn't arbitrarily confined to linguistic sense plus reference assignment and disambiguation. On the other hand, we need constraints on the process of enrichment of the linguistic sense in building the explicature of the utterance, to ensure that the explicature is not overextended so as to include information properly understood as implicit. However, while it is instructive to consider such criteria, they might well be seen as rather superficial, descriptive principles, if not *ad hoc*. It would be more satisfying to find that they are consequences of some more explanatory psychological principle or principles. This is indeed so; they follow from a single principle directing utterance interpretation, the principle of relevance, which is itself embedded in a general theory of human cognition and communication, the relevance theory of Sperber & Wilson (1986);[3] so they need not be separately stated. In the light of the relevance-theoretic framework I reconsider some examples standardly treated as generalised conversational implicatures and show them instead to be cases of explicature. One nice outcome of this reanalysis is that a previously intractable problem for the semantics/pragmatics distinction dissolves, having been caused by the erroneous implicature analysis. And, finally, this work brings into high relief the mistaken assumption of many truth-theoretic semanticists that the proper domain of truth conditional semantics is natural language sentences, rather than mental language sentences. A distinction must be made between linguistic semantics and truth-theoretic semantics.

2   Implicatures

Let's start with conversational implicature, which is what has galvanised work in the new field of pragmatics. Grice established the idea first by setting up a few compelling examples rather than by attempting to define the notion. One of these is given in (2) in the rather informal way that he gave it:

(2)   A: Smith doesn't seem to have a girlfriend these days
      B: He's been paying a lot of visits to New York lately

B implicates that Smith has, or may have, a girlfriend in New York, an assumption he must be taken to believe in order to preserve the assumption that he is observing the maxim of relation 'Be relevant' (Grice 1975: 51). This example seems clear since, whatever problems we might have in clarifying the notion of explicature, we surely don't think that the assumption that Smith has a girlfriend in New York is explicitly conveyed by B's utterance. That message is conveyed implicitly, indirectly, and is clearly dependent on the particular context which includes A's preceding utterance. If the context were different, say A's preceding utterance had been 'I believe Smith's looking for a new job', then this implicit message would not be conveyed by B's utterance. This property of cancellability without creating contradiction is one of the characteristics of implicature to which Grice gives particular emphasis.

A second important property is the calculability of implicatures, that is, something isn't an implicature if it's not possible to give an account of a reasoned derivation of it based on the assumption that the speaker is observing pragmatic principles. Sperber & Wilson (1986) have developed an account of the non-demonstrative inference processes involved in the derivation of implicatures. These processes will not be explained here but one example will indicate what has to be explained:

(3)   A: Have you read Susan's book?
      B: I don't read autobiographies
      implicated premise: Susan's book is an autobiography
      implicated conclusion: B hasn't read Susan's book

A similar distinction can be made for (2):

      implicated premise: If Smith's been paying a lot of visits to New York lately he's probably got a girlfriend there.
      implicated conclusion: Smith's probably got a girlfriend in New York.

There are two kinds of implicature involved in the derivations: implicated premises and implicated conclusions. Once the implicated premise has been recovered, the conclusion follows by a straightforward deductive inference rule, taking the implicated premise and the explicature of the utterance as input. The real work lies in accounting for the recovery of the implicated premise in terms of a non-deductive process of hypothesis formation and confirmation.[4]

The obvious but important point here is that the explicature is distinct from the implicatures of the utterance; they do not overlap in content. In (3) the truth conditions of 'Susan's book is an autobiography' are independent of the truth conditions of 'B doesn't read autobiographies'. Implicatures have distinct propositional forms (see note 2 of this chapter) with their own truth conditions and they function independently of the explicature as the premises and conclusions of arguments. So we have a further property of any assumption conveyed by an utterance that we would want to call an implicature: as well as cancellability (without contradiction) and calculability, there is the independent functioning of these forms in the inferences involved in deriving the full import of an utterance. Any such requirement on implicatures naturally places an identical requirement on the explicatures of the utterance. They too are assumptions which occupy independent roles in the mental life of the hearer (and no doubt of the speaker as well): they must function as autonomous premises in inferential interactions with other assumptions and must be stored in memory as separate assumptions. In fact this is the crucial property, since cancellability and calculability are properties of any and all aspects of utterance meaning which are derived pragmatically rather than via a process of linguistic decoding. Thus the results of disambiguation and reference assignment, which are standardly acknowledged as involved in establishing the explicature of an utterance, are also cancellable and calculable. This functional autonomy property decides in favour of extending the explicature of (1) to include the explanation of what Jane didn't get enough units for and what she cannot continue, since otherwise the explicature is entailed by the implicature and thus is redundant, playing no independent role in inference. This third property proves decisive later when we face problem cases, one of which is exemplified by the casual connection between the conjuncts in (1).[5] However, in the end, this property is no more than a useful heuristic, as we shall see in section 5.

Having introduced the pragmatic maxims and the notion of conversational implicature by using these highly context-dependent cases (particularised conversational implicatures), Grice went on to consider the group he calls generalised conversational implicatures. While particularised implicatures are 'carried by saying that p on a particular occasion in virtue of special features of the context,' generalised implicatures are those 'normally carried by saying that p' no matter what the context is (Grice 1975: 56). A set of familiar instances of these, some of which will be reconsidered in this paper, is given in (4)–(9). In each case (a) is the sentence uttered by the speaker and (b), or (b) and (c) in (9), is the generalised conversational implicature which would be standardly conveyed by an utterance of the sentence.

(4) a. She gave him her key *and* he opened the door
     b. She gave him her key and then he opened the door

(5) a. Mr Jones has been insulted *and* he's going to resign
     b. Mr Jones has been insulted and as a result he's going to resign

(6) a. Mrs Smith has *three* children
     b. Mrs Smith has no more than three children

(7) a. *Some* of the students passed the exam
    b. Not all of the students passed the exam

(8) a. She's a *competent* pianist
    b. She's not a brilliant pianist

(9) a. Bill is ill *or* he's working at home
    b. Bill isn't both ill and working at home
    c. The speaker doesn't know whether or not Bill is ill

Grice was interested in a pragmatic explanation for these aspects of meaning as a counter to the prevailing tendency at the time to postulate a large number of distinct but related senses for a word, multiple ambiguities. Given the notion of generalised conversational implicature he could maintain that the semantics of natural language *and* is identical with logical conjunction.

3 *And*

Let us first remove the lexical ambiguity view from the debate on the appropriate treatment of these *and* cases by quickly running through some evidence against it. Firstly, if one is going to go for ambiguity, then *and* is going to be many more than three ways ambiguous and some of these ways are actually going to contradict one another:

(10) a. Mary was in the kitchen and she was listening to the radio
     b. He fell into a deep sleep and dreamed that he was flying
     c. We investigated the problem and it was far more complex than expected

If we consider the examples in (10) together with the two we already have in (4) and (5) we find three different temporal notions: successivity in (4), simultaneity in (10a) and some sort of temporal containment in (10b). Then in (10c) there is some sort of resultant sense as there is in (5), but they are different: in (5) the one event is a cause of the other or at least gives a reason for the other. But in (10c) the fact that the problem proved far more complex than expected isn't caused by our investigating it, and our investigating it isn't a reason for its being more complex than expected. The more such examples one looks at, the less plausible it seems that what we have here are a range of subtly different meanings of the word *and*. Rather, these meanings are the result of the way our minds organise information into connected scenarios or scripts, making a variety of connections amongst events and states of affairs in the world (that variety doubtless determined by innate constraints on our powers of conceptualisation). So we relate events temporally, causally and for that matter spatially (in (10a), for example, we naturally assume that the listening of the radio was going on in the kitchen) whenever it seems reasonable to do so. It seems that this must be the outcome of general properties of the mind rather than the meaning of *and*, since if we take out all the *and*s in the examples and put in instead a full-stop or a pause, we find ourselves making exactly the same temporal and causal connections.

This strongly indicates that the account of the temporal, etc., connotations be a pragmatic one. Grice has given such an account explicitly for the temporal case invoking the submaxim, 'Be orderly', of the general maxim of Manner, 'Be perspicuous'. He says '. . . if what one is engaged upon is a narrative (if one is talking about events), then the most orderly manner for a narration of events is an order that corresponds to the order in which they took place. So the meaning of the expression "He took off his trousers and he got into bed" and the corresponding expression with a logician's constant "&" would be exactly the same' (Grice 1981: 186). That is, both acquire, by the act of utterance, the implication that the event related in the first conjunct took place before that related in the second one. Grice does not discuss the further causal sense of examples such as (5) and (1) and it's less easy to see how the explanation would go using his maxims. A co-operative speaker should not present a hearer with a sequence of events which any normal human being would assume to be causally connected if she does not intend this assumption to be made. A more substantial explanation than this is desirable and is possible with a properly developed principle of relevance (see section 5).

Grice has undoubtedly established a strong case for the pragmatic treatment of these aspects of conveyed meaning; it tends to be assumed that they are therefore implicated. Linguists, such as Gazdar (1979), Horn (1972, 1984) and Levinson (1983), who took up Grice's principles, have written as if any meaning not derived by linguistic decoding must be implicated. However, everyone acknowledges that deriving the explicature depends on reference assignment and disambiguation; as several people have pointed out (Katz 1972, Walker 1975 and Wilson & Sperber 1981), these are processes which are just as dependent on context and pragmatic principles as is the derivation of implicatures. So there simply is not a neat correlation between a semantics/pragmatics distinction and an explicating/implicating distinction. The (tacit) assumption of most pragmatists then is that there IS a small gap between sentence sense and explicature, but that it is entirely filled by disambiguation and reference assignment. Why should this be so? It seems a rather arbitrary and unprincipled assumption and will be shown to be in fact false. Given that the maxims make SOME contribution to determining the explicature, it is an open question how great their contribution is. In particular, given that we are rejecting the semantic ambiguity account of conjoined utterances, it is an open question whether those aspects of their interpretation that are pragmatically determined are explicated or implicated. It seems that an account at either level is possible.

A pragmatic account at the explicature level might go as follows. In determining what the speaker of (4a) has explicated, the hearer must assign a reference to each of the referring expressions, including the past tense *gave* and *opened*. Just as pragmatic principles are employed in ascertaining the referents of *she* and *he*, so they are used in assigning temporal reference. The hearer goes beyond the strict semantic content of the sentence uttered, and on the basis of contextual assumptions and pragmatic principles (say the maxims of relation and manner) recovers from (4a), at the level of expli-cature, a representation such as (11):

> (11) She$_1$ gave him$_2$ [her$_1$ key]$_3$ at *t* and he$_2$ opened the door at *t+n* using [the key]$_3$

Now this is a conceptual representation whose properties can be shown only roughly by this index-boosted linguistic representation. The indexed pro-nouns should be understood as indicating uniquely referring concepts rather than as simply showing coreference; one could replace the pronouns by proper names, say *Mary* and *Bill*, but, although these are more specific referring expressions than pronouns, some further means of indicating the particular Mary and the particular Bill would be necessary. *t* is some more or less specific time prior to the time of utterance and *t+n* is some more or less specific time, later than *t*. The temporal ordering of the events described in conjuncts is thus treated as a by-product of the reference assignment process involved in determining the explicature.

The representation in (11) might reasonably be taken to imply that (4a) contains some linguistic devices referring to instants of time analogous with pronouns that make particular references. Pierre Jacob (personal com-munication) says that it is not at all clear that the way tensed verbs refer to times is comparable to the way pronouns refer to persons, and that (4a) does not express conjoined singular propositions with respect to times but rather existentially (hence general) conjoined propositions as in (12):

> (12) ($\exists$ *t, t'*) (She$_1$ gave him$_2$ [her$_1$ key]$_3$ at *t* and he$_2$ opened the door at *t'* with [the key]$_3$ and *t* precedes *t'*)

It seems to me that this will depend on the particular context of utterance; (12) is the least specific possibility, derived in a context where all that matters is the order of some events. More often, though, hearers will narrow down the time spans to some probable period along the line from the begin-ning of time to the moment of utterance.

Partee (1973) finds a range of parallels in the use of pronouns and tenses. Discussing the example *I didn't turn off the stove* she says 'When uttered, for instance, halfway down the turnpike, such a sentence does not mean that there exists some time in the past at which I did not turn off the stove or that there exists no time in the past at which I turned off the stove. The sentence clearly refers to a particular time – not a particular instant, most likely, but a definite interval whose identity is generally clear from the extralinguistic context' (Partee 1973: 602–3). As she acknowledges in a footnote, the nar-rowing down to the relevant time is explainable pragmatically, so it is not the sentence that picks out the time interval but the explicature of the utterance. The most reasonable construal of Jacob's suggestion, then, is that it concerns the linguistic sense of the sentence, which should be taken to include these time variables bound by an existential quantifier, that is (12) above without the indices and without the clause specifying temporal ordering, and that it is left to pragmatic considerations whether and to what extent the time span is specified. In this respect the semantics of tense is parallel with that of indefinite pronouns rather than personal pronouns: *Someone has eaten the cake* might be understood as some specific person, say Bill, in some contexts, and as simply indefinite in others. The linguistic device of tense does not prescribe the accessing of particular times but nor does it preclude the possibility. It may well be that neither (11) nor (12) captures this satisfactorily. However, this is a notational problem which arises whether one opts for an explicature or an implicature analysis of temporal connotations and as such does not affect the possibility of an explicature analysis.

Finally, notice that we also understand (4a) as saying that the key *he* used to open the door is the one *she* gave him, although this too goes beyond the linguistically given sense. This is simply the most plausible interpretation to give the second conjunct since the speaker has chosen to conjoin it to the first one. If she hadn't meant us to understand this, she should have supplied the information that another key was used. This completion of sense is similar to that proposed for (1), and is discussed further below.

So once the semantic ambiguity analysis is ruled out there are two pragmatic accounts possible. We need to see if there is any reason for preferring one to the other. Let's return to the traditional implicature account for (4a) and consider what the explicature of the utterance is on such an account. It must be either (11) or (12) minus the specification of $t+n$, or t', as later than t. Then, assuming that the implicature is a conceptual representation with a propositional form, the explicature is entailed by the implicature. If the implicated assumption is stored in memory the explicated assumption need not be, since all the information given by the latter is also given by the former. Further, whatever role the explicated assumption might play in chains of reasoning the implicated assumption could also play, as well as giving rise to the extra possibilities hinging on its encoding of the temporal ordering. In other words whatever the explicature can do, so can the implicature plus more. The explicature has no function in mental life that can't be played by the implicature. By the criterion of functional independence proposed earlier, the explicature analysis of temporal sequence is favoured. It will shortly be shown that this conclusion is supported by relevance theory predictions too and that it sweeps away a problem that the implicature analysis creates.

The question now arises whether this analysis extends to the causal connotations that often accompany uses of *and*, as in (1) and (5). While some theorists seem to be willing to grant the treatment of the temporal ordering as above they baulk at the further enrichment of explicit content so as to include the causal relation between the events related in the conjuncts. The reason for this is that the former can be seen as a by-product of the reference assignment process which is necessarily involved in deriving the explicature of the utterance. Ambiguities and referring expressions can be seen as instructions given by the grammar to carry out some process of choosing or specifying in order to derive a propositional form. There is no grammatical device in (5) that sets up a further slot to be filled, or that directs any fuller articulation of the relation between the events of the two conjuncts, which might lead to the specification of a causal relation. The assumption that the relation exists is a result of general world knowledge about human feelings and behaviour, mentally represented as scripts about the nature and effects of insults and of resigning from jobs. So it might well be felt that the causal relation is implicated and not part of the explicature. We could dub the assumption guiding this decision the 'linguistic (or grammatical) direction' principle. It should be distinguished from the linguistic encoding of conceptual content. Linguistic direction includes this but also covers cases such as pronouns, tenses, and empty grammatical categories which are indicators delivered by the grammar that some pragmatic work is needed to derive some conceptual content from the context. On this principle, the causal connection is implicated because the grammar does not deliver a relational variable instructing the hearer to find a relevant connection. This is clearly at odds with the prediction made by the criterion of functional independence, which, again, would favour an explicature analysis. Before pronouncing further on this case, which raises more problems than the temporal one, let us retreat a few steps and consider a little more closely what is meant by an explicature and whether explicatures in general respect the linguistic direction principle.

4 Explicatures

As already noted, most pragmatists working in the Gricean framework have adopted as a working principle the view that any pragmatically determined aspect of utterance interpretation, apart from disambiguation and reference assignment, is necessarily an implicature. The explanation for cutting things this way lies with the further assumption that the explicature must be truth-evaluable; so Grice and the Griceans are prepared to let in just whatever is necessary in addition to linguistically determined content to bring the representation up to a complete propositional form, that is, something capable of bearing a truth value. On this basis even the temporal ordering information is not strictly part of the explicature, since a truth-evaluable proposition is derived without it: (4a) can be said to be true provided the two events took place at some time in the past, never mind the order of the events. However, as a consequence of reference assignment it might be countenanced as part of the explicature.

In general the linguistic direction principle and the minimally truth-evaluable criterion coincide, the one reflecting a more linguistic turn of mind, the other a more philosophical; both assume that the domain of grammar, sentences, and the domain of truth-conditional semantics, propositions, are essentially the same. I want to argue that neither of these is an appropriate principle for a PSYCHOLOGICALLY plausible theory of utterance interpretation, that they give only a sufficient condition for some pragmatically derived meaning to be an aspect of the explicature, not a necessary one, and that the domains of grammar and of truth-conditional semantics are not the same.

As soon as one looks at real utterances, it becomes apparent that pragmatic principles may have much more to do in establishing what has been explicated than just assigning reference and disambiguation. Supplying ellipsed material is an obvious case of under-specification by linguistic meaning, so phrasal or lexical utterances such as *On the table*, *Telephone*, are standardly instantly understood as conveying complete propositions – a large portion of which has clearly been pragmatically derived. It can be argued that this is in line with the truth-evaluability requirement and the linguistic direction requirement, since linguistic decoding might well deliver up a representation such as (13):

(13) $_S[_{NP}[\text{ e }]\ _{VP}[\ _V[\text{ e }]\ _{PP}[\text{ on the table}]]]$

thereby directing the supply of further material by pragmatic processing. The completion of (1) could be directed in the same way, if the verb *continue* is subcategorised for a following NP.

For my purposes the more interesting cases are those which have the following three properties: linguistic meaning, reference assignment and disambiguation DO supply a complete (hence truth-evaluable) proposition, the grammar does NOT generate variables instructing further filling in, and yet the proposition is still too underspecified to be taken as the explicature of the utterance:

(14)   a.   The park is some distance from where I live
        b.   It will take us some time to get there

Consider (14a); the logical form of this is existentially quantified over distances and requires just reference fixing (of *I* and *the park*) to be fully propositional, that is, capable of bearing a truth value. It's doubtless generally true that there is a distance (of some length or other) between the speaker's home and the park referred to, but it's very unlikely that that's what a speaker wants to convey on a given occasion of utterance or that that's what a hearer would take her to be explicating. This is what linguistic decoding and reference assignment alone retrieve but it is seldom going to be a claim worth making; it wouldn't tell a hearer anything he didn't already know. If this was all the speaker was saying, she wouldn't be observing pragmatic principles which enjoin relevance and informativeness. The particular proposition expressed by (14a) will depend on the particular context, which must be such that it is worth remarking on the distance. One possibility is that the speaker thinks the hearer is underestimating it, in which case the explicature would be something like 'The park is further away from where I live than you think' or 'The park isn't a walkable distance from my house'.

Philosophers and pragmatists who subscribe to the principles above want to stop at the weakest propositional form with determinate truth conditions, so in the case of (14a) this would simply be the truth that there is a distance between the park and my house, and any other conveyed meaning is an implicature. But what function then does the explicature have in the mental life of the hearer? It is entailed by the implicature: if the park is further away from my house than the hearer had been assuming, it follows that it is some distance or other from my house. When this entailment relation holds between putative implicature and explicature the probability of functional independence of the two propositional forms is very low. What the hearer is going to remember from this utterance is some estimate of the distance involved, not the fact that there is a distance, and any inferences he draws on the basis of the utterance will involve the proposition concerning this amount of distance, rather than the basic proposition concerning the existence of a distance, a truism which has long been an assumption he has subscribed to. So, again in conformity with the functional independence criterion, this more fully specified proposition must be understood as explicated. The same argument applies to (14b). It's difficult to see any justification for a principle along the lines of 'use the maxims just in order to get a minimally truth-bearing vehicle'. This is to ignore the nature of communication and of cognition in general in the interests of a formal principle which has absolutely no bearing on human psychology.

As Diane Blakemore has impressed upon me, the building in of extra information of one sort or another is quite pervasive; consider the following examples:

(15) a.   He ran to the edge of the cliff and jumped
      b.   I went to the exhibition and ran into John
      c.   She took the gun, walked into the garden and killed her mother
      d.   I had a holiday in Austria and did some cross-country skiing

The interpretation of (15a) in most contexts of utterance will include the understanding that he jumped over the cliff although there's no linguistic expression there telling us this or requiring us to fill in a prepositional phrase. The verb *jump* is not subcategorised for an obligatory following PP. Similarly, in (15b) we would most likely assume that the place where I ran into John was the exhibition, in (15c) that the killing of the mother was with the gun and took place in the garden, and in (15d) that the skiing referred to took place in Austria, although, again, the linguistic content of the utterances does not supply this information or direct its retrieval. The same point can be made regarding the PP *with a key* which is supplied in the interpretation of (4). In each case this is simply the most natural interpretation to give and a speaker who didn't intend this would simply not be observing the maxim of relation. Since the form with the additional prepositional phrase entails the form without in each case, the criterion of functional independence would again choose the enriched form as the explicature of the utterance rather than as an implicature.

It does not seem, then, that the pragmatically derived enrichments of the linguistically given meaning are confined to following instructions delivered by the grammar, such as finding pronominal or temporal referents. Given this, the absence of a linguistic device directing retrieval of a causal relation in (5a) need not deter an enrichment along these lines in determining the explicature of the utterance. Although it is truth-evaluable without our supposing any particular connection between the events, the most natural interpretation, in the vast majority of contexts, is one in which these events are part of a scenario in which they are both temporally and causally connected. We might represent this causal connection as in 16 (which would also of course have to be temporally specified as in (11) or (12) above):

(16)   [[Mr Jones]$_1$ has been insulted]$_p$ and because of p [he's]$_1$ going to resign

As with (4) there are two possible pragmatic analyses. The cancellability and calculability criteria apply to all pragmatically derived material, whether at the level of explicature or implicature, so cannot help us. The tacitly assumed criteria for determining explicatures (or what is said) do not help either: both the minimal truth-evaluability criterion and the linguistic direction criterion have been shown insufficient to account for a range of cases; fulfilling them places only a lower bound on the process of enrichment. Again the functional independence criterion makes a decision: it dictates that the causally enriched (16) be understood as the explicature, since if it is taken as an implicature of the utterance the explicature is rendered redundant as it is entailed by the implicature. The same line of reasoning applies to the relation between the conjuncts in (1) when it is understood that Susan cannot continue university studies *because* she didn't pass enough course units.[6]

As Kempson (introduction, this volume) points out, the indexicality of natural language has proved far more extensive than truth-theoretic semanticists originally allowed. The term indexical is usually understood as referring to linguistic expressions whose value is dependent on the context in which they are uttered. As the last few examples show, the recovery of the proposition expressed by the utterance of a linguistic form has an even stronger degree of context-dependence than indexicality; some content supplied by the context receives no direction at all from linguistic expressions.

Sperber & Wilson (1986: 182) say that 'an assumption communicated by an utterance U is *explicit* (that is, is an explicature) if and only if it is a development of a logical form encoded by U'. The logical form of the linguistic expression uttered is the semantic representation (or sense) assigned to it by the grammar and recovered in utterance interpretation by an automatic

process of decoding. As we have seen, in a range of examples this logical form
is frequently not fully propositional, and a hearer then has the task of completing it to recover the fully propositional form that the speaker intended to
convey. While any communicated assumption is either an explicature or an
implicature, it is clear that an explicature may be more or less explicit since it
is a combination of linguistically encoded and contextually inferred features.
There is always a linguistic contribution, but this contribution varies from
near total determination of the explicature to a very small role, as shown by
the following examples:

(17) a.   The sun will rise at 5.25 am on May 15 1990
      b.   Susan's performance isn't good enough
      c.   She took it
      d.   At home
      e.   Later

Understanding these requires various amounts of disambiguation, reference
assignment, enrichment (e.g. not good enough for what, in (b)) and completion, in accordance with the pragmatic principles. The explicature in (17a) is
highly explicit while that in (c) is much less so and (e) even less.[7]

We might worry a little about what constitutes a development of a
logical form. A list of allowed developments could be made: reference assignment, disambiguation, specification of vague terms, supplying empty grammatical categories with conceptual content, building in certain relations
between events and states. Obviously, though, it would be better if we could
find something more explanatory to say than this. The temporal and causal
connections standardly derived in interpreting conjunctions such as (4) and
(5), which were formerly treated as generalised conversational implicatures,
now fall under the definition of explicature. What is to stop all elements of
communicated meaning being interpreted as parts of the explicature? Whole
further assumptions might be tacked on: for instance, it might be claimed
that the explicature of (3) is 'I don't read autobiographies and Susan's book
is an autobiography' (referring expressions more fully specified of course).
This surely is a development of the logical form of the utterance. In other
words, while truth-evaluability sets a lower bound on the process of development there doesn't seem to be an upper bound. We might try setting up
constraints, such as prohibition on any development which involves a logical
form independent of the original one and so has a range of entailments of its
own distinct from those of the original logic form of the utterance. Alternatively, we might exclude any development which is entirely detachable by
a logical rule such as *and*-elimination. It is unlikely that these will be fool-
proof: although 'I don't read autobiographies' and 'Susan's book is an autobiography' do have largely distinct entailments they may have some in
common, 'Autobiographies exist' for instance, and in general such a constraint is likely to be too strong. While a development involving adding the
proposition 'Susan's book is an autobiography' is detachable by *and*-

elimination, it may be argued that the proposed explicature need not be understood as a conjunction: 'I don't read autobiographies of which Susan's book is an instance'. However, playing around any further with these possibilities is unnecessary, since the principle of relevance which drives the interpretation process can be shown to impose the supposed missing upper bound. I turn to that now.

5   The principle of relevance

One of Grice's maxims is the instruction to speakers to 'Be relevant'. He recognised that much work needed to be done to develop this principle; Sperber & Wilson (1986) have done this work. Only the merest indication of their theory can be given here (see note 3 of this chapter).

Utterances are one of a great range of stimuli that impinge on humans; they have the special property of being ostensive, that is, they call attention to themselves in a particular way. Ostensive stimuli make evident to a receiver the intention of the communicator to make it evident that she intends to inform the receiver of something. So an addressee is justified in expecting some significance from ostensive stimuli that he cannot expect from non-ostensive stimuli which he may attend to. He cannot expect an ostensive stimulus to achieve a certain level of *relevance*.

A phenomenon is said to be relevant to an individual if it has certain cognitive effects for that individual. There are three kinds of such cognitive effects: (1) interaction with assumptions in the individual's mental context to yield new implications (Sperber & Wilson call this *contextual implications*), (2) contradiction of an existing assumption which leads to its being abandoned, and (3) providing additional evidence for an existing assumption and so strengthening the individual's confidence in it. Clearly, then, relevance is a matter of degree: the more cognitive effects a phenomenon has the more relevant it is. This is offset, however, by a factor of processing costs: one doesn't go on endlessly processing a new piece of information, checking through all one's existing assumptions to see if it interacts with them, but abandons the endeavour when the returns threaten not to offset the effort. So there are two parts to defining relevance: the more cognitive effects a phenomenon has the more relevant it is, and the less the effort required to process a phenomenon the more relevant it is.

Utterances, and ostensive stimuli in general, come with a guarantee of *optimal relevance*: a guarantee that the cognitive effects the speaker intends the stimulus to have are sufficiently great to make it worth the hearer's while to process it, and that the stimulus is the least costly in terms of processing effort that the speaker could have chosen to have these effects. Finally, then, the *principle of relevance* states: every act of ostensive communication communicates a guarantee of its own optimal relevance. In comprehending an utterance a hearer must find an interpretation which is *consistent with the principle of relevance*, where this is defined as an interpretation which 'a rational communicator might have expected to be optimally relevant to the addressee' (Sperber & Wilson 1986: 166). The first interpretation which the hearer finds to be consistent with the principle of relevance is taken to be the correct one, the one intended by the speaker. Obviously the first interpretation arrived at is the least costly one in terms of processing effort so, provided it has an adequate range of cognitive (or contextual) effects and it could have been intended by the speaker,[8] it is the only interpretation consistent with the principle of relevance. There is always at most one interpretation consistent with the principle of relevance. Sperber & Wilson (1986) show that this single principle, resting on a general theory of relevance, is sufficient to account for all pragmatic aspects of utterance interpretation and that it subsumes Grice's maxims.[9]

Let us consider how this principle might constrain the process of developing logical forms into explicatures so that they are not over enriched, encroaching on the territory of implicature. Firstly, we need some idea of what's involved in incurring processing costs. Linguistic decoding takes variable amounts of processing effort dependent on length and structural complexity of the expressions used. Interpreting an utterance requires the setting up of a context of assumptions within which to assess the cognitive impact of the utterance (some subset of the set of all our pre-existing assumptions and perhaps others constructed on the spot). The processing effort required for this varies from individual to individual and from utterance to utterance, the less accessible the assumptions needed, the more the effort involved in assembling them. The interaction of the context and the explicature involves a variable number of applications of a variable number of inference rules, the more of each the greater the processing costs.

We made the reasonable assumption above that the speaker in uttering (3) was implicating the assumption that Susan's book is an autobiography and the conclusion that she hasn't read it; surely if anything qualifies as implicature these do. But the definition of explicature that we have seems to allow the attachment of these to the logical form of the utterance as part of the development process. It might seem that we need to define the notion *development of a logical form* more closely. However, this is unnecessary. The rule that derives the implicated conclusion is a synthetic one, that is, a rule which takes two separate assumptions as its input, a universal of the form 'All X are Y' (in this case, a property is predicated of all autobiographies) and a singular of the form 'n is X', where n picks out an individual (in this case, a particular autobiography). If the explicature had been developed into a conjunction of the enriched logical form and the retrieved assumption that Susan's book is an autobiography, the conjuncts would simply have to be detached by a rule of *and*-elimination for the inference to go through. Nothing would have been gained by this development of the logical form of the utterance and a certain amount of effort would have been expended to no end, that is, the attachment of the assumption immediately followed by its detachment. Since the utterance comes with a guarantee of optimal relevance, no hearer will waste effort in this fashion when the same effects are achievable more economically. Furthermore, a hearer might well go on to draw some conclusions of his own for which the speaker can't be held responsible: for instance, he might be privately of the opinion that people who write autobiographies are egotists and thus conclude that Susan is an egotist. Once again, arriving at this conclusion depends on the independence of the assumption that Susan's book is an autobiography.[10] A wider range of cases is considered in Carston (forthcoming) to demonstrate that the principle of relevance quite generally ensures that redundant overextensions of the explicature do not occur.

Let us consider now the two pragmatic analyses of the temporal connotations of (4a): the one treating (4b) as the explicature of the utterance, the other taking it as an implicated assumption. On an implicature analysis we have a situation in which, schematising, the explicature is 'P & Q' and the implicature is 'P & then Q', that is, the implicature entails the explicature, so that any role that the explicature might have in memory or in reasoning processes could almost certainly be performed by the implicature, which is richer in content. So the principle of functional independence favours taking 'P & then Q' as the explicature of the utterance. The same goes for the causal connotations of (5a): the explicature is either 'P & Q' or 'P & then as a result Q', with the latter favoured by functional independence.

What does the criterion of consistency with the principle of relevance have to say about these cases? It is clearly more economical to derive the single assumption 'P & then Q' rather than both 'P & Q' and 'P & then Q', and whatever contextual effects 'P & Q' gives rise to so will 'P & then Q', as well as having the potential for more. Let us suppose that on a given occasion of utterance the most accessible context for interpreting (4a) is one which contains an assumption of the form 'If Q then R', say 'If he_2 opened the door he_2 must have seen the dead man' then the conclusion R, 'He_2 must have seen the dead man', is derived as a result of *and*-elimination performed on either 'P & Q' or 'P & then Q' with the appropriate detached assumption and the contextual assumption functioning as premises in an application of modus ponens. Let us suppose further that in deriving an adequate range of effects the proposition concerning the sequence of events is crucial, interacting with a contextual assumption of the form 'If P & then Q then S' to give the implication S. In general, whatever constitutes an adequate range of contextual effects, they can be derived entirely from the single assumption 'P & then Q', which is more economical to derive and manipulate than the two assumptions. In fact if 'P & then Q' were understood as an implicated assumption the derivation of S would follow from contextual assumptions alone. Then it would not qualify as a contextual implication since a contextual implication is defined as following from the propositional content of the utterance and the propositional content of the context together, but from neither alone (Sperber & Wilson 1986: 107–8). So it would not count as a contextual effect involved in establishing the relevance of the utterance, which, however, it clearly is. So not only does the criterion of consistency with the principle of relevance predict that the explicature of the utterance is 'P & then Q' the relevance-theoretic framework actually precludes an implicature analysis.

The argument for the inclusion of the causal connotations at the level of explicature will run in exactly the same way as will any case in which a putative generalised conversational implicature renders the putative explicature of the utterance functionally inert. Clearly then the guarantee of optimal relevance subsumes the predictions of the earlier functional independence guideline. In all aspects of utterance interpretation considerations of optimal relevance play a vital constraining and enriching role.

6 A problem solved

McCawley (1981: 6–10) points out that a question such as:

(18) Did John get up and fall down?

might be answered either *Yes* or *No* if the hearer knows that John in fact first fell down and then got back up. His choice would depend on whether the speaker is taken to have asked a symmetric-*and* question (Did John perform these two activities?) or a consecutive-*and* question (Did John perform these two activities in that order?), a choice dependent on context. McCawley, by the way, saw this as evidence for a lexical ambiguity at work, since a standard test for ambiguity at that time was to see if a sentence could be said to be simultaneously true and false with regard to exactly the same condition in the world. We are assuming that the semantic ambiguity of *and* is no longer a viable position, and will argue in the final section that this ambiguity test does not work: truth-conditional ambiguity cannot be used to establish the semantic ambiguity of a word, resting as it does on a conflation of natural language sentences with propositional forms. Horn (1984) recognises the pragmatic processing involved in deriving the temporal connotations but, being of the pragmatic=implicature persuasion, says that a negative answer to the question must be construed as taking into account the conversational implicature associated with *and*. But this is an odd sort of thing for the answerer of a question to do. In effect, what Horn is saying is that the hearer answers an implicated question rather than what he takes to be asked at the explicit level. The relevance-theoretic treatment of such a case would of course take the asymmetric conjunction to be the explicature and the answer *No* to be addressed to the question explicitly asked.

Grice (1967) noted a similar problem with the implicature account.[11] On that account, a denial of a conjoined utterance would sometimes apply only to what has been implicated and not to what has been explicated.

Taking an adaptation of his example (2), consider the following exchange, where (19a), in context implicates (20):

(19) a. A: Jones has made a lot of visits to New York lately
      b. B: No he hasn't

(20) Jones probably has a girlfriend in New York

The question is whether (19b) could be taken to bear, not on the explicit content of (19a), but only on its implicature (20), leaving the truth of (19a) intact. Surely the answer is no. Yet the implicature analysis of conjunctions predicts that denials can sometimes bear only on what is implicated. So consider (21b) and (21c) as replies to (21a), for example:

(21) a. A: She gave him the key and he opened the door
      b. B: No. He opened the door before she gave him the key
      c. B: No. He opened the door and then she gave him the key

On the implicature analysis the denials in (21b) and (21c) would bear not on what has been explicated but on the alleged implicature. Both (21b) and (21c) concede that the two actions occurred, and deny only the alleged implicature that her action preceded his. Again this doesn't seem right. Only the explicature analysis of the temporal connotations, predicted by relevance theory, satisfies the intuition that these cases of denials and answers to questions do not refer to implicatures alone, totally ignoring explicit content, and it does so without having to attribute an unwarranted ambiguity to the lexical item *and*.

However, although the point holds for these particular examples it may well be that when we take a detailed look at denials there are instances where it is the implicature of an utterance that has the main relevance and that a denial response generally refers to the most highly relevant propositional form conveyed by the utterance.[12] The strongest evidence against an implicature analysis, usually presented by those who favour a lexical ambiguity, takes a slightly different form. It seems that the alleged implicatures of conjoined utterances fall within the scope of such logical operators as negation, disjunction, comparison and conditionals. Even advocates of the implicature approach, including Grice, have seen such cases as very worrying:

(22) a. If the old king died of a heart attack and a republic was declared Sam will be happy, but if a republic was declared and the old king died of a heart attack Sam will be unhappy

                                            (adapted from Cohen 1971)

      b. He didn't steal some money and go to the bank; he went to the bank and stole some money

                                            (adapted from Gazdar 1980)

      c. It's better to meet the love of your life and get married than to get married and meet the love of your life

                                            (D. Wilson)

   d.   Either she became an alcoholic and her husband left her or he
        left her and she became an alcoholic; I'm not sure which

   As Cohen (1971) has pointed out, if *and* is simply truth-functional and
the temporal and causal connotations are captured by implicatures, then
(22a) and (22b) should be contradictory at the level of explicit content
(instantiating 'If P then Q but if P then not Q', and 'Not P; P' respectively).[13]
Similarly, (22c) should be a nonsensical (equivalent to 'It's better to P than
P') and (22d) redundant (equivalent to 'either P or P'). However, these
examples are not understood as contradictory or redundant. Those who wish
to maintain an implicature analysis have to say that the alleged temporal and
causal implicatures contribute to the truth conditions of the utterance in
which they occur, that is, to the explicit content (what is said) since they
follow Grice in the view that the explicature is another term for the truth-
conditional content of the utterance. This conclusion sits uneasily in his
general framework, where the sole determinants of explicit content are supposed to be the sense of the sentence uttered, disambiguation and reference
assignment. It looks as if the implicaturist is driving himself into a corner in
which the only position left to him is that the implicatures of conjoined
subordinate clauses contribute to the meaning of *sentences* – not just
utterances – in which they occur. This looks like a *reductio ad absurdum* of the
implicature analysis.

   Pragmatists generally see only two ways in which to try to cope with
these facts: either to reject the implicature analysis and to find a semantic
solution, the ambiguity one or Cohen's (1971) boosted semantic account (see
note 13 of this chapter); or to assume that, since the implicature analysis
MUST be right, some solution to the problems it raises has to be sought.
However, as this chapter shows, there is a third option: a pragmatic account
in which the temporal and causal connotations of conjoined utterances, along
with many other aspects of nonlinguistically determined meaning, are
recovered at the level of explicit content. Given this position the problems we
have been contemplating disappear: if these connotations are determined at
the level of explicature, then it is not surprising to find them falling within the
scope of denials, negation, conditionals, disjunctions, etc., and contributing
to the truth conditions of complex utterances in which they occur. Happily,
as we've seen, this explicature position is independently supported and
predicted by the pragmatic principles of relevance theory.

7   Generalised quantity implicatures?

I have concentrated in this paper on a very small range of examples but the
point is intended to be quite general. Pragmatic processing makes a far
greater contribution to determining explicit content than has generally been
assumed. One consequence for pragmatics is that it should not automatically
be assumed that every pragmatically determined aspect of utterance mean-

ing is an implicature. Many examples of generalised conversational implicature should be reconsidered in the light of relevance theory; there is not space here to deal adequately with examples (6)–(9), though a brief discussion will indicate the direction a full analysis would take.[14] The standard approach is represented by Horn (1972) who has a notion of scales of predicates arranged in order by degree of informativeness or semantic strength:

    (23) a. ⟨ . . . few, some, many, most, all⟩

          b. ⟨ . . ., three, four, five . . .⟩

          c. ⟨or, and⟩

A simple sentence containing an item on the scale entails another simple sentence which differs from the first only in containing an item lower on the scale. The reverse is not the case. So (24a) entails (24b) and (24b) does not entail (24a). However, when used in conversation such sentences frequently strongly suggest the negation of sentences in which a word is replaced by an item higher on the scale, so (24a) strongly suggests (24c), though this is cancellable as in (24d):

    (24) a. Mrs Smith has three children

          b. Mrs Smith has two children

          c. Mrs Smith does not have four children

          d. Mrs Smith has three children; indeed she has four altogether

A semantic ambiguity theorist would have to treat all number terms in all languages as having two senses: 'at least x' and 'exactly x' so that in (24d) the 'at least' sense is being used, while in (24a) it is the 'exactly' sense, thus entailing (24c). I reject this for the familiar reasons. On the pragmatic approach of Horn and others, number terms have one sense only, 'at least x', and in many contexts utterances containing them must be understood as implicating 'at most x' in order to preserve the assumption that Grice's Quantity maxim (Be as informative as required) is being observed: the two propositions together give the meaning 'exactly x'. Again this approach is based on the assumption that anything pragmatically derived (apart from reference assignment and disambiguation) is an implicature, an assumption that simply cannot be maintained as I have argued above. We have here another case where an alleged implicature entails the explicature of the utterance: 'Mrs Smith has exactly three children' entails 'Mrs Smith has at least three children', which should immediately alert us to the possibility that the supposedly implicated material is actually part of the explicature. This is the line I would wish to pursue, taking all the numerals as having a single sense, neither an 'at least', an 'at most' nor an 'exactly' sense, these being determined pragmatically at the level of explicit content. This line is again supported by examples of numerical sentences falling within the scope of logical operators:

    (25) a. If there are three books by Chomsky in the shop I'll buy them all

          b. Mrs Smith doesn't have three children; she has four

          c. Mrs Smith does have three children; in fact she has four

Understood as 'exactly three books by Chomsky' the utterance in (25a) may be true while understood as 'at least three' it may be false, in the same set of circumstances. This is no problem for the explicature analysis, indeed it is predicted, while it creates an apparently unresolvable problem for the implicature approach as shown in the previous section. Similarly, the implicature approach leads to the paradox that both (25b) and (25c) are consistent statements, although at the explicit level in both cases *three* has to be understood as 'at least three'.[15] Again there is no paradox in the explicature approach, since the sense of *three* is simply augmented differently at that level in the two cases.

The same line of reasoning leads to a reanalysis of the alleged implicatures in (7)–(9) as aspects of explicit content.

8   Two kinds of semantics

Grice introduced the maxims governing conversation and giving rise to implicatures in order to channel off as much of utterance meaning as possible into pragmatics, leaving as spare a semantics as possible. The semantics at issue was the sense of words in natural language such as *and, or, if,* quantifiers, etc. which seemed to diverge from that of their counterparts in formal logic. A second interest of his was to distinguish the truth conditional content of an utterance from the non-truth-conditional, that is, to determine that on the basis of which the speaker can be judged to have spoken truly or falsely. So, for example, two sentences of the forms: '*P* and *Q*' and '*P* but *Q*', are taken to have identical truth conditions although there is clearly some crucial difference in linguistic sense between the two (see note 7 of this chapter). Not all grammatically given information, then, is part of the logical form of the utterance. For Grice the first concern is simply a part of the second, so that if it can be shown that some aspect of meaning is pragmatically derived, such as the temporal and causal connotations of *and*, it is not to be attributed to the semantics of the term but is an implicature and makes no contribution to the truth conditions of the sentence/utterance.

It should be clear by now that this equation of linguistic sense with truth-conditional semantics simply won't work, that while linguistic sense makes a crucial contribution to truth conditions it almost never supplies a truth evaluable propositional form. As long as linguistic sense and truth-conditional semantics are not distinguished, Grice's two concerns are at odds with each other, pulling in opposite directions: disambiguation, reference assignment, recovery of ellipsed material are all pragmatically driven processes, so the content derived by them should not contribute to the truth-conditional content of the utterance, but if this is so then most utterances do not have any truth conditions, a conclusion which no one would endorse.

Pragmatists in the Gricean tradition have generally followed his example, more or less equating linguistic sense and truth-conditional content (Gazdar 1979, 1980; Levinson 1983; Posner 1980) and, assuming the formula 'pragmatics=meaning – truth conditions'. But faced with examples such as (22a) to (22d), where implicatures seem to contribute to truth conditions, Gazdar (1980: 11) says: 'There is increasing evidence that the semantic component of the theory [of meaning] must sometimes have access to the pragmatic properties of constituent clauses when assigning the truth conditions of compound sentences. This evidence indicates that the semantic component is not autonomous with respect to the pragmatic component.' This is certainly so where by semantics we mean truth-conditional semantics and provided 'pragmatic properties' are not equated with implicatures. Nor is it confined to examples like (22); the truth conditions of the vast majority of utterances depend on input from pragmatic processes, as practically every example above demonstrates.

However, talk of *the* semantic component is misleading, since as we've seen the semantics of a lexical item such as *and* may be unitary and unvarying while the connotations it acquires in utterances may be several and variable, those connotations contributing to the truth-conditional content of utterances. It seems then that we must distinguish two kinds of semantics, linguistic and truth conditional, the former naturally figuring only in a theory of utterance meaning, the latter taking as its domain propositional forms, whether of utterances or unspoken thoughts. Linguistic semantics is autonomous with respect to pragmatics; it provides the input to pragmatic processes and the two together make propositional forms which are the input to a truth-conditional semantics. Once this distinction is made, the compulsion to treat all pragmatically derived meaning as implicature subsides; there is no reason why pragmatics cannot contribute to the explicature, the truth-conditional content of the utterance. Whether some particular pragmatically derived meaning is an implicature or not will fall out from the process of finding the interpretation consistent with the principle of relevance.

What does it mean to give a semantic interpretation of an expression in a language? For the truth theorist the answer is obvious: if the expression is a sentence, it is to give its truth conditions; if subsentential, it is to specify the contribution it makes to the truth conditions of sentences. In discussing what constitutes the proper subject matter of semantics, Cresswell (forthcoming) asks the question what sort of ability it is that demonstrates that a speaker knows the meanings of the expressions in a given language, and answers 'The most promising candidate for such an ability seems to be the ability to distinguish situations in which a sentence is true from those in which it is false.'

Sperber & Wilson (1986: 173) take a wider view: 'A formula is semantically interpreted by being put into systematic correspondence with other objects: for example, with the formulas of another language, with states of the user of the language, or with possible states of the world.' Since we are distinguishing natural language sentences and the propositional forms they may be used to express as two different kinds of entity, we might consider the semantics of each individually. Speakers and hearers map incoming linguistic stimuli onto conceptual representations (logical forms), plausibly viewed themselves as formulas in a (mental) language. The language ability – knowing English – according to this view, is then precisely what Lewis and others have derided (see Kempson's introduction): it is the ability to map linguistic forms onto logical forms matching to a high degree the mappings made by a certain group of others (the speakers of English). In theory this ability could exist without the further capacities involved in matching these with conditions in the world. A computer might be programmed so as to perform perfectly correct translations from English into a logical language without, as Lewis and Searle have said, knowing the first thing about the meaning (=truth conditions) of the English sentence. Distinguishing two kinds of semantics in this way – a translational kind and the truth conditional – shows further that the semantic representation of one language may be a syntactic representation in another, though the chain must end somewhere with formulas related to situations and states of the world or possible worlds.[16]

It may be a biological fact about humans that the two abilities develop in tandem, or that the linguistic ability depends on the other perceptual and pragmatic capacities for its development, but that does not make them the same ability. Cresswell is probably right that the best way to demonstrate that one has knowledge of a language is to show that one can correctly pair up utterances in that language with situations in the world. This does not of course expose the particular abilities involved in this demonstration. The main argument of this paper has been to show that a hearer must do a lot of pragmatic work (which involves quite distinct abilities from his linguistic ones),[17] on the basis of the logical form derived from the linguistic form of the utterance, before he has a representation which is truth-evaluable, and that there is even more to be done before he has THE truth-evaluable propositional form he can reasonably take the speaker to have intended to convey.

Cresswell (1982: 69) gives the following as his 'most certain principle' in the field of semantics: if we have two sentences, A and B, and A is true and B is false in exactly the same situation in the world, then A and B do not mean the same. However, this is simply not true of natural language sentences:

(26) a. Mary hit Bill and Bill fell
     b. Bill fell and Mary hit him

The linguistic semantics of these is identical, given an unambiguous truth-functional semantics for *and* and the standard principle of semantic compositionality, yet a speaker demonstrating her knowledge of language in the way Cresswell prescribes will almost certainly judge them as not both true in the one situation (say, a situation in which Mary hit Bill and as a result he fell over). If there is any doubt about this, embedding them so that they fall within the scope of logical operators as in (22), should dispel it. So it seems that Cresswell's most certain principle is not one concerning linguistic entities but rather the propositional forms which linguistic forms may be used to express. Similarly, the truth-conditional ambiguity test mentioned in section 6, takes as its domain propositional forms rather than natural language sentences, and cannot lead to conclusions about lexical ambiguities.

The picture we end with has a clear semantics/pragmatics distinction, where semantics is understood as translations of linguistic forms into logical forms, partially articulated conceptual representations which are the output of the grammar. Natural language semantics, then, is autonomous and provides the input to pragmatics, which plays a major role in determining the explicature of an utterance as well as determining implicatures, both of which are distinct and complete propositional forms, and as such are the domain for truth-conditional semantics.[18]

NOTES

1 For the sake of a simple clear distinction between explicature and implicature I consider only literal assertions in this paper. Thus questions and imperatives are ignored, as are such figurative uses as metaphor and irony. Sperber & Wilson (1986) use the term *propositional form of the utterance* for what I am calling the explicature. Explicatures are assumptions which have two properties: they are explicitly conveyed and the speaker wants to make them manifest to the hearer (that is, available to him as assumptions he can represent to himself as true). An utterance generally has a set of explicatures: this includes the propositional form of the utterance in the case of literal assertions but does not in the case of tropes or non-assertive speech acts.

2 The term proposition is a notoriously slippery one. I sidestep the ontological issues it raises and use the term *propositional form* in the sense of Sperber & Wilson (1986: 72–3). A propositional form is a well-formed formula which (a) undergoes formal logical (truth preserving) operations determined by its structure, and (b) is semantically complete in that it is capable of being true or false.

3 For summaries of relevance theory see Wilson & Sperber (1986b), Sperber & Wilson (forthcoming) and Wilson & Sperber in this volume.

4 The problem of where this implicated assumption comes from is the central unanswered question raised by the calculability requirement; it is confronted in Wilson & Sperber 1986a and in Sperber & Wilson 1986 (193–202).

5 Another characteristic mentioned by Grice is that of the indeterminacy of implicatures, which is indeed a property which distinguishes them from explicatures. The implicit import of an utterance need not comprise solely fully determinate assumptions each of which was individually communicated by the speaker. For example, the hearer of (3) might have a readily accessible assumption that people who don't read autobiographies are not much interested in other people's lives, and conclude on that basis that B isn't much interested in other people's lives. This is not a conclusion that the speaker can be held to have communicated to the hearer; while the indirectness of her answer has encouraged the hearer to access further assumptions and draw further conclusions, the hearer has the primary responsibility for the particular assumptions made and conclusions drawn.

6 In most contexts, then, an utterance of (5a) has the same propositional content as utterances of sentences in which the causal connection is recovered by linguistic decoding: for example, *Mr Jones has been insulted and as a result (or: because of this) he is*

going to resign. More interesting is the case of *and so* discussed by Blakemore (1987 and this volume). She argues that the meaning of *so* cannot by analysed in terms of conceptual content but rather in terms of a processing instruction to the hearer and that the causal connection frequently derived from a use of *so* illustrates one way in which an explicature may be enriched so as to satisfy that instruction.

7 Certain linguistically given (hence explicit) aspects of the utterance are not part of the explicature of the utterance because their role is not to supply conceptual content but to guide the hearer's *processing* of the utterance. They may place constraints on the sort of context in which the explicature is to be processed or direct the inferential role of the explicature in the context. Examples of such linguistic expressions are *but, after all, anyway, so*. They have been studied in detail by Blakemore (1987).

8 Note that it's not enough that the interpretation is optimally relevant to the addressee: a hearer might hit on a readily accessible interpretation with a good range of contextual effects but have to dismiss it as what the speaker intended, perhaps because he knows that the speaker couldn't possibly have the beliefs that this interpretation depends on.

9 Wilson & Sperber (1981) deals specifically with this.

10 Furthermore, since B has chosen to answer A in this indirect way rather than simply saying *No*, which would have saved him the effort of accessing the assumption and deducing the conclusion, it follows by the principle of relevance that she is encouraging him to access further assumptions and draw further conclusions. She must have expected this indirect response to yield cognitive effects not derivable from the direct answer which would compensate for the extra processing costs. For instance she might know that A is in the throes of writing an autobiography and that he can thereby arrive at the implication that she will not read his book.

11 Grice actually raises the problem in connection with his analysis of *if*, but it carries over intact to the analysis of *and*.

12 The most likely counterexamples to a general statement that denials must refer to explicatures are ironical and metaphorical statements. See footnote 1. It remains to be seen whether the generalisation could be salvaged by tightening it up along the lines that a denial cannot refer to an implicature alone when the propositional form of the utterance is an explicature.

13 Given this sort of counterexample to the implicature approach Cohen (1971) advocates a semantic solution, though not the ambiguity one. He wants a single complex lexical entry for *and* incorporating temporal, causal and other features, with some (pragmatic) mechanism for cancelling features in particular contexts. Posner (1980) discusses problems with this meaning-maximalist position.

14 For a more detailed reanalysis of a range of examples standardly treated as generalised quantity implicatures see Carston (forthcoming).

15 Horn (1985) tackles this problem by analysing the negation here as metalinguistic. This looks like a promising approach and may well replace the explicature treatment in some cases; this is considered in Carston (forthcoming) where a broader notion of metarepresentation is advocated.

16 In addition to a linguistic semantics mapping linguistic forms onto concepts and a truth-conditional semantics relating propositional forms to the real world there is a third kind of semantics, a logical or conceptual role semantics, concerned with relations of entailment, contradiction, etc., amongst logical and propositional forms.

17 Fodor (1983) and Sperber & Wilson (1986) take the language processing system
    to be a specialised automatic decoding system. The pragmatic processing of
    utterances employs relatively unspecialised inferential processes and encyclopedic
    knowledge which are involved in processing all incoming information, whether
    linguistic or perceptual, and in general thought processes.
18 Even more than usual this paper has benefited from the ideas and advice of
    Deirdre Wilson to whom I am very grateful. Thanks also to Diane Blakemore,
    Max Cresswell, Pierre Jacob, Ruth Kempson, Ewan Klein, and François
    Recanati for comments on an earlier version.

REFERENCES

Blakemore, D. 1987. *Semantic constraints on relevance*. Oxford: Blackwell.
Carston, R. forthcoming. A reanalysis of some generalised quantity implicatures.
    Ms., University College London.
Cohen, L.J. 1971. The logical particles of natural language. In Y. Bar-Hillel (ed.)
    Pragmatics of natural language. Dordrecht: Reidel.
Cresswell, M.J. 1982. The autonomy of semantics. In S. Peters & E. Saarinen (eds.)
    Processes, beliefs, and questions. Dordrecht: Reidel.
Cresswell, M.J. forthcoming. Basic concepts in semantics. In A. von Stechow (ed.)
    Handbook of semantics.
Fodor, J.A. 1983. *Modularity of mind*. Cambridge, Mass.: MIT Press.
Gazdar, G. 1979. *Pragmatics: implicature, presupposition and logical form*. London:
    Academic Press.
Gazdar, G. 1980. Pragmatics and logical form. *Journal of Pragmatics* 4:1–13.
Grice, H.P. 1967. Logic and conversation. William James lectures. Harvard Univer-
    sity. Unpublished.
Grice, H.P. 1975. Logic and conversation. In P. Cole & J. Morgan (eds.) *Syntax and
    semantics, vol. 3: speech acts*. New York: Academic Press.
Grice, H.P. 1981. Presupposition and conversational implicature. In P. Cole (ed.)
    Radical pragmatics. New York: Academic Press.
Horn, L.R. 1972. On the semantic properties of logical operators. Ph. D thesis,
    University of California, Los Angeles.
Horn, L. 1984. Ambiguity, negation and the London school of parsimony. In C. Jones
    & P. Sells (eds.) *Proceedings from NELS XIV*.
Horn, L. 1985. Metalinguistic negation and pragmatic ambiguity. *Language* 61:
    121–74.
Katz, J.J. 1972. *Semantic theory*. New York: Harper and Row.
Levinson, S. 1983. *Pragmatics*. Cambridge: Cambridge University Press.
McCawley, J.D. 1981. *Everything that linguists have always wanted to know about logic but
    were afraid to ask*. Oxford: Blackwell.
Partee, B. 1973. Some structural analogies between tenses and pronouns in English.
    The Journal of Philosophy 70: 601–9.
Posner, R. 1980. Semantics and pragmatics of sentence connectives in natural
    language. In J. Searle, F. Kiefer & M. Bierwisch (eds.) *Speech act theory and
    pragmatics*. Dordrecht: Reidel.
Sperber, D. & Wilson, D. 1986. *Relevance: communication and cognition*. Oxford:
    Blackwell.
Sperber, D. & Wilson D. forthcoming. Precis of relevance theory. In *Behavioral and
    Brain Sciences*.

Walker, R. 1975. Conversational implicatures. In S. Blackburn (ed.) *Meaning, reference and necessity*. Cambridge: Cambridge University Press.

Wilson, D. & Sperber, D. 1981. On Grice's theory of conversation. In P. Werth (ed.) *Conversation and discourse*. London: Croom Helm.

Wilson, D. & Sperber, D. 1986a. Inference and implicature in utterance interpretation. In T. Myers, K. Brown & B. McGonigle (eds.) *Reasoning and discourse processes*. London: Academic Press.

Wilson, D. & Sperber, D. 1986b. Pragmatics and modularity. In *Parasession on pragmatics and grammatical theory*. Chicago: Chicago Linguistics Society.

8
'So' as a constraint on relevance[1]

DIANE BLAKEMORE

1 Introduction

Grice's theory of conversation (Grice 1975) is generally associated with an attempt to maintain an approach to semantics according to which the meanings of all linguistic expressions can be analysed in terms of their contribution to the truth conditions of the utterances that contain them. Indeed, the idea that there are aspects of utterance interpretation that are determined by general pragmatic principles has often led to the conflation of linguistic semantics and propositional (or truth-conditional) semantics so that on the one hand, it is assumed that linguistic meaning cannot determine non-truth-conditional aspects of utterance interpretation, while on the other, it is assumed that pragmatic principles cannot play a role in determining the propositional content of utterances.

In fact, neither of these assumptions can be maintained. The second was challenged by Wilson & Sperber (1981) when they showed that pragmatic principles must play a part in disambiguation, reference assignment, the resolution of vagueness, and the recovery of ellipsed or unexpressed material. More recently, this idea that there are many aspects of propositional content that are pragmatically determined has been taken up by Carston (1983, and this volume) who shows that there is evidence which suggests that the temporal and causal connotations of conjoined utterances should be analysed in this way.

Carston's proposals for the analysis of conjoined utterances play an important part in the account of the role of *so* developed in this chapter. However, the implications of this account are mainly for the first assumption – that is, the assumption that all linguistic meaning can be defined truth conditionally. It will be recalled that Grice himself questioned this view when he introduced the notion of conventional implicature. His (tantalisingly brief) comments concerned the use of *therefore* in (1):

> (1)   He is an Englishman; he is, therefore, brave

According to Grice's analysis, this use of *therefore* indicates that his being brave is a consequence of his being an Englishman, but that the utterance would not be false should the consequence in question fail to hold.

The problem with this account is that 'consequence' can refer either to a causal effect or to a logical conclusion. Did Grice mean that *therefore* indicates that his being brave was caused by his being an Englishman or that it indicates that the fact that he is an Englishman is a reason for believing that he is brave? In other words, does the use of *therefore* in (1) indicate a causal relation between states of affairs in the world or an inferential relation between propositions?

It seems to me that what Grice meant was that the proposition he is brave is a logical consequence of the proposition he is an Englishman, and that *therefore* signals an inferential relation between the two propositions in much the same way as *after all* and *moreover* are used to signal inferential relations in (2) and (3):[2]

    (2)   He is an Englishman; he is, after all, brave

    (3)   He is an Englishman; he is, moreover, brave

In (2), as in (1), there is a relation of logical consequence. However, in this case the proposition that he is an Englishman is suggested to be a consequence of the proposition that he is brave. In (3) the propositions are not suggested to be related as premise and conclusion, but rather as premises: the proposition he is brave is suggested to be an additional premise for the deduction of whatever conclusion is derived from the proposition he is an Englishman.

In this paper I wish to discuss the role of just one of these inferential connectives – *so*. That *so* can be used to express an inferential connection between two propositions is evident from the examples in (4):

    (4) a.   There was $5 in his wallet. So he hadn't spent all the money

         b.   She's your teacher. So you must respect her

Like *therefore*, *so* introduces a proposition which is deducible from the preceding one. However, it is not clear that these two expressions always play the same role in the interpretation of the utterances that contain them. In the first part of this paper I shall outline Sperber & Wilson's (1986) account of the role of inference in utterance interpretation generally, and, on the basis of this, account for the differences which can be shown to exist between utterances with *so* and utterances with *therefore*. I shall argue that the meaning of *so* (and, indeed, the meanings of all these inferential connectives) cannot be analysed in terms of its contribution to the proposition expressed by the utterance that contains it but must instead be analysed in terms of a constraint on the inferential computations that proposition may enter into – or, in other words, its relevance.[3]

However, it seems to me that *so* is not always used to express an inferential connection. For example, it seems that in (5a) and (b) the proposition introduced by *so* will be interpreted as a causal consequence of the state of affairs described by the first proposition:

    (5) a.   Tom ate the condemned meat. So he fell ill

         b.   Bill insulted Mary. So she left

In the second part of the paper I shall reconcile these two uses of *so* not by conflating the notions of cause and effect and logical consequence, but by showing that the use of *so* in (5), as in (4), indicates that the hearer is expected to establish an inferential connection between the two propositions presented. The point is that in order to establish this connection the hearer of the utterances in (5) must assume that the state of affairs represented by the proposition introduced by *so* is a causal consequence of the event represented by the first proposition.

According to this account, the meaning of *so* must be analysed in purely non-truth-conditional terms. Its sole function is to guide the interpretation process by imposing a constraint on the inferential (or pragmatic) computations a proposition may enter into. However, as we shall see, when *so* is used in a co-ordinate utterance the inferential connection it expresses may fall under the scope of logical operators. Such examples might seem to suggest that we must either abandon the original analysis altogether or attribute to *so* a further truth-conditional sense. On the other hand, considered from the point of view of Carston's analysis of conjoined utterances (see chapter 7 in this volume), they do not illustrate a truth-conditional meaning of *so*, but rather the way in which the propositional content of an utterance may have to be enriched so that it reaches a satisfactory level of relevance.

2 Constraints on relevance

Sperber & Wilson (1986) have argued that an account of utterance interpretation must be based on a general cognitive theory of information processing. The basic idea underlying their theory is that in processing information, people generally aim to bring about the greatest improvement to their overall representation of the world for the least cost in processing. That is, they try to balance costs and rewards. Obviously, not every addition of information counts as an improvement. A hearer's representation of the world will not necessarily be improved by the addition of information that it already contains. Nor will it be improved by the presentation of information that is unrelated to any of the information it already contains. The hearer's aim is to integrate new information with old, or in other words, to recover information that is relevant to him. Notice, too, that a hearer is not simply interested in gaining more information about the world: he is also interested in obtaining better evidence for his existing beliefs and assumptions. The point is, that in every case his search for relevance leads him to process new information in a context of existing assumptions.

In this theory computing the effect of a newly presented proposition crucially involves inference. That is, the role of contextual assumptions is to combine with the content of an utterance as premises in an argument. There is no space here to outline the nature of the inferential abilities that Sperber & Wilson believe to be involved in utterance interpretation. However, it is important to recognise that in this theory propositions are treated not just as logical objects but as psychological representations, and that inferences are psychological computations performed over those representations. Their basic claim is that assumptions about the world come with varying degrees of strength, and that logical computations assign strength to conclusions on the basis of the strength of the premises used in deriving them.

There are three ways in which an inference system plays a role in assessing the impact of a new item of information on an existing representation of the world. First, since an inference system can be used to test for inconsistencies in the propositions submitted to it, it can play a role in the hearer's decision to abandon an existing assumption in favour of the information that has been presented to him. Secondly, the fact that conclusions inherit their strength from the premises from which they are derived means that inference rules can be used to assess the extent to which an existing assumption is confirmed or justified by a new item of information. Finally, since the propositions which are taken as premises may be derived from the hearer's existing representation of the world, an inference system may play a role in the identification of what Sperber & Wilson call contextual implications. That is, it enables the hearer to add to his existing representation of the world by processing new information in a context of old information.

Given the role of deduction in the assessment of contextual effects, it should not be surprising that the use of a word which expresses a relation of logical consequence should be associated with proof or justification. When, as in the case of (1), the second of two propositions is marked as a conclusion, the speaker is understood to be indicating that its strength is based on the strength of the proposition in the preceding clause. When, as in the case of (2), the second of two propositions is marked as a premise, it is understood as evidence or proof for the proposition expressed in the previous clause.

While it may be clear why a word that expresses a relation of logical consequence should play such a role, it may not be clear from the point of view of a theory of utterance interpretation why there should be such words. Obviously, neither *therefore* nor *after all* contribute to the truth-conditional content of the utterances that contain them. Both (1) and (2) will be understood as expressing the propositions in (6):

    (6) a. He is an Englishman
          b. He is brave

On the other hand, it is evident that the use of these expressions affects the way that these propositions are understood to be connected. That is, whereas in (1) the proposition in (6a) is relevant as evidence for the proposition in (6b), in (2) it is the proposition in (6b) that is relevant as evidence for the one in (6a). Notice that in neither case can the connection between the two propositions be established unless a further assumption is supplied from the context. For example, in (1) the hearer must supply the assumption in (7):

    (7)   All Englishmen are brave

This suggests that the effect of using these words in an utterance is to constrain the hearer's choice of context for its interpretation.

Why should there be linguistically specified constraints on contexts? Recall that the cases of contextual modification that are of most concern to a theory of pragmatics are those in which the hearer combines the proposition presented with a subset of his contextual assumptions. Since the impact of an utterance may depend on the context, the hearer must have some principle by which he chooses the particular contextual assumptions he brings to bear. For logically speaking, any of his beliefs and assumptions may be brought to bear on the interpretation of an utterance, which means that from this point of view, his interpretation isn't constrained at all. Since successful communication does occur and hearers often interpret utterances in the way they are expected to, the hearer's choice of context must be one that can be exploited and manipulated by the speaker.

According to Sperber & Wilson, what the speaker manipulates is the hearer's search for relevance. Intuitively, it is clear that the greater the impact a proposition has on the hearer's representation of the world the greater its relevance. On the other hand, accessing contextual assumptions and using them to derive contextual effects involves a cost, and the cost of deriving contextual effects in a small, easily accessible context will be less than the cost of obtaining them from a larger, less accessible context. A hearer who is searching for relevance will process each new item of information in the context that yields a maximum contextual effect for the minimum cost in processing. Obviously, it is in the interests of a hearer who is searching for relevance that the speaker should produce an utterance whose interpretation calls for less processing effort than any other utterance that he could have made. But equally, given that the speaker wishes to communicate with the hearer, it is in his interests to make his utterance as easily understood as possible. This means that the hearer is entitled to interpret every utterance on the assumption that the speaker has tried to give him adequate contextual effects for the minimum necessary processing, or, in other words, that the speaker has aimed at optimal relevance. Sperber & Wilson call the principle which gives rise to this assumption the principle of relevance.

Now, in some cases the speaker will have only very general grounds for thinking that his utterance is consistent with this principle. That is, he will not have any specific expectations as to the contextual assumptions that the hearer will bring to bear. For example, if you ask me the time, I will assume that my answer will be relevant to you even though I may have no idea of the conclusions you will draw from it. However, a speaker who has a specific interpretation in mind may direct the hearer towards that interpretation by making a certain set of contextual assumptions immediately accessible thus ensuring their selection under the principle of relevance. For example, in the dialogue in (8) speaker B is exploiting the hearer's assumption that his reply conforms to the principle of relevance in order to convey the proposition in (9):

(8) A: Is Tom very rich?
     B: ALL lawyers are rich

(9)   Tom is rich

Notice that in order to maintain his assumption that B was being relevant the hearer must supply the contextual assumption in (10):

(10)   Tom is a lawyer

Clearly, this step requires processing effort that would not have been required had B produced the direct answer in the first place. How, then, could his utterance be said to be consistent with the principle of relevance?

The fact that B has forced the hearer to access this assumption and use it to derive (9) as a contextual implication may be explained if the processing effort these steps require is offset by the recovery of contextual implications that would not have been derivable from the direct answer. In other words, the extra information must be relevant in its own right.

This is an example of a nonlinguistic or pragmatic means of constraining the hearer's choice of context. In the case of the linguistic constraints illustrated in (1) and (2) the speaker cannot be said to have added to the information that the hearer is expected to process for relevance, since neither of these expressions contributes to the content of the utterances that contain them. Rather, their use minimises the hearer's processing costs by guaranteeing that the information conveyed by the utterance that contains them is relevant in a specific context. Thus for example, the use of *therefore* in Grice's example in (1) indicates that the hearer is expected to process the utterance in a context in which the first proposition can be construed as evidence for the second. In other words, these expressions provide an effective means for constraining the hearer's interpretation of utterances in discourse in accordance with the principle of relevance.

Now, we have seen that like *therefore*, *so* also expresses a relation of logical consequence. However, unlike *therefore*, *so* is not always associated with proof of justification.[4] Compare, for example, the acceptable use of *so* in (11) with the unacceptable use of therefore in (12):

(11)   There's $5 in my wallet. So I didn't spend all the money then

(12)   There's $5 in my wallet. ?? Therefore I didn't spend all the money then

The addition of sentence final *then* in these examples indicates that the second proposition must be construed as the specification of the significance or relevance of the first proposition rather than as a proposition whose truth is proven by the first proposition. In other words, *so*, but not *therefore* can be used to indicate that the relevance of the proposition it introduces lies in the fact that it is a contextual implication of the first proposition.

In (11) the speaker has used *so* to specify a contextual implication of a proposition that has been deliberately communicated in an utterance. However, it seems that *so* contrasts with *therefore* in that it can be used to introduce a proposition which does not have a linguistic antecedent. Imagine, for example, that I have arrived home laden with parcels. In this situation it would be appropriate for you to produce the utterance in (13) but not the one in (14):

(13)   So, you've spent all your money

(14)   ?Therefore, you've spent all your money

Clearly, *so* is not being used in (13) to indicate that the proposition it introduces is proven by what has just been said. No one has said anything. More generally, for a proposition to provide proof it must itself come with a guarantee of factuality, and only communicated propositions come with a guarantee of factuality. If the speaker of (13) is not trying to prove anything, then why has he indicated that the proposition expressed by his utterance is a logical consequence?

Let us assume that a speaker has come upon an item of information *P* from which he has derived a contextual implication *Q*. Let us assume further that he has grounds for thinking that although *P* is available to the hearer together with the contextual premises needed to derive *Q*, he has not actually combined these propositions to obtain *Q*. If in this situation the speaker wishes the hearer to recognise that he may derive *Q* as a contextual implication of *P*, then he must respect *Q* as a contextual implication of *P*. Since he has grounds for thinking that *P* is already highly accessible to the hearer, then he does not have to present *P* himself. Thus in the situation described in the previous paragraph you may produce the utterance in (13).

The problem with this account is that there may be a number of different propositions available to me in this situation. For example, in addition to the fact that I am laden with parcels I may be aware that my feet hurt or that you are smoking a pipe. Yet I will interpret your utterance in (13) only as a contextual implication of the proposition that I am laden with parcels. The explanation for this follows from the principle of relevance together with the meaning of *so*. The fact that you have prefaced your utterance with *so* entitles me to assume that the proposition it expresses is a contextual implication of a proposition that is already available to me. Although the proposition expressed by (13) may in principle be derived from the proposition that my feet hurt or that you are smoking a pipe, the costs incurred by these derivations will be greater than those incurred by the derivation of this proposition from the proposition that I'm laden with parcels. Since the principle of relevance entitles me to assume that you have tried to give me adequate contextual effects for the minimum cost in processing, I may conclude that you meant (13) as a specification of the relevance of this proposition rather than any other.

The final difference between *so* and *therefore* is provided by those (rather too familiar) situations in which a hearer is unable to see the significance of what someone has said. The typical response made in such a situation is, of course, 'So?' or 'So what?' – but never 'Therefore?'. Notice that the hearer's problem here is not that he cannot understand the content of the remark but rather that he cannot see what it implies – or at least, that he cannot see that it implies anything worthwhile. The response 'So?' is, then, a request for the speaker to specify the contextual implications of his remark or, alternatively, the contextual premises required in order to obtain them. Sometimes a hearer may think that he has grasped the significance of a remark but not be sure. In this situation he may ask for confirmation. Thus for example, if you tell me that you have $5 in your wallet and I respond with the utterance, 'So you DIDn't spend all your money', I am not proving to you that you didn't spend all your money – (I assume that you believe this) – but simply checking that this is what you were implying.

3 *So* in conjoined utterances

The suggestion of the previous section was that *so* constrains the relevance of the proposition it introduces by indicating that it must be interpreted as a contextual implication of some immediately accessible proposition – for example, the proposition most recently expressed – or, in other words, that it expresses an inferential relation between two propositions the significance of which can be explained in terms of the role that inference rules play in the identification of contextual implications. However, as we have already seen, there are examples which suggest that *so* is not always used to introduce a logical consequence. In the utterances in (5) (repeated here below) it appears to indicate that the event described by the proposition it introduces is a causal consequence of the event in the first proposition:

(5) a.   Tom ate the condemned meat. So he fell ill
     b.   Bill insulted Mary. So she left

This suggests that unless we are prepared to conflate the notions of causal effect and deductive consequence, then we must accept that *so* is ambiguous between a causal meaning and an inferential meaning – a position which is contrary to the Gricean spirit of the pragmatic framework accepted here.

Causal connections between events/states of affairs are often left implicit, as, for example, in (15a) and (b):

(15) a.   Tom ate the condemned meat and he fell ill
      b.   Bill insulted Mary. She left

As is well known, the fact that these causal connotations are carried by 'full-stop' utterances as well as by conjoined utterances shows that they cannot be due to the meaning of *and*, but must be pragmatically determined. In Gricean analyses this is generally taken to mean that they must be analysed as conversational implicatures arising from the assumption that the Manner maxim has been observed. The same argument has been applied to the interpretation of the temporal connotations of utterances such as those in (16):

(16) a.   The king raised his glass and drank
      b.   He ran over to the cliff and jumped

However, this implicature account has been found unsatisfactory on the grounds that, unlike genuine implicatures, these suggestions can fall within the scope of logical operators.[5] Carston (this volume) does not construe this as evidence for a semantic account of these connotations, but instead points out that since pragmatic principles have been shown (by Wilson & Sperber 1981) to play a role in the recovery of various aspects of propositional content – for example, reference assignment, disambiguation, the recovery of ellipsed or unexpressed material – there is every reason to suppose that they are involved in the recovery of other aspects of propositional content as well.

Recall that according to Sperber & Wilson, any act of communication comes with the communicator's guarantee that the hearer will be able to derive adequate contextual effects for the minimum cost in processing. Obviously, this guarantee may be based on a misapprehension (for example, about the hearer's processing resources). However, the point is that the principle of relevance entitles the hearer to go ahead and recover the proposition which yields adequate contextual effects in the smallest and most accessible context.

In the case of conjoined utterances it seems that the hearer receives a further – or more specific – guarantee. For a speaker who is aiming at optimal relevance cannot expect the hearer to undertake the processing entailed by his use of *and* unless he believes that the conjoined proposition his utterance expresses has relevance over and above the relevance of its conjuncts taken individually. What otherwise would have been the point of conjoining the two propositions in the first place? This means that although each conjunct may have its own individual relevance, it is only their conjunction which is consistent with the principle of relevance – or, in other words, whose relevance is guaranteed.[6]

We may interpret the basic idea underlying Carston's account of the temporal connotations of conjoined utterances as a claim that the hearer's search for relevance may lead him to recover a conjoined proposition whose second conjunct contains information based on the interpretation of the first. This account proceeds from the quite standard assumption that an utterance describing an event is interpreted as expressing a proposition which contains a value for a time index determined on the basis of the context. Her point is that given his background beliefs and the principle of relevance, a hearer can go beyond the linguistic meaning of utterances such as (16a) and (b) and recover values for the time index in each conjunct so that if the value in the first conjunct is t, then the value for the index in the second conjunct is $t+n$. In particular, the most relevant proposition that can be recovered from a conjoined utterance may go beyond the linguistic content of the utterance in that its second conjunct may include information that is determined by the interpretation of the first conjunct. As Carston demonstrates, this approach allows us to account for a wide range of suggestions recovered from conjoined utterances.[7] However, most important from the point of view of the present paper is that it allows us to account for the interpretation of utterances like those in (15).

The fact that an event occurred does not entail that it had a cause. Nevertheless, the most relevant proposition expressed by a conjoined utterance may be one whose second conjunct contains a causal predicate – an AS A RESULT OF predicate whose argument is based on the interpretation of the first conjunct. For example, the hearer of (15a) will recover the proposition represented in (17):

(17) [Tom$_i$ ate the condemned meat]$_j$ and because of that$_j$ he$_i$ fell ill

Now, it has been suggested that in (5a) and (b) *so* indicates that the hearer is expected to interpret the second proposition as a representation of a causal consequence of the event described by the first proposition. Does this mean that the use of *so* in the conjoined utterance in (18) indicates explicitly that the hearer is expected to recover a conjoined proposition of the type in (17)?

(18) Tom ate the condemned meat and so he fell ill

If *so* does perform this rule, then it should be possible to use it to make the causal connotations of any conjoined utterance explicit. For example, it should be possible to use *so* in order to indicate that the hearer of (19) is expected to recover the conjoined proposition in (20):

(19) Tom ate the condemned meat and he fell ill thirteen and a half hours later

(20) [Tom ate the condemned meat] and because of that he fell ill thirteen and a half hours later

However, while this causal interpretation of (19) is plausible, in normal circumstances the utterance of (21) is odd:[8]

(21) Tom ate the condemned meat and so he fell ill thirteen and a half hours later

(21) would, of course, be acceptable to a hearer who believed that anyone who ate the condemned meat would fall ill thirteen and a half hours later. In contrast, the causal interpretation of the conjoined utterance in (19) is not dependent on such an assumption.[9]

The role played by this contextual assumption is the role played by any contextual assumption in utterance interpretation: it is a premise. But, significantly, it is a premise that enables the hearer to deduce the second proposition of (21) from the first. In other words, the role of *so* in (18) and (21) is identical to the role discussed in the previous section. It indicates that the second proposition is a contextual implication of the first, or, that the second proposition is a proposition that the hearer can be expected to deduce from the first. Obviously a hearer will recognise one proposition as a contextual implication of another only if he has access to the contextual premises needed to complete the argument. The only thing that distinguishes the utterance in (18) from the ones discussed in the last section is that the premises which the hearer is expected to supply in order to establish the inferential relation between the two propositions presented express generalisations about causal relations between events of the type represented in the first proposition of the type represented in the second.[10]

There is, however, a different respect in which the uses of *so* discussed in this section differ from those in the last. This difference is quite independent of the causal flavour of these utterances, and derives instead from the fact that *so* is being used to express a connection between the conjuncts of a conjoined utterance. As the earlier examples in (5) show, the inferential connection expressed by *so* may depend on a causal premise when it is not part of a conjoined utterance. Moreover, as the example in (22) shows, *so* may be used in a conjoined utterance when the inferential connection it expresses does not depend on a causal premise:

(22) Conjoined utterances convey suggestions of temporal sequence and so *and* is not truth functional

I have argued that the hearer's aim, when he is presented with a conjoined utterance, is to recover a maximally relevant conjoined proposition – one that has relevance over and above that of its individual conjuncts. If this is right, then the role of *so* in utterances like (18) and (22) cannot be to indicate that the proposition it introduces is relevant as a specification of the relevance of the first proposition. For then the two propositions would have to be consistent with the principle of relevance individually. In other words, in these examples *so* cannot be analysed as imposing a constraint on the relevance of the proposition it introduces, but rather must contribute to the interpretation of the conjoined proposition as a whole. Thus in (22) the hearer is expected to interpret the whole argument as being consistent with the principle of relevance.

But this would seem to suggest that in such examples the inferential connection expressed by *so* is part of the propositional (that is, truth-conditional) content. And, indeed, this seems to find support in the fact that in certain cases this connection may fall under the scope of logical operators. Consider, for example, the conditional in (23), where the inferential connection may be indicated explicitly or left implicit:

(23) If conjoined utterances convey suggestions of temporal sequence and (so) *and* is not truth functional, you will have to revise your theory

If the two conjuncts of the antecedent are both true but it is not the case that the second follows from the first, then even if it is true that the addressee has to revise her theory, the conditional will be false.

This is not to say that *so* is ambiguous between the non-truth-conditional sense discussed in the previous section and a further truth-conditional sense. The use of *so*, as always, instructs the hearer to establish an inferential connection. The fact that this connection is interpreted as part of the propositional content of (23) is due to the same factor that leads any hearer to enrich the content of a conjoined utterance – the assumption that it expresses a conjoined proposition consistent with the principle of relevance.

NOTES

1 Many of the ideas in this paper are developed further in my book, *Semantic constraints on relevance*. I would like to thank Robyn Carston, Ruth Kempson, Andy Spencer, and Deirdre Wilson for discussing them with me.

2 Kempson (1975) claims that Grice's analysis is mistaken on the grounds that since its meaning can fall within the scope of logical connectives it must contribute to truth conditions. However, it seems that her examples are acceptable only to the extent that *therefore* can be given a causal 'as a result of that' interpretation rather than the more usual inferential one.

3 The fact that there are linguistic structures and expressions whose use imposes constraints on the contexts in which utterances containing them can occur was recognised by Stalnaker (1974), and Karttunen & Peters (1979). However, because their proposals were not accompanied by an adequate account of the selection and role of the context in utterance interpretation they were not able to explain why there should be such structures.

4 It will be recognised that *so* is often used as a less formal means of conveying the connection expressed by *therefore*. However, here I am concerned only with those uses of *so* in which it cannot be substituted by *therefore*.

5 See Cohen (1971) and Carston (1983) for examples.

6 This idea is presented in more detail in Blakemore (1987).

7 This approach allows us to account for the entire range of the suggestions listed by Posner (1980).

8 I am grateful to Andy Spencer for this example.

9 In order to underline this point further consider a hearer who has been presented with just the first conjunct of (22). Given the normal expectations about the result of eating condemned meat he might respond with the utterance in (i). However, the response in (ii) would only be made by a speaker who was aware of a causal link between eating condemned meat and falling ill thirteen and a half hours later:
   (i)   And so did he fall ill?
   (ii) And so did he fall ill thirteen and a half hours later?

10 This is not to say that *so* never expresses a causal connection. However, in these cases it seems that *so* functions more like an anaphor, a role analogous to the one played by *that* in phrases such as because of *that*. Thus for example, it seems that the hearer will interpret the utterance in (i) as expressing the proposition represented in (ii):
   (i)   If Susan threw the brick and so broke the window, then she will be arrested
   (ii) $Susan_i$ [threw the brick]$_j$ and by doing so_j she_i broke the window

REFERENCES

Blakemore, D. 1987. *Semantic constraints on relevance*. Oxford: Blackwell.

Carston, R. 1983. 'Semantic and pragmatic analysis of *and*.' Unpublished ms.

Cohen, J. 1971. Some remarks on Grice's views about the logical connectives of natural languages. In Y. Bar-Hillel (ed.) *Pragmatics of natural languages*. Dordrecht: Reidel.

Gazdar, G. 1979. *Pragmatics: implicature, presupposition and logical form.* New York: Academic Press.

Grice, H.P. 1975. Logic and conversation. In P. Cole & J. Morgan (eds.) *Syntax and semantics,* vol. 3: *speech acts.* New York: Academic Press.

Karttunen, L. & Peters, S. 1979 Conventional implicature. In C. K. Oh & D. Dineen (eds.) *Syntax and semantics.* vol. 11 *Presupposition.* New York: Academic Press.

Kempson, R. 1975. *Presupposition and the delimitation of semantics.* Cambridge: Cambridge University Press.

Posner, R. 1980. Semantics and pragmatics of sentence connectives in natural language. In J.R. Searle, F. Kiefer & M. Bierwisch (eds.) *Speech act theory and pragmatics.* Dordrecht: Reidel.

Sperber, D. & Wilson, D. 1986. *Relevance: communication and cognition.* Oxford: Blackwell.

Stalnaker, R. 1974. Pragmatic presupposition. In M. Munitz & P. Unger (eds.) *Semantics and philosophy: studies in contemporary philosophy.* New York: New York University Press, 197–213.

Wilson, D. & Sperber, D. 1981. On Grice's theory of conversation. In P. Werth (ed.) *Conversation and discourse.* London: Croom Helm.

V

The language faculty and cognition

9

On the grammar–cognition interface:
the principle of full interpretation

RUTH M. KEMPSON

1 The problem: Universal Grammar and central cognitive processes

This chapter draws out the consequences of relevance theory taken in conjunction with the claims about Universal Grammar (UG) made within the Government and Binding (GB) paradigm. I shall take in turn the principle of full interpretation, the theta criterion, and the projection principle, construe them in terms suggested by relevance theory, and then use these new formulations as a basis for posing the following question:

If for any principle *A* of Universal Grammar we can establish that it is a consequence of some general cognitive constraint, does it follow that *A* is not a characteristic of Universal Grammar, but merely a consequence of the interaction between Universal Grammar and general cognitive faculties?

While my answer will turn out to be orthodox, the route I take to get to it and the conclusions I draw from it are not.

2 The principle of full interpretation

The principle of full interpretation (FI) (Chomsky 1986) is a principle which requires that every construct of a level which interfaces with a system of language use must be externally licensed by being assigned an interpretation appropriate to that interface. In Chomsky's paradigm this takes the form of the requirement that 'every element of PF (Phonological Form) and LF (Logical Form) taken to be the interface of syntax (in the broad sense) with systems of language use, must receive an appropriate interpretation – licensed in the sense indicated. None can be simply disregarded ... We cannot have sentences of the form

(1) *I was in England last year the man
(2) *John was here yesterday walked
(3) *Who John saw Bill
(4) *Every everyone was here [Chomsky's examples 88(i)–(iv)]'

Chomsky uses this principle to conclude that it would be 'flat wrong' to include a grammar of English rules that specifically bar examples of the sort (1)–(4) in particular the vacuous quantification in (3) and (4) as such rules 'would simply restate in a complex way facts that follow from quite general syntactic properties of human languages'. Having outlined so-called external licensing conditions for logical form, Chomsky remarks 'we might look forward to the possibility of their being expressed in a more organised manner relating to some broader theory of semantic interpretation'.

Relevance theory immediately suggests such a 'broader' theory of semantic interpretation. According to relevance theory, the concept of interpretation provided by the grammar is the mapping onto expressions of the language of thought, each sentence being paired with some incomplete configuration of the language of thought as its logical form. Each logical form is the result of specifications of content associated with individual lexical items which compositionally induce the logical form (see section 3 of this chapter for a discussion of the theta criterion in these terms). The logical form then provides the hearer with a basis for forming a hypotheses about the proposition expressed by any utterance of the sentence in question. So the main task of the content associated with a lexical item is to act as a constraint on the propositional content expressible by sentences containing it. The concept of linguistic content is not, however, exhausted by the contribution an item makes to the logical form of sentences (and hence indirectly to their propositional content). For some lexical items contribute rather to the selection of context a hearer is to make (Blakemore this volume argues this in detail). So we arrive at the following general characterisation of linguistic content. The relevance-theoretic concept of linguistic content is a set of constraints on the process of inference intrinsic to utterance interpretation.

However, if we apply the principle of FI to this interpretation procedure, now construed in terms of constraints on utterance interpretation, then we are faced with a claim which is much stronger than that posed by Chomsky himself, for the level subject to interpretation on relevance assumptions is that of S-structure. So the claim now takes the form that all expressions at S-structure 'must receive an appropriate interpretation – licensed in the sense indicated' (Chomsky 1986) – must in other words make a nonempty contribution to constraining the process of utterance interpretation.

2.1 Expletives
Such a construal of the principle of FI would successfully preclude Chomsky's examples (1)–(4). But the immediate apparent counter-examples to it are the constructions whose defining property is supposedly their lack of intrinsic content – the expletive. Indeed Chomsky argues for an application of move α operating at LF in order to guarantee that expletives are not present at the level to which the principle of FI applies. However, I shall argue that on the relevance-defined concept of content, the only counter-examples are the idiomatic weather verbs.

Expletives in English are of three types:
(i) existential constructions

    (5)   There's a man outside

(ii) the *it*-S configuration of extraposition structures

    (6) It's annoying that Mary isn't here

(iii) the weather verbs

    (7) It's raining

2.1.1 Existential constructions Existential constructions in English and other languages are associated with a so-called 'definiteness effect' which precludes definite NPs from occurring in the complement position of the verb. This definiteness effect is realised in slightly different ways in different languages.[1] For example the Dutch existential construction can be formed using the adverbial pronominal form *er* with all verbs, transitive as well as intransitive, as long as any NPs directly associated with the verb as part of its complement are indefinite (an NP inside a PP associated with this verb is not subject to the restriction). (See Bennis 1986 for a detailed account.)[2]

    (8)   dat er   een jongen in de tuin   liep
           that there a   boy   in the garden walked

    (9)   *dat er   de jongen in de tuin   liep
           that there the boy   in the garden walked

  (10) ??dat er   niemand het gekocht heft
           that there nobody it   bought has

  (11) dat er   niemand/*Jan een olifant/ *hem gezien heeft
           that there nobody/ *Jan an elephant/him seen has

This definiteness restriction has been analysed in different ways, some syntactic, some semantic. Given the approach to lexical content intrinsic to relevance theory these constructions will not be precluded by the principle of FI as long as the definiteness effect can be analysed in terms of the contribution they make to utterance interpretation. And it is precisely this mode of explanation which several semantic accounts of the definiteness effect proffer. For example Rando & Napoli (1978) analyse *there*-insertion as a transformation designed to provide a dummy theme or topic. And Bennis (1986) analyses *er* constructions in terms of a requirement that any associated NPs are nonthematic.

    Such requirements are straightforwardly stateable in this framework as a predictable type of intrinsic lexical content – content that constrains how the utterance is interpreted. The content of the existential *er* pronominal of Dutch for example can be analysed as imposing a restriction on propositional form assignment that any logical arguments associated with the given predicate be not part of what is immediately accessible from any information given prior to the processing of that constituent.[3] More formally:[4]

$$[er \; V \; COMP] \rightarrow V' \; (\, (a_i) \,) \, (a_j)$$
$$a_i, a_j \notin C_{x<v}$$

V'=logical translation of V

C_x=information accessible in processing X

This type of approach has been described by Safir (1984). His criticisms are on the one hand that such explanations are functional and therefore unable to explain structural idiosyncracies of specific languages – for
example that, in Dutch, the definiteness effect does not apply to NPs inside
PPs; and on the other hand that the definiteness effect arises in structures
lacking an expletive and so cannot be explained by an analysis specific to the
expletive. Such criticisms do not stand up to scrutiny.[5] The analysis is
functional only in that the content of the expression is directed towards
constraining how an utterance containing an expression is interpreted. It is a
constraint on interpretation associated with a specific lexical item in a certain
type of configuration, and as such can be sensitive to details of the configuration. PPs in particular are no problem, as long as we assume they are not part
of the argument specification of a given predicate but are adjuncts (cf.
Grimshaw 1986 for the distinction between adjuncts and arguments). As
adjuncts, they will not be relevant to the satisfaction of restrictions on the
argument structure of a given predicative construction. Thus in this account
of the Dutch examples (12) and (13) invoked by Safir:

(12)   *dat er   door   de deur het kind kwam
        that there through the door the child came

(13)   dat er   aan het kind gedacht werd
        that there of   the child thought was

het kind is an argument of *kwam* in (12) but not of *gedacht* in (13).

As for Safir's second argument, just as two configurations may have the
same s-selection requirements, so there is no reason to preclude two syntactic
configurations from sharing the same argument-restriction. So the fact that
the definiteness effect arises in two types of structure is of no consequence.
What is offered here is an account of the intrinsic content of existential
constructions in terms of a systematic restriction they impose on propositions
expressible by them. This is not disturbed by the existence of other constructions which impose similar restrictions, as long as such a restriction can
either be imposed from the lexicon, or is a consequence of general pragmatic
principles.[6] Furthermore, and most important of all, the analysis HAS
attributed intrinsic content to the existential construction taking as an example the Dutch existential involving the pronominal *er*, for restrictions on
proposition construction and context selection are part of the specification of
lexical content, given relevance assumptions. So such dummy pronominals
are therefore compatible with the principle of FI. An exactly similar analysis
pertains to the English existential construction *there* except that there is an
additional restriction on the type of verb it syntactically requires.

Moreover, the assumptions specific to relevance theory explain a
phenomenon completely inexplicable on most other accounts. Despite the
supposed preclusion of definite NPs from existential constructions, they are
in fact possible, as are names – both with a marked effect. So we find
(14)–(15):

(14)   There's John to consider

(15)   (Who else should we invite?) There's the man who lives at no. 38

This is inexplicable in any analysis of existentials stated either in terms of syntactic configuration or in terms of the semantic distinction between indefinite and definite NPs. The effect of such supposedly marked structures is that the individuals in question would not be thought of independent of their introduction into the discourse by use of the existential construction. An analysis of the content of existential constructions in terms of a restriction on contextual accessibility provides just what is needed. The concept of accessibility which considerations of relevance trade on is not a fixed concept, dependent on constant and total access to memory (either shared by the two participants as 'mutual knowledge' or even for a single individual). On the contrary, all processing with assumptions of relevance is constrained by the need to obtain inferential effects with as little processing cost as possible. This is the constraint called 'maximising relevance'. So the concept of accessibility to constructs stored in memory is heavily inhibited by the processing-cost filter. What is accessible to a hearer at any point in a discourse is only the sources of information more-or-less immediately available to him – not his total memory stock. Hence the definiteness restriction on NPs in existential constructions does not absolutely preclude definite NPs or names, but allows their use with the implication that mention of the individuals referred to is new or unexpected in the discourse.[7]

It is of some interest that despite the difference in approach, in effect this analysis reconstructs the Chomskian 1986 account of expletives. In Chomsky's view, there is an application of move α at LF moving the complement NP to the position of the expletive, providing an LF configuration

$NP_i \ldots e_i \, XP$

from the S-structure configuration

expletive $\ldots NP_i \, XP$

According to the view sketched here, the S-structure configuration

expletive $\ldots NP_i \, XP$

is mapped onto a logical form structure with the expletive replaced as the first argument of the predicate by the logical translation of the complement NP. By both analyses then, there is no expletive at the level of logical form. On this analysis this conclusion falls out from general principles: the language in which logical forms are stated is an inferentially transparent system, and expletives having no inferential role are not members of such a system.

2.1.2 Extraposition structures Extraposition structures have no such definiteness restriction reflecting the intrinsic linguistic content of the expletive. These structures are associated with predicates which allow clausal subjects, such clauses often being placed as complements of the predicate with a dummy pronoun in subject position:

(16)   That Mary's at home is annoying

(17)   It's annoying that Mary's not at home

There is no restriction on the semantic relation between the predicates and complement, the relations ranging from an implication of presupposed truth, and asserted truth, to no implication of truth:

(18)   It's annoying that Mary can read

(19)   It's true that Mary can read

(20)   It's obvious that Mary can read

(21)   It's unlikely that Mary can read

The only restriction is that imposed by the predicates themselves, precluding non-clausal complements:

(22)   *It's true the book

(23)   *That Joan will come is unlikely the party

It might seem that such expletive pronouns merely have the function of fulfilling a language-specific requirement that the subject always be explicitly realised, and in having no intrinsic content of their own must be examples which provide the lie to the assumption of a principle of FI applying at S-structure. From the point of view of propositional content, they indeed contribute nothing: (16)–(17) are synonymous, true in all the same worlds. However, on relevance assumptions, dummy subjects DO alter the utterance interpretation process. The process of constructing a hypothesised proposition+context set of premises involved in utterance interpretation is in principle operative from the beginning of an utterance (cf. Sperber & Wilson 1986, chap. 4). Every lexical item used makes accessible its associated concept on the basis of which the speaker progressively chooses a context set. Thus whatever information the speaker presents the hearer with *ab initio* will be immediately considered as accessible for this process. The effect of a dummy pronoun in subject position inhibits this process, for the information associated with the argument of the predicate is withheld. In other words, in making such a selection, the speaker is deliberately not conveying any indication as to what to use as a basis for constructing a context set of premises. (Contrast this with the use of a definite NP or pronoun in subject position, expressions whose interpretation at the level of propositional form depends on such accessible information.)

Such information does not need to be specified as part of the intrinsic content contributed by the pronoun. All that is required is a rule of interpretation associated with the structure mapping a complement S̄ into the argument position provided by the pronoun: given its S-structure position, the pronoun will have the effect of contributing to the inferential process of utterance interpretation without any intrinsic specification. So on the assumption that what is critical to a satisfaction of the principle of FI is not truth-theoretic content but contribution to the inferential process of utterance interpretation, even dummy expletive pronouns do not violate such a principle applying to S-structure.[8]

As in the case of existential constructions, the effect of Chomsky's 1986 analysis is achieved without specification of move α. The syntactic configuration provides one more NP than imposed by the logical specification of the verb. Thus the mapping from S-structure to logical form involves a reduction of the number of NP-translations by one.

2.1.3   Weather expressions   The only type of example remaining is the weather-verb, and these are genuine exceptions to the principle that every element at S-structure make a non-empty contribution to utterance interpretation. Their subjects are dummy pronouns and the sole function of these is to fill the subject slot for a predicate with the apparent exceptional property of not requiring an argument, even logically. However, the predicates are exceptions to all theories of predication, and the structures idiomatic. Moreover, these empty pronominal subjects play a part in control structures (Chomsky 1981) and, possibly, in anaphoric relations:

(24)   It sometimes rains after snowing

(25)   It rained incredibly hard and it soaked even my vest

Examples such as these, particularly (24), provide some slight evidence that the weather *it*'s are carried over as elements of the logical form – i.e. are expressions of the language of thought. I therefore assume that in learning such structures a child simply learns them, as wholes, lexically stipulated like other idioms as a whole phrase. The overall evidence then is that expletives do not seriously disturb the claim that all expressions of surface-structure configurations contribute in some systematic way to the process of utterance interpretation.

At this juncture, a sceptic might counterargue that it is not necessary to make such a strong claim. The application of the principle of FI to S-structure could be side-stepped by assuming that the relevance-theoretic logical form configuration is an interpretation of the GB-defined level of LF, the grammar specifying for each sentence the levels D-structure, S-structure, PF, LF, and Logical Form. I prefer here to adopt the more minimalist stance that LF and Logical Form are complementary. In support of this stance is evidence that the binding principles and the theta criterion are satisfied NOT on natural language configurations but on language of thought configurations, and moreover, that the binding principles are a set of constraints on the pragmatic process of proposition construction not even implemented at a level articulated by the grammar (Kempson forthcoming). But the binding principles and the theta criterion are the properties which motivate the GB-defined concept of LF. If these conclusions are correct, the only motivation for a level of LF is removed. These arguments do not apply to the relevance-theoretic logical form, leaving it as the level which provides interpretations

for S-structure configurations. I do not have space to argue for these conclusions here (which are presented in detail in Kempson forthcoming); so
metatheoretical aesthetic grounds for preferring the simpler account will
have to suffice here.

In summary, this relevance-theoretic version of the 'broader theory of
semantic interpretation' that Chomsky 'looked forward to' in Chomsky 1986
as substantiating the principle of full interpretation has two properties:

(i) Linguistic content both for lexical items and syntactic configurations is specified as the contribution the item or configuration makes to the
inferential process involved in utterance interpretation, contributing either to
the truth-theoretic content of propositional forms by being part of the logical
form of a sentence, or by constraining the type of context a hearer may select
to pair with its propositional form.

(ii) This process of interpretation of S-structure configurations is formalised as a mapping onto formulae of the language of thought by a compositionally induced mapping from lexically specified contents. It is this process
which the principle of FI constrains, and, as we shall see immediately, the
theta criterion is an implementation of this constraint.

3   The theta criterion

This construal of the principle of FI by mapping each natural language
configuration onto another mode of representation matches the syntactic
spirit in which Chomsky construed it despite its application to S-structure;
for Chomsky's licensing conditions, said to interpret LF-structures, are syntactic in nature. They fall into two types, the licensing conditions for maximal projections and those for nonmaximal projections. The conditions for
maximal projections are that 'each such phrase A must be licensed
"externally" as either an argument or the trace of an argument, a predicate
or an operator. If an argument, A must be assigned a T-role [theta role]; if a
predicate, A must assign a T-role; and if an operator, A must bind a variable
(which, furthermore, must be strongly bound)' (Chomsky 1986: 101). These
conditions could be straightforwardly reconstrued as restrictions on a mapping from S-structure configurations onto configurations of the language of
thought:

If A is an argument in the syntax of the natural language, the interpretation of A must provide a logical argument of some predicate.

If A is a predicate in the syntax of the natural language, the interpretation of A must have associated arguments.

If A is an operator in the syntax of natural language, the interpretation
of A must bind a variable (whose domain must be immediately recoverable).
The first and second of these conditions are transparently related to the theta
criterion, in its simplest form (Chomsky 1981) stated as:

Each syntactic argument is assigned one and only one theta-role and each theta-role is assigned to one and only one syntactic argument.

With the interpretational aspect of the theta criterion covered in this way by the principle of FI, Chomsky redefines the theta criterion to make explicit the link between theta theory and case theory (cf. the introduction to this volume and Brody & Manzini for discussion). But it is the earlier interpretational aspect of the theta criterion on which I shall focus here.

Chomsky's licensing conditions on interpretation are suitable, as stated, for maximal projections only. The nonmaximal projections on Chomsky's view by contrast are not assigned external licensing conditions directly but 'are licensed relative to their maximal projections'. Construing these licensing conditions as constraints on the mapping into the language of thought, makes this restriction of 'external' licensing conditions to maximal projections quite arbitrary, a mere consequence of the theta criterion being stated only with respect to verbs and adjectives and their corresponding syntactic arguments. A generalisation of the theta criterion to cover maximal and nonmaximal projections is provided by Higginbotham (1985).

Higginbotham assumes that every lexical item which has the semantic role of predicate (requiring one or more arguments) has an associated theta-grid indicating the number and nature of these arguments, in particular what mode of combination they require. This generalisation of the application of the theta criterion immediately leads to the problem that the specification of theta roles and their assignation is not restricted to verbs and their syntactic NP arguments – for example the theta-role associated with what is a predicate *man* in *the man* is not assigned to any syntactic argument. Accordingly Higginbotham generalises the theta criterion as follows:

Higginbotham's theta criterion

(1) Every thematic position is discharged.

(2) An argument of X must be assigned a role that is present in the thematic structure of X.

(3) If X discharges a thematic role in Y, then it discharges only one. The process of discharging theta-roles, as Higginbotham calls it, is a combinatorial process carried out progressively up a syntactic tree in one of a number of ways as specified in the theta-grid associated with the lexical item of the point in the configuration. I sketch out four examples. (i) V–NP sequences. These are interpreted as before by assignment of the theta-role associated with the verb to that argument (the NP), and hence 'discharging' the theta-role. (ii) Det–N sequences. These are interpreted by what Higginbotham calls 'theta-binding' in which the determiner provides the theta-role for the noun; so the expression *man* is interpreted as 'man (x)' for some 'x'. (iii) Adj–N sequences. These sometimes merely require identity of arguments for the adjective and the noun, and in such cases, the theta-grid

associated with the configuration guarantees that any argument assigned to
the phrase assigns the same argument to the Adj and the N. Thus *an empty
bucket* is interpreted as 'empty (x) and bucket (x)' for some 'x'. (iv) Some Adj–
N sequences, however, require the introduction of a comparison class for the
adjective, and these have a more complex theta-grid assigned to the adjective, among other things guaranteeing that the adjective expresses a relation
of which the content of the head noun provides the second argument. From
this more complex grid, *a big butterfly* is interpreted as 'butterfly (x) and big-
for-a-butterfly (x)' for some 'x'. And so on. I leave all details on one side. All
that is required for my purposes is that the satisfaction of the theta criterion
involves carrying out various semantic modes of combination up the tree as
stipulated by varyingly complex theta-grid specifications associated with the
lexical items.

Higginbotham himself construes the projection of these theta-grids as
providing real semantic values directly in a Davidsonian spirit, but suppose
we construe them in the spirit of relevance theory. On this construal, theta-
grids associated with lexical items specify the logical structure required for
that predicate and associated constructs of the logic that the predicate must
combine with. And paired with each node in a tree is a mapping rule
determining at each stage what the associated logical configuration must be.
Construed like this, the requirement of external licensing conditions imposed
by the principle of FI is not restricted to maximal projections but applies
quite generally to all nodes in a tree. Each node in a tree must have associated with it an instruction determining what type of logical structure it maps
onto (induced even in the case of maximal projections from the logical
structure assigned lexically to the head of the phrase). Moreover if we
assume, like Higginbotham, that the assignment of theta-roles is not a purely
syntactic process but provides a semantic interpretation, this here being
some mapping into a formula of the language of thought, then as part of the
principle of FI, the theta criterion according to Higginbotham can now be
reconstrued:

The theta criterion:

(1) Every logical argument associated with expression X as a theta-role
must be discharged.[9]

(2) Every syntactic argument of X must be used to provide a logical
argument in satisfaction of some theta-grid specification of X.[10] The theta
criterion is thus a constraint on the mapping from S-structure to logical form.

I demonstrate this reconstrual of the theta-grid specifications and the
theta criterion with the simplest type of example first:

(26)   John liked Mary

I assume the following theta-grid specifications associated with the lexical
items, with a lambda calculus as the language of thought (X' representing
the logical correlate of the natural-language category X):

John: $\lambda P[P(j)]$
Mary: $\lambda P[P(m)]$

like: $\lambda y \lambda x[\text{like}'(y)\,(x)]$

past: $\lambda \text{VP}'\,\lambda x[\text{past}'(\text{VP}'\,(x))]$

The only critical difference between this use of the lambda calculus and its use in Montague 1974 is that the output logical representation is assumed here to be ineliminable. (Problems of intentionality I ignore.) These lexical specifications are driven by the theta criterion to induce a logical form:

past' (like' $(\lambda P[P(m)])$ (j))

The NPs *John* and *Mary* must be used to build the specified logical form for not to do so would leave the theta-grid specifications unsatisfied and would make no use of the NPs in building the logical form. Both the theta criterion and the principle of FI would thus be violated.

The aspect of the theta criterion which this revision does not incorporate is the uniqueness requirement. This requirement is of considerable significance since according to Brody (1984) the major argument for distinguishing D- and S-structure is that D-structure is a pure representation of the grammatical functions associated with theta-roles. In particular D-structure provides the simplest characterisation of the theta criterion in that the uniqueness requirement which has to be stipulated at S-structure is an immediate consequence of the theta criterion stated at D-structure (given Chomsky's definition of D-structure). However, there is reason to think that this uniqueness requirement is a consequence of a much more general principle which I state as follows:

The uniqueness principle:

For any linguistic entity A and every domain of application of some subsystem S in which A has a value V, it must only have one such value V.

The informal intuition behind this is that rules (or subsystems of constraints) apply within a certain domain; and any expression within that domain has just one value with respect to the rule in question. This is a definitional property of linguistic rules if we construe these to be function–argument in structure. Any input to a rule is either a function or an argument to some function, and whichever of these it is, it can only be one of them. The restatement of rules as interacting subsystems of constraints makes no essential difference. Whatever subsystem an expression plays a role in for any given domain in which that subsystem applies, it cannot play more than one such role at a time. The application of the theta criterion is just one example of this general principle. If A is a predicate which assigns, say, its patient role to some NP, it cannot also assign a patient role to some other NP within a single functional complex (cf. Chomsky's concept of 'complete functional complex (CFC)', Chomsky 1986). If A is an argument to some predicate, it cannot be more than one argument to that predicate. The small clause examples such as (27)–(28)

(27) John left the room angry

(28) I like milk cold

are not counter-examples to this. There are two possible modes of explanation of this type of case. On the one hand one might argue that the sentence contains two functional complexes, provided by the main clause and small clause respectively, and the expression *John* contributes uniquely in each subsystem. This is not a contradiction. The uniqueness principle as stated does not preclude such double contributions. What it precludes are double contributions within a single functional complex. On the other hand, one might argue that small clauses provide additional predicates to the head predicate (either VP$'$ or N$'$) forming a compound predicate requiring only a single argument in satisfaction. I leave this issue open. Either way there is no violation of the uniqueness principle.

The restriction of uniqueness is completely general: examples can be culled from any subsystem of the grammar. No expression can be simultaneously a variable bound by some quantifier P and yet also be some second variable bound by some other quantifier Q. No quantifier can be mentioned once but be assumed to separately quantify any number of expressions in the sentence expressions in the sentence in question.[11] (30) cannot mean (29):

  (29) Few men like currants in buns
  (30) 'Few men like few currants in few buns'

No expression can be both a variable and a binder within the same domain.[12] No NP can have more than one case assigned to it. Nor can a verb assign any one case to more than one NP.[13] And so on. Quite generally, expressions have a fully determinate value within the domain of application of each subsystem of grammar–case, theta, binding, etc. – and no single expression (simple or complex) can be construed as being assigned more than one such value within a given domain.[14] The only examples where a single NP apparently can play two roles in the same complex are cases where there are grounds for suggesting that the relation in question is between the individual denoted by the NP and a property. These are the PRO cases provided by such verbs as *want* and *try*:

  want: [__VP] , $\lambda VP' \lambda x[\text{want}' \ (VP' \ (x)) \ (x)]$
  try: [__VP] , $\lambda VP' \ \lambda x[\text{try}' \ (VP' \ (x)) \ (x)]$

Assuming the format of the lambda calculus, the double provision of the two-subject argument places by the one surface subject has to be a lexically stipulated exception to the uniqueness principle. If we adopted the richer property logic, IL*, advocated by Chierchia (1984), these would no longer be counterexamples for even at the level of logical representation, the subordinate VP would be represented as an individual correlate of a property, not requiring an argument. For the time being, however, I allow lexical exceptions to the general principle. With this caveat of allowing lexically stipulated exceptions, the uniqueness restriction holds for all applications of general principles. This being so, we do not need to stipulate uniqueness as part of the theta criterion.

  This conclusion, if correct, has immediate consequences for D-structure. The statement of the theta criterion is now just as simple to state at S-structure over chains, for the uniqueness requirement intrinsic to D-structure theta-role assignment but supposedly requiring stipulation at S-structure is independently motivated as a quite general property of rule statements. This undermines the motivation for D-structure as a level of grammar. Moreover, if the theta criterion is a constraint on 'external' interpretation (i.e. translation into the language of thought), it applies only to the mapping between S-structure and LF. If we grant with Brody that S-structure is the basic level, and D-structure justified by its contribution to the specification of the theta criterion, then given an independent uniqueness principle and the construal of the theta criterion just given, it is arguable that D-structure makes no essential contribution to the grammar at all.

Suppose then that S-structure are directly generated with only an associated mapping onto logical forms as induced from the lexicon. How can one capture the restriction in a D-structure/S-structure analysis that the head of a chain must be in $\bar{\text{A}}$ position, and the foot of a chain in A position? This, I propose, is captured by the interaction of the theta criterion, the principle of FI and the principle of uniqueness. I take the following examples:

(31) John seems to admire Mary

(32) *John believed to have admired Mary

In (31), standardly an $\bar{\text{A}}$–A chain, *admire* and *seem* have associated subcategorisation restrictions and theta-grids:

admire: [__NP], $\lambda y\lambda x[\text{admire}'\ (y)(x)]$

seem: [__VP], $\lambda VP'\lambda x[\text{seem}'(VP'(x))]$

The theta-grid of *seem* specifies that the concept *seem'* is a propositional operator. By the theta criterion, both theta specifications must be discharged. By the principle of FI, every element at S-structure must play a non-empty role in the inference process of utterance interpretation (here contributing to the logical form of the sentence). These restrictions jointly guarantee that *admire* must have its theta specifications fulfilled by expressions contained in the sentence, and that the surface subject, *John* will be construed as argument of *admire'*. Otherwise we would have simultaneous violations of the theta criterion and of the principle of FI as in (26). The effect is to have NP movement in reverse operating at logical form.

In (32), where the double argument chain between the two subject positions must be precluded, *believe* has two associated subcategorisation frames

[__NP VP]

[__$\bar{\text{S}}$]

and only one theta-grid specification

$\lambda\bar{\text{S}}'\ \lambda x[\text{believe}'\ (\bar{\text{S}}')\ (x)]$

In other words the concept *believe'* is a two-place relation between an individual and a proposition (never between an individual and a property). These requirements are not satisfied by (32). If the subject *John* in (32) were

used only to satisfy the open position in the embedded VP, the theta criterion
would be violated (in both parts). If it were used only to satisfy the subject of
believe, the theta-grid specification of *believe'* would be violated. And if the
subject were used to provide logical arguments to two discrete predicates
(one with the additional argument providing a propositional argument for
the other), it would play two entirely discrete roles within a single complex in
violation of the uniqueness principle, with no grounds available for postulat-
ing the construction of a compound property (unlike the small clause cases of
(27)–(28)). As in the case of *want*, a more direct explanation is available if we
adopt the Chierchia stance that infinitives are individual correlates of
properties. For then the constraint that *believe* expresses a relation between an
individual and (the individual correlate of) a proposition is sufficient to
preclude (32) directly. Either way, (32) is impossible. I therefore conclude
that the characteristic property of chains as to A and Ā distribution can be
explained in this framework without the postulation of D-structure by the
interaction of a number of principles, all of them universal. The only stipula-
tions that have to be made, if any, are lexical specifications.

4   The projection principle

One immediate consequence of assuming direct generation of S-structure as
the basic level with only a mapping onto the interpretational logical form is
the status of the projection principle. The projection principle is the requirement that 'representations at each syntactic level are projected from the
lexicon in that they observe the subcategorisation properties of lexical items'
(Chomsky 1981). The substance of the projection principle is twofold. It
embodies the claim (i) that syntactic representations are projected from the
lexicon, and (ii) that such representations are present at all levels. As a
constraint on a model containing three levels within a single syntactic mode
of characterisation, this second part is a particularly strong form of what
Chomsky has called the recoverability principle.

   However, with no D-structure, the force of the projection principle is
very much reduced. Given the revised form of the theta criterion in which it
is reconstrued as a constraint on the mapping of syntactic arguments onto
logical arguments, the projection from syntactic argument structure to logical structure does not require separate specification. And the reverse
dependency that logical arguments must be expressed as syntactic arguments, faces counter-examples in implicit argument examples such as (33):

   (33)   (What fools John and Joan were.) Yesterday's attacks on each
          other's work were mutually destructive

I have suggested elsewhere (Kempson forthcoming) that these are cases
where the logical structure is projected from the lexicon directly without
syntactic realisation (cf. also Brody & Manzini this volume).[15] Moreover a

number of people have argued for the necessity of event variables at the level of LF, whose motivation at other levels is obscure at best (cf. Higginbotham 1985 and Williams 1985). These data suggest that in so far as the second half of the projection principle can be maintained, it reduces to the theta criterion. Thus if the status of D-structure is severely undermined, all that remains of the projection principle is its first part – the restriction that the syntactic properties of an S-structure configuration are projected from the lexical specification of its terminal elements. So on the analysis suggested here, both the sentential S-structure configuration and its associated logical form are induced from the lexicon by restrictions imposed by the joint syntactic and logical requirements of the lexical items, the former driven by the projection principle, the latter by the theta criterion.

This analysis is tentative, as detailed evaluation of D-structure as an independent level against the joint requirements of relevance theory and GB theory has yet to be made. One attraction of this model in the mean time, despite the abandonment of D-structure and much of the substance of the projection principle, is that it instantiates in a particularly direct way the central claim of Chomsky's approach to language acquisition that, apart from parameter fixing, all the child has to learn is a lexicon. For on this view both syntactic and semantic properties of expressions of the language are projected from the lexicon. If, furthermore, as Chomsky has claimed, the subcategorisational requirements of a lexical item (c-selection) largely follow from its logical specification (s-selection), then the acquisition of a grammar follows almost in toto from learning what concepts the individual lexical items name.

5 The link between principles of grammar and relevance constraints

I have so far argued for revisions of the principle of FI, the theta criterion and the projection principle, and proposed an independent uniqueness principle. On the basis of these revisions, I wish to consider the relation between such principles and the concept of relevance. Given the widespread methodological assumption that considerations of pragmatic theory are irrelevant to the articulation of formal syntactic properties, it might seem that any such relation would be of no consequence for syntactic theory. However, relevance theory does not merely provide a theory of utterance interpretation but a theory of cognition. So this assumption, though true, is itself irrelevant. Consideration of arguments for the form of one's grammar imposed externally by general constraints on cognition may not be fashionable, but few linguists other than Katz (1981) reject them out of hand. And the concept of relevance by claim imposes a constraint on the entire cognitive mechanism that all cognitive processes are geared towards maximisation of relevance – geared towards the least processing cost for suitable inferential reward. The burden of this section, then, is to establish the link between this constraint and the constraints specific to the language faculty (UG).

5.1 The principle of full interpretation (FI)

It is easy to demonstrate that there is some link between the principles of UG and the goal of maximising relevance, even if indirect. If there were no principle of FI, no theta criterion, no uniqueness principle, no projection principle, the grammar would overgenerate wildly *vis à vis* what a speaker takes to be acceptable, and every act of utterance interpretation would present an immense ambiguity problem, most readings having to be rejected pragmatically. However, the grammaticality facts of (1)–(4) (repeated here) could not be made to follow from a purely pragmatic explanation.

(1)   *I was in England last year the man
(2)   *John was here yesterday walked
(3)   *Who John saw Bill
(4)   *Every everyone was here

Such an exclusively functional explanation would predict that there might be interaction between contextual effects of one sort or another which could lead to establishing some proposition expressed by these strings. But there is no such interaction. There are no conditions under which more than one NP can be construed as discrete, unco-ordinated subjects (as in (1)), or a chain of ⟨NP,e⟩ be simply not used at LF (as in (3)). Nor are there any circumstances under which a speaker can knowingly slip in an extra quantifier as in (4), or an extra verb as in (2), relying on the hearer to ignore such extraneous expressions in constructing the proposition expressed as not worth the trouble. These are grammaticality data, to be prohibited by rule or constraint operating at some point in the explanation.

Suppose, however, we take the data as providing evidence for wellformedness conditions on the logic of the central cognitive mechanism – that vacuous quantification is disallowed, that each expression of the logic have one and only one function, that all predicates must be assigned the appropriate number of arguments. The deviance of the examples in question, (1)–(4), does now follow directly from the constraint of maximising relevance. Inferential reward is achieved by constructing propositions, wellformed formulae of the language of thought. So sentences of the natural language will be viable strings of the language only if they can be used to construct wellformed formulae. A sentence must therefore have associated with it a logical form which can provide the basis for constructing a wellformed logical expression. And this expression of the logic must be constructible from the words selected, at minimal processing cost. Any words which have no contribution to make to the processing of the utterance are excluded (they involve processing cost with no associated reward), and any words which together guarantee that the complex expression has no associated wellformed formula of the logic are excluded – they too involve a processing cost with no possible reward. Indeed, for a speaker to choose such a string would be doubly misleading because he would be deliberately causing his hearer the processing cost of figuring out why such an aberrant form had been used – all to no avail. Hence by the principle of relevance (3) is out, (4) is out, and so on.

From general relevance considerations, we have now derived the effect of the principle of FI that every expression must play some non-empty role in the inferential process of utterance interpretation. All this predicted by the constraint of maximising relevance. No cognitive system obeying this constraint would tolerate the processing cost involved in computing some expression which would systematically provide no reward in the effort of understanding utterances. So the principle of FI is a direct consequence of the assumption that the cognitive mechanism is constrained to maximise relevance – as long as we assume that vacuous quantification, unique argument selection, assignment of appropriate numbers of arguments to a predicate are wellformedness conditions associated directly with the logic of the central cognitive mechanism. Since these are definitional properties of familiar systems of representation for which a syntactic account of inference is given, I take it this assumption is uncontroversial. The underlying premise behind this assumption is that general restrictions on quantifier binding and complement selection (what Chomsky calls s-selection) are taken as evidence of wellformedness constraints on the associated logic, an entirely plausible view. In any case, as we shall see shortly, the existence of these constraints on the logic is predicted from general principles.

5.2   The theta criterion

The theta criterion has here been construed as determining the map from the natural language to the appropriate argument structure of the logic via theta-grids associated with the lexical items and the structural configuration. These grids specify the logical structure required by each lexical item; the theta criterion requires that these be fulfilled. Suppose there were no such requirement. Then some mappings might fail to provide arguments for any given predicate (i.e. violate the first part of the theta criterion). And some mappings might provide arguments not directly recoverable from the string in question in violation of the second part (e.g. mapping *John likes Mary* onto 'Mary likes John'). But both these possibilities are excluded by relevance requirements. If some predicate failed to get an argument altogether, the resulting logical expression would be illformed; and as we've just seen, mappings onto illformed expressions are excluded in principle as totally fruitless (they involve processing cost with no possible inferential reward). And the production of a sentence which required a mapping from the sequence *John likes Mary* onto 'Mary likes John' as its interpretation would violate the principle of relevance. No speaker could intend a hearer to recover the information that Mary likes John from *John likes Mary* because to expect the hearer to ignore the syntactic argument specification in constructing some proposition when a form is available which provides the intended meaning directly from its syntactic argument specification would be a violation of the principle of relevance – it would require the hearer to ignore his/her internalised constraint of maximising relevance in a particularly flagrant way. Hence both aspects of the theta criterion *sans* uniqueness are direct consequences of the constraints imposed by relevance.

5.3   The uniqueness principle

I argued in section 3 that the uniqueness principle was independent of and more general than the theta criterion. This principle is certainly not a direct consequence of the principle of relevance. After all, it might be more economical to say a word once and be able to assume it could be used more than once in constructing the argument structure of a string. What more economical way of expressing that John hit himself could there be than by saying *John hit*, given that the very mention of John guarantees that this information is accessible for construing as the second argument of 'hit'. Nevertheless, the assumption of uniqueness of syntactic function greatly reduces the indeterminacy associated with interpreting a string. The leap between processing the string and deciding what proposition it expressed would be vast indeed if every expression could be used several times over in a single functional complex or more than one expression be assumed to satisfy a single requirement. Furthermore, the uniqueness requirement is not particular to natural languages. It is certainly a wellformedness condition of the associated logic. No expression of any logical string can have more than one inferential role in the string. The system is strictly function–argument in structure and this by definition imposes a uniqueness requirement on all combinatorial operations. In this respect, the natural language restriction parallels the internal representational system, a parallelism which guarantees a straightforward mapping between the two. Thus the uniqueness restriction, as a definitional property of the two rule-governed systems, certainly contributes to the general cognitive goal of maximising relevance.

5.4   The projection principle

With direct generation of S-structure configurations and only the mapping onto logical forms to interpret them, only a skeleton of the projection principle remains – the requirement that the properties of an S-structure configuration are projected from the lexical specification of its member constituents. However, the projection principle and the theta criterion jointly guarantee a closeness of match between S-structure configurations and logical configurations, weakened as in the case of expletives by the sometimes conflicting requirements of constraining the context–selection process. The manipulation of such a system, with S-structure configurations providing reliable indication of the logical form configurations, certainly satisfies the processing cost requirements imposed by relevance. However, since by assumption the brain is hard-wired with the detailed specification of the language faculty, there would be nothing in principle to preclude a complex and opaque mapping between the two levels. Indeed, part of Fodor's argument for the isolation of input mechanisms is the asymmetry between the speed with which such mechanisms operate and the complexity of the process involved (cf. Fodor 1983).

Nevertheless, there is an unambiguous functional motivation for semantic and syntactic properties of a grammar being inducible from the lexicon if we take into account the language-acquisition process. If we assume that the major burden involved in learning a language is in learning the specifications associated with lexical items, then it dramatically reduces the difficulty involved in learning if the specification of syntactic argument structure matches as closely as possible the specification of logical predicate-argument structure. This need not be so. The lexicon is finite. It could be learnt piecemeal, and in some sense has to be. In principle a child could learn his lexicon via an assumption that n-place syntactic predicates randomly map onto m-place predicates of varying logical type, each such mapping having to be learned without any basis for generalisations across the mapping process. And for some lexical entries this is indeed the case. Items such as *sell* have one-place, two-place or three-place realisations:

(34)   The books sold easily
(35)   John sold the books
(36)   John sold the books to Mary

But it is obviously in the child's interest that this should not be so across the board. Thus functional motivation for the implementation of a two-level analysis with both levels being inducible from the lexicon is found in the ease such an account brings to the process of language acquisition.

6   Cognition and Universal Grammar: the reductionist question answered

So we come finally to this question: If the principle of FI, the theta criterion, the projection principle and the uniqueness principle are all mechanisms whose underlying motivation can be explained in terms of the general cognitive constraint of seeking to maximise relevance, does it follow that they are not part of UG, the innate faculty specific to the task of learning and speaking a language? I can think of four types of answer, on the assumption that we make a distinction between UG and the grammar the human constructs on the basis of the constraints imposed by UG (Core Grammar). I give first the two most extreme forms of answer only to dismiss them.

Answer 1: The articulation of properties of UG is quite independent of other faculties, so nothing follows from consideration of relevance as a constraint on general cognitive mechanisms. External motivation is irrelevant: principles of UG are justified solely in terms internal to the vocabulary of the theory irrespective of external criteria. I assume the rejection of this view should be an article of faith for anyone working in the Chomskian paradigm. The central tenets of Chomsky's philosophy are that languages are psychological constructs and that the goal of linguistics is to explain the cognitive problem of how children learn their first language – more specifically what are the characteristics particular to the language-specific faculty that enable them to do so. No one working in the Chomskian paradigm can afford to ignore claims made about other aspects of cognition in so far as any such claims appear to overlap with the language faculty. So I dismiss this isolationist view out of hand.

Answer 2, which we might call the Radical Pragmatics view, is that any language phenomenon which can be shown to be a consequence of constraints of the general cognitive mechanism is a performance consideration (broadly construed) and so not a property of grammars at all, either UG or Core. So (1)–(4) excluded by the principle of FI are evaluated as wellformed by processes of the grammar but excluded merely in virtue of their being logically illformed. This won't do either. If the strings in question were grammatical, one would predict that hearers would use one of two strategies. They might simply ignore that part of the string that presents them with such an unfruitful processing task. So (37) could be processed as either (38) or (39):

(37)   Which man did you see the mouse?

(38)   'Which man did you see?'

(39)   'Did you see the mouse?'

the remainder in either case being ignored as not worth the effort. Or they would treat such strings as incomplete and interpret them as elliptical expressions via information accessible to them, according to the principle of relevance. Neither prediction is correct. (37) cannot be interpreted by ignoring one argument (as in (38) or (39)), nor can (40) be interpreted by ignoring the quantified expression.

(40)   Most houses Bill wrote to Mary

And they cannot be construed as elliptical either – (40) for example cannot be interpreted as (41), even in circumstances in which Bill's worrying about whether some set of houses needs reroofing is highly accessible information:

(41)   'Bill wrote to Mary about the fact that most houses needed to be reroofed'

So these strings never provide an input to the process of having some interpretation assigned. And this is a language-specific fact. Something must determine that strings which violate the goal of maximising relevance in this particular way are filtered out as ungrammatical. So the Radical Pragmatics view has to be rejected.

There are two possible answers remaining to the question posed, which lie on a scale between these two extremes. On the first of these, the third form of answer overall, UG is by definition the specification of those properties uniquely characteristic of the language faculty. Any property which can be shown to be a consequence of some other faculty is not a property of UG. According to this view, the principle of FI, the uniqueness principle, the projection principle and the theta criterion would have to be analysed as not being an intrinsic part of UG, if their functional motivation demonstrated that they were not characteristics exclusive to grammars of natural languages. They would have to be analysed either as part of the general cognitive faculty directly, or as some consequence of the interaction between UG and that general faculty. In either such case they would still be predicted to play an essential role in determining the form an individual core grammar may take, but they would not be part of UG itself.

The fourth form of answer is less reductionist, allowing duplication of mechanisms of UG and constraints on the central cognitive mechanism. The argument for this view is that the constraint of maximising relevance is not yet another faculty. It is a constraint underlying all cognitive faculties; and it does not necessarily follow that a domain-specific implementation of the constraint is not a property of that faculty. This view assumes that the innate language faculty would be predicted to have properties shared by the language of thought precisely because natural languages are vehicles for articulating propositions of the language of thought. The two are wired in parallel. Thus the principles of FI, the theta criterion, uniqueness principle and projection principle could all be properties of UG despite their functional motivation. Indeed, the resulting parallelism in wellformedness conditions in the two languages (*vis à vis* vacuous quantification, uniqueness of syntactic function, etc.) would be seen as a consequence of the one being an interpretation of the other. Thus, unlike the reductionist view, but as in the GB orthodoxy, these principles would be properties of every core grammar because they are a property of UG itself.

These two forms of answer to the question of the status of functionally-motivated universal principles of grammar might seem indistinguishable, since they both assume that the four principles in question apply to each Core Grammar. However, they are distinct, for the more reductionist view attributes less content to the innate faculty of Universal Grammar. The correct answer, I suggest, is a mixture of the two. Consider the vocabulary available to the innate language faculty, and the vocabulary in terms of which these four principles are expressed. The innate language faculty provides a set of restrictions specific to the task of grammar construction and with which a child constructs his Core Grammar. The vocabulary used in articulating this faculty is thus essentially specific to the domain of grammars. On this assumption we have a means of evaluating the status of these four principles by posing this question: To what extent is the way in which each of these principles is expressed necessarily specific to natural language grammars? The answer is clear-cut. The principle of FI and the uniqueness requirement are not. They can be restated as:

The general principle of full interpretation
In every cognitive system, every construct C must be interpreted according to the licensing conditions provided by some given system of interpretation.

The general principle of uniqueness
For any construct C in any domain of application of some subsystem S in which C has a value V, C must have only that one value V.

The principle of FI we know has to apply at least to phonological constructs; and the principle of uniqueness clearly applies there also. But these principles have a broader domain of application than that of the language faculty. They constitute definitional properties of the concept of representation and as such apply to all representations manipulated by the cognitive mechanism.

The assumption that these two principles constrain all representations has an immediate consequence – both the wellformedness conditions on S-structure configurations and the wellformedness conditions of the logic of the central cognitive mechanisms must preclude vacuous quantification and the duplication of arguments for a single predicate. These restrictions were argued to be consequences of these principles. Since S-structure configurations and propositions in the language of thought are both representations (the first interpreted by logical form structures, the second interpreted by some form of truth-theoretic semantics (cf. Fodor 1982, 1986)), the principles of FI and uniqueness apply equally to both. So this duplication of restrictions is not merely a happy coincidence which facilitates translation between the two systems of representation. It is explained, with no stipulation. So this theoretical framework, like that of Chomsky's, predicts the ungrammaticality of examples (1)–(4) on the basis of the principle of FI – but by a rather different route, and without any stipulation at all.

In contrast to these two principles, the theta criterion and the projection principle are essentially specific to the domain of grammars. The projection principle is the principle which determines the compositionality of natural language structures, predictable from the syntactic properties of their parts. And the theta criterion induces the compositionality of the interpretation of those natural language structures from the constraints on proposition construction imposed by their parts. At this point a radical reductionism becomes tempting. As Fodor has pointed out, the language of thought has all the properties of systematicity and indefinite extendability of natural language. From this it follows that the language of thought has a compositional syntax and a compositional semantics (see Fodor 1986 for explicit arguments to this effect). If systematic compositionality is a property of thoughts, then the easiest hypothesis for a child learning a first language is to assume that the language he is confronted with has the same properties as that of his central representational system. This is in effect the very argument by which I justified the functional basis of the projection principle. But, so the argument goes, this implies that the projection principle and the theta criterion are strictly unnecessary as a specification of UG: they would be predicted to be a property of all grammars directly from the joint assumptions made by the child that (i) grammars are input systems, (ii) maximisation of relevance controls the central cognitive device, and (iii) communication is controlled by the principle of relevance. For the easiest assumption for the child to make is that any acts of communication made to him have the compositional properties that his internal representation system does.

However, functional motivation is not a sufficient argument for functional reductionism. To make this assumption is to miss the point that over time input mechanisms may come to have hard-wired properties which facilitate the mapping process onto central system representations. The functional motivation of such mechanisms is of no necessary consequence for their status as part of the cognitive mechanism. Indeed, it would be surprising if processes of the input mechanism were not efficiently constructed for the purpose for which they are designed. What is critical is whether they have to be stated in a vocabulary specific to the particular input mechanism.

The functional motivation for the projection principle and the theta criterion is of precisely this type. The specific properties of compositionality intrinsic to both are an essential premise to the natural language acquisition process. The child has to assume both that a natural language constitutes an input mechanism and that the properties of the language to which he is exposed can be inferred from the assumption of systematic compositionality. And these are not hypotheses each child has to construct anew upon facing the problem of first language acquisition: his cognitive mechanism is hard-wired only to construct hypotheses consonant with these constraints. The vocabulary-specific statement of both principles in the form needed is not in doubt – the theta criterion in particular providing the child with the basic principles of translation which enable him to acquire the language he does on the assumption of its being a vehicle for expressing propositions of the language of thought. This mapping is unique to the input mechanism provided by the language faculty. No nonhuman cognitive mechanism shares it. If the mapping process and its associated constraints were not hard-wired, there would be no reason in principle why other higher-order animals should not reason the same way and therefore naturally acquire language. But they do not. The specification of the theta criterion and the projection principle are therefore essential to the language faculty system. Despite their characterisation as a means of fulfilling relevance considerations, they are irreducible.

After a rather tortuous route, we have got from a simple question to an unsurprising answer. The question was:

If some purported principle A of UG is a consequence of some general cognitive strategy, does it follow that A is not a characteristic of UG?

Answer: There is no a priori answer. In some cases it does, in some it does not. The issue as to whether some such principle A is a defining characteristic of UG is an empirical one, turning on the properties of the principle itself. The more specific answers I have given to instantiations of this question are slightly less uncontroversial. They are that the principle of FI and the principle of uniqueness are not defining properties of UG but the theta criterion and the projection principle are. In all four cases, these principles are grounded in the constraint imposed by the central cognitive system that all its activities are directed towards the goal of maximising relevance.

All of these claims, in the form I have made them, turn on details which could not be exhaustively followed through within the confines of a single paper. But at the very least this paper demonstrates the rich results to be harvested from putting the fruits of GB and relevance together in a single basket.[16]

NOTES

1 Ken Safir has drawn my attention to the French *il*-construction and examples such as *Il a tiré sur le bateau*. This has the same definiteness restriction as Dutch *er* (also not imposed on NPs within a PP) and the analysis of *er* here will carry over straightforwardly. The *il* construction displays the additional problem of not requiring any arguments, but this is not relevant here.

2 The examples are from Bennis 1986 and are all in subordinate-clause verb-final form.

3 This analysis assumes that a constituent marked as definite is an instruction to the hearer that the logical representation to be associated with that constituent is immediately accessible to him/her. I have argued for this analysis in several places elsewhere (Kempson 1984a, 1987, forthcoming). The restriction here is in effect a condition that complements of existential constructions should not be definite in this sense.

4 Equivalently:

$$a_i, a_j \notin \{\beta_1, \beta_2, \beta_3, \ldots\}$$

beta variables being associated with anaphoric elements whose value is restricted to such immediately accessible information (cf. the introduction to this volume and Kempson 1986). The specification of the syntactic source for the arguments a_i, a_j, is unnecessary because this is guaranteed by the theta criterion cf. section 3.

5 Safir's account has two awkward features: (i) it requires that an NP in an existential construction is simultaneously both a predicate and a referring expression; (ii) it forces an unmotivated distinction between the subject in a nonexistential construction and the subject in its existential congener, only the latter being in part a predicate nominal.

6 A definiteness restriction on postverbal subjects in Romance (Rita Manzini personal communication) would for example presumably have to be stated as a restriction on the thematic grid associated with the predicate.

7 I have no explanation for why definite NPs can only occur in complements of *be*, not the other existential predicate *appear*.

8 Expletive *it* with an adjacent complement sentence in object position is a problem for this analysis. In my dialect examples such as *I regret it that she's not here* are questionable in status, but for those dialects in which they are acceptable, they would have to be analysed as examples of apposition.

9 I have not specified what the theta-roles must be discharged by in view of examples such as *The boat was sunk to recover the insurance*, where the theta-grid requirements of the verb are not discharged by any syntactic expression (cf. Brody & Manzini of this volume). Examples such as these and the data from pro-drop languages without a rich inflectional system suggest that the theta criterion may be satisfiable at the level of propositional form only. But I shall not pursue this possibility here.

10 Syntactic arguments are expressions in subcategorised positions, plus subjects. The only definition of syntactic argument is therefore an inferential one – syntactic arguments are expressions which provide logical arguments. The second part of the theta criterion is thus definitional.

11 A single quantifier binding more than one variable as in some analyses of the so-called donkey sentences is not a counterexample. Such double-binding of variables is a single binding operation that binds all variables free in the restrictive clause of the operator (cf. Lewis 1975).

12 *Every* provides a quantifier and an argument variable, and therefore in one sense has two language of thought expressions simultaneously assigned as values. But this apparent counterexample is notational and hence artificial. On alternative analyses of natural language quantification, e.g. that suggested by Fine 1984, such quantifying expressions map onto arbitrary names and so are not split between quantifier and variable.

13 Apparent counterexamples are double object constructions in which the verb appears to assign syntactic (objective) case twice over. However, alternative analyses of these constructions are available – in particular one that assumes case is assigned once under government, the other NP having inherent case assignment. Significantly, no such pairs of expressions are ever assigned the same thematic role (cf. Baker 1986) for discussion of these constructions in a range of languages.

14 This principle of uniqueness precludes a priori Safir's analysis of NPs in existential constructions as being simultaneously a predicate and a referring expression.

15 Brody & Manzini argue for an asymmetry between subject and object arguments which must be explicit, and oblique arguments which need not be, and they weaken the projection principle accordingly. This asymmetry is then explained in terms of interaction of case theory and the projection principle. I have nothing to say here about case theory and I leave this problem on one side. Given examples such as (33) and the existence of object pro-drop languages (e.g. Chinese, Portuguese) and languages which allow subjectless intransitive passives (e.g. Turkish), I assume merely that the issue remains open.

16 This paper was funded in part by ESRC Research project HR8635. I am grateful for comments from participants at the Cumberland Lodge conference, in particular to Isobel Haik, Jim Higginbotham, Robert May and Ken Safir. I also wish to thank Diane Blakemore, Robyn Carston, Annabel Cormack and Rita Manzini for helpful discussions. In particular Rita was kind enough to play devil's advocate with me for the opening sections of the paper, to its considerable improvement.

My warmest thanks have, however, to be reserved for Deirdre Wilson for the continuing intellectual sustenance she provides me, in conversations, teaching and work together. None of these people can be guaranteed to agree with me about anything.

REFERENCES

Baker, M. 1985. Incorporation: a theory of grammatical function changing. Ph.D thesis, Massachusetts Institute of Technology.

Bennis, H. 1986. *Gaps and dummies*. Dordrecht: Foris.

Blakemore, D. 1986. Semantic constraints on relevance. Ph.D thesis, University of London.

Blass, R. 1985. 'Cohesion, coherence, and relevance'. Ms., London.

Brody, M. 1984. On contextual definitions and the role of chains. *Linguistic Inquiry* 15: 355–80.

Chierchia, G. 1984. *'Topics in the syntax and semantics of infinitives gerunds'*. Ph.D thesis, University of Massachusetts, Amherst.

Chomsky, N. 1981. *Lectures on government and binding*. Dordrecht: Foris.

Chomsky, N. 1986. *Knowledge of language: its nature, origin and use*. New York: Praeger.

Fine, K. 1984. *Reasoning with arbitrary objects*. Oxford: Blackwell.

Fodor, J.A. 1982. *Representations*. Cambridge, Mass.: MIT Press.

Fodor, J.A. 1983. *Modularity of mind*. Cambridge, Mass.: MIT Press.

Fodor, J.A. 1986. Individualism and supervenience. *Proceedings of the Aristotelian Society Supplementary Volume* LX: 235–62.

Grimshaw, J. 1986. 'Nouns, arguments and adjuncts: Ms., Brandeis.

Higginbotham, J. 1985. On semantics. *Linguistic Inquiry* 16: 547–94.

Kempson, R. 1984a. Anaphora, the compositionality requirement and the semantics–pragmatics distinction. In C. Jones & P. Sells (eds.) *Proceedings of the North-Eastern Linguistics Society* XIV: 183–206.

Kempson, R. 1984b. Pragmatics, anaphora and logical form. In D. Shiffrin (ed.) *Meaning, form and use in context*. Georgetown: Georgetown University Press, 1–10.

Kempson, R. 1987. Grammar and conversational principles. In F. Newmeyer (ed.) *Cambridge Linguistic Survey* 2: 139–63.

Kempson, R. 1988. 'Reconstruction and logical form'. Ms. London.

Kempson, R. forthcoming. Logical form: the grammar–cognition interface. *Journal of Linguistics*.

Lewis, D. 1975. Adverbs of quantification. In E. Keenan (ed.) *Formal semantics of natural language*. Cambridge: Cambridge University Press, 3–15.

Montague, R. 1974. *Formal philosophy* ed. R. Thomason New Haven: Yale University Press.

Rando, E. & Napoli, D.J. 1978. Definites in *there*-sentences. *Language* 54: 300–13.

Safir, K. 1984. 'What explains the definiteness effect?' ms. Rutgers.

Sperber, D. & Wilson, D. 1986. *Relevance: communication and cognition*. Oxford: Blackwell.

Williams, E. 1985. PRO and the subject of NP. *Natural Language and Linguistic Theory*, 3: 297–315.

INDEX

A-binding, 94, 100, 106
A'-binding, 85, 86, 90, 93, 94, 95, 97, 100,
    102, 215, 223
absorption, 100
accessibility, 18, 141, 142, 144, 170, 178, 187,
    189, 191, 203, 204, 216, 218, 222; of
    subject, 106, 107
A-chain, 120, 125
A'-chain 125, 126
acquisition, language, 4, 213, 218, 221;
    grammar, 213, 217, 219; lexical, 14, 205,
    213, 217; semantic, 15, 16, 30; by
    parameter setting, 77, 78
adjunction, 91, 92, 95, 96, 99
agent, 105, 110, 113, 114, 116, 126; implicit,
    112, 113, 115, 119, 120, 124
ambiguity, 20, 31, 38, 68, 91, 94, 98, 116,
    159, 160, 162, 163, 193, 214; lexical, 171,
    172, 178; truth-conditional, 171, 179
analytic, 32, 33; *see also* implication, analytic
anaphor, 8, 20, 106, 108, 129; lexical, 113,
    114, 126
anaphora, 22, 87, 222; bound variable, 85,
    86, 89, 90, 91, 93, 95, 97, 99, 100, 102
and, 52, 158–63, 175, 183, 190, 181; causal
    interpretation of, 160, 162, 163, 166, 167,
    170, 173, 178, 192, 193; consecutive, 171;
    symmetric, 171; temporal interpretation
    of, 159, 161, 167, 170, 172, 173, 190, 193
answers to questions, 149, 151, 171, 172, 188
argument, 185, 192, 202, 206, 208, 209, 212,
    216, 217, 220, 223; implicit, *see* implicit
    argument; logical, 9, 20, 201, 206, 208,
    212, 215, 222; syntactic, 9, 105, 119, 120,
    122
argument position (A-position), 11, 86–7,
    127, 211, 212
assumptions, 135, 166, 168, 169, 170, 178,
    185, 186; background, 69, 138, 140, 186;
    contextual, 161, 170, 185, 186, 187, 192;
    explicated, 162; implicated, 162, 169,
    170, 178; strength of, 186
attitude, propositional, 134, 135, 139, 149,
    151, 152
attributive, 38, 39
autonomy, functional, *see* independence,
    functional

belief, 19, 134, 135, 140, 185, 187, 191; as an
    event, 14
bijection principle, 86, 98
binding, 4, 86, 97, 105, 107, 124; *see also* A-
    binding, A'-binding; crossed, 100, 101,
    102; long distance, 108; quantifier, *see*
    A'-binding
binding principles, 9, 99, 205

case, 4, 9, 22, 117, 118, 119, 125; inherent,
    118, 119, 123, 126, 223; structural, 118,
    123
case absorption, 120
case assignment, 117
case linking, 107
case marking, 117, 120
case projection principle, 118
c-command, 9, 64, 74, 80, 87, 89, 90, 92, 96,
    99, 101, 108; and implicit arguments,
    113
chains, 9, 107, 125, 211, 212, *see also* A-
    chains, A'-chains; clitic, 127, 129;
    expletive-argument, 120, 121, 123, 125,
    126; foot of, 120, 211; heads of, 9, 121,
    123, 125, 126, 211; implicit argument,
    126, 127, 128, 129
clitic, 127, 128; zero, 106
communication, 16, 40, 136, 137, 139, 140,
    165, 191
competence, 3, 4, 46
compositionality, 6, 7, 34, 43, 200, 206, 220,
    221
computation, inferential, 184, *see also*
    inference; constraint on, 185
concept, 15, 16
conclusions, 186; implicated, 157, 169, 170,
    184
conditional, 34, 40, 54, 172
conjunction, 51, *see also and*
connections, speaker's, 13
consequence, logical, 184, 186, 188, 190
constraint, cognitive, 199, 220–2;
    conventional, 14; structural, 53, 54, 55
content, explicit, 155, 156, 173, 184; implicit,
    22, *see also* implicature; lexical, 45, 69,
    200, 201, 206, 208, 212; linguistic, 11,
    12, 13, 15, 17, 18, 23, 31, 32, 35, 156,